# THE
# AMERICAN SECRETARIES OF STATE
# AND THEIR DIPLOMACY

## VOLUME XVIII

# THE AMERICAN SECRETARIES OF STATE AND THEIR DIPLOMACY

ROBERT H. FERRELL, *Editor*

SAMUEL FLAGG BEMIS, *Advisory Editor*

COOPER SQUARE
NEW YORK

VOLUME XVIII

# CHRISTIAN A. HERTER

*by*
G. BERNARD NOBLE

PUBLISHERS, INC.
1970

PUBLISHED BY COOPER SQUARE PUBLISHERS, INC.
59 FOURTH AVENUE, NEW YORK, NEW YORK 10003

LIBRARY OF CONGRESS CATALOG CARD NO. 67-24039

PRINTED IN THE UNITED STATES OF AMERICA
NOBLE OFFSET PRINTERS, INC., 419 LAFAYETTE ST., NEW YORK, N. Y. 10003

# VOLUME XVIII

# TABLE OF CONTENTS

vi

# PREFACE TO VOLUME XVIII

"**P**OLITICS is not good clean fun!" So remarked Governor Herter at a college commencement where, on the occasion of his receiving the customary gubernatorial honorary degree, a fellow recipient expressed the hope that he could take in hand the politicos clustering and festering around the golden dome of the State House in Boston. Only the questioner used a stronger word than politicos.

But Christian Herter himself was an outstanding example of the good clean man in politics—the type of public servant that commencement orators extol and urge upon the mortarboards and tassels before them. From the moment of receiving his Harvard degree of Bachelor of Arts until his death as a former Secretary of State he epitomized the hardworking public servant who never personally fouled a play, whether in his twelve years in the Massachusetts State Legislature, his early apprenticeship in the Foreign Service, his association with the humanitarian work of Herbert Hoover, or his work as Under Secretary of State and Secretary of State under President Eisenhower, where he was called upon to take over the high office when death beckoned to John Foster Dulles. Nor did he flinch despite a painful physical handicap when in the succeeding Democratic Administration, President Kennedy asked him to head the American delegation in the long, complicated and tiresome Geneva negotiations on tariff and trade, the so-called Kennedy round, leading to the signature of the multilateral treaty of 1967. He died in patriotic harness.

Herter's period as Secretary of State was short, but it came in a specially critical period of the cold war when old threats to American security and to international peace were maturing and new ones were coming into play. The Secretary and other administration leaders could only hope to find temporary palliatives that could postpone disaster until time and piecemeal adjustments might reduce international tensions and hasten peaceful counsels.

An obstinate believer in the system of the United Nations, Herter might have said of his problems in New York and Geneva that it was not good clean fun.

A good clean man, all the way along.

While preparing this volume Dr. Noble had the advantage of close contact with Mr. Herter and his papers, both officially and then privately, right up to the very week of his death. Bernard Noble has been a gallant soldier and public servant in time of war and a proficient diplomatic historian in time of peace. It would be difficult if not impossible to find a historian better fitted to write this volume.

SAMUEL FLAGG BEMIS
*Advisory Editor*

New Haven, Connecticut
VIII.15, 1969

# ACKNOWLEDGMENTS

For assistance in making possible the writing of this book I am deeply indebted to the American Philosophical Society and to the Charles T. Estes Memorial Foundation. Their contributions greatly facilitated the completion of the work. My warmest appreciations to both.

I am indebted also to many persons who worked closely with Secretary Herter, or knew him well otherwise, who in interviews gave me valuable information and interpretative insights. A remarkable fact is the unanimity of judgments as to the Secretary's outstanding character. I had the good fortune to have many talks with the Secretary and profited greatly from these. He also read and discussed with me more than half the manuscript. He permitted me to have access to his papers. These were the richest of all source materials, and provide the basis for many statements which cannot be footnoted.

On Mr. Herter's death Livingston T. Merchant, Under Secretary for Political Affairs, and closest adviser to the Secretary, kindly undertook to read the entire manuscript and give me the benefit of his advice, which was invaluable and is deeply appreciated. Gerard C. Smith, then head of the Department Policy Planning Staff, read a number of chapters and was very helpful. Many other officers of the Department, and some from other agencies, past and present, were kind enough to read chapters relevant to their respective fields of responsibility. In all cases they were concerned primarily with the facts, though willing to discuss interpretations. Space does not permit listing all these names.

Appreciations are due to Warren Henderson, Paul Washington, and Harry Brock, in the Communications Center of the Executive Secretariat for their valuable cooperation in making available relevant materials. Fred W. Shipman, Department Librarian, and his able staff have been most accommodating in facilitating the use of Library materials. Mr. Shipman has read many chapters and given wise counsel regarding them. Mrs. Virginia Hartley, Special Assistant in International Organization Affairs, has also been a helpful critic. Arthur Kogan, of the Historical Office, has kindly read several key chapters covering subjects in areas of his special research. Miss Elizabeth Ann Brown, Office Director, U.N. Political Affairs, ably assisted in reading proofs. I am also grateful to my wife, Matilda, and her two sisters, Thurzetta Ross and Effie Ray Elliott, for their services in helping to move the work along.

G. BERNARD NOBLE

Washington, D.C.
1970

CHRISTIAN A. HERTER

Christian A. Herter

# CHRISTIAN A. HERTER

## 1959-1961

### CHAPTER ONE

### ACROSS THE YEARS

ARLY IN THE AFTERNOON of April 22, 1959, many dignitaries crowded into the White House Cabinet Room to see Christian A. Herter sworn in as the fifty-third Secretary of State. President Eisenhower stood by Herter's side, solemn and unsmiling, his thoughts apparently dominated by concern for his stricken friend, John Foster Dulles. In handing Herter his commission as Secretary of State, the President said they both knew how they had hoped and prayed "for Foster's early recovery," so that he might come back. "You also know," he added, "that he and I were one in deciding that you were the man best qualified to take over the office of Secretary of State."

"As you undertake this mission, God bless you—and I am sure the people of the United States join me in that feeling." Obviously moved by the President's remarks, Mr. Herter grasped the President's hand and said, "You can't know how much it means to me to have your confidence."[1]

After the brief ceremony and congratulations from friends, the new Secretary returned to the Department of State. There he was surprised to be welcomed by a gathering of some 600 members of the Department staff (*quorum pars fui*) who greeted him with enthusiastic acclaim. These staffers had gotten

1

wind of the swearing-in ceremony and were aware of the embarrassing delay in reaching, or announcing, the decision to appoint Herter after the resignation of Secretary Dulles. They therefore wanted to manifest their confidence in the new Secretary and their genuine satisfaction with the decision.

Herter descended from his car, supported by elbow crutches owing to an arthritic condition, and expressed his surprise and pleasure, remarking: "All I can say is that this is completely unexpected, and I can't tell you how touched I am. As one who began public life in the State Department, it is, of course, a tremendous thrill to be allowed to feel that I can now perhaps help all of us who are working as a team together, in the tremendously important job we all have, to try to keep this country at peace and the world at peace. I only wish I had time now to shake hands with every one of you. I'm sorry I can't do it. But I want you to know that my heart is very warm at this moment, and I am hoping that in the days to come I will have a chance to see each of you and thank you all for this very fine reception."[2] The words were expressive of the attitudes which characterized his tenure of office throughout his Secretaryship: team play, friendliness, and deep concern for the maintenance of peace in our country's relations.

1

Christian A. Herter's birth in Paris on March 28, 1895, of American parents, and his first nine years in France—three of them school years in the Ecole

Alsacienne—did not predestine him to become a leading figure in American international relations. But that formative period broadened his perspectives and became a fitting background for a career which, though changing direction from time to time, was always influenced and ultimately determined by an underlying and developing interest in international affairs.

His father, Albert, was a famous painter of murals, portraits and tapestry cartoons. His murals adorn interiors of public buildings from Paris to Los Angeles. His mother, the former Adele McGinnis, was an accomplished portrait and still-life painter. Almost inevitably Christian Herter's interests developed in the field of the arts. On coming to the United States with his parents, he continued his education in the Browning School of New York City, from which he graduated at the age of 15, but because of his youth he remained another year, after which he—a gangling youth, six feet four—entered Harvard University. In line with his heritage, he went in for fine arts and graduated in 1915 cum laude. He manifested his literary endowments at Harvard by writing a part of the book and lyrics for the 1915 Hasty Pudding Club show, "The Fattest Calf."

Herter then enrolled in the School of Fine and Applied Arts in New York to study architecture and interior decorating. The following year, 1916, attending a class reunion at Harvard, he met a former classmate, Lithgow Osborne, later Ambassador to Norway, who gave him a glowing account of life in Berlin as a diplomatic attaché. The story struck fire in Herter's mind. "Gosh, I wish I had an opportunity like yours," he said. Osborne replied, "Do you really mean it?" The answer was "yes." An exchange of cables to Berlin ensued. A week later the course of his life had changed, and he was off to Berlin under a Diplomatic Service appointment.

His service in Berlin was chiefly notable for the acquaintances he made in the Berlin Foreign Office. Outstanding among these was friendship with Kurt Hahn, a great humanitarian and postwar founder of boys' schools in England, Scotland, Wales and Germany, impregnated with the principle of a "moral equivalent of war." At the close of hostilities Hahn rendered invaluable service in reporting to Herter on desperate food conditions in Germany and giving helpful advice.

In December 1916, Herter was sent on detail to Brussels where the United States, Spanish and Dutch missions remained as protectors of the Commission for Belgian Relief. During Minister Brand Whitlock's illness he became acting United States Minister to Belgium for six weeks, at the age of 22. It was his responsibility to watch the German deportation of Belgians and to write the final report on this saddening episode to the State Department. He was still in Brussels when, in February 1917, the United States broke relations with Germany. He wanted to rejoin the Berlin Embassy staff but was sent home by way of Switzerland.

Waiting to change trains in Mainz en route to Switzerland, he was arrested by the military as a suspected spy and taken before the Commandant whom he could not convince of his *bona fides*. He was deprived of baggage and marched off three miles to jail; kept there overnight, sharing the one chair with his guard; taken the next morning at eleven, without breakfast and brought before a group of officers, whose commander had a pile of papers that apparently told of his every move since arriving in Berlin; had his pipe rudely knocked out of his mouth while smoking in an effort to appear nonchalant; was released after the interrogation and taken to a restaurant by a friendly soldier, whose bread card he shared; was then arrested by civil authorities as a suspicious foreigner who had spent the night in Mainz without permission. When they learned that he had been jailed, interrogated and released by the military, they made a ceremony of expunging his name from the police blotter and then escorted him to the train for Switzerland.

En route home via La Coruna, Spain, and across the Atlantic to Havana on the uncomfortable and malodorous ship, *Infanta Isabel*, Herter and his friend, Osborne, were in charge of the month-long tour of ninety-six Americans and thousands of pieces of baggage. Among the diplomatic passengers was the erstwhile Ambassador to Germany, James W. Gerard. Herter and Osborne drilled daily with the Ambassador's firearms, with a view to affording such protection as might be possible if deemed necessary. These two passengers particularly welcomed the end of the voyage.

The loss of his elder brother, Everit, at Chateau Thierry with the American Expeditionary Force, caused Herter to resolve to make the achievement of peace his lifetime mission. On returning home he made repeated unsuccessful tries at enlisting—twice at Plattsburg, one three-month training course at Harvard, and an attempt to get into the regular army. Then he was drafted, but on account of his height, underweight (33 pounds) and bad hips, the army classified him as 5-C, a category presumably limited to "imbeciles, idiots, morons and habitual criminals."

Herter, on August 25, 1917, married Mary Caroline Pratt, whose grandfather had founded Pratt Institute in Brooklyn after retirement from the oil business. Her father devoted all his life to the Institute.

That autumn young Herter accepted an invitation from Secretary of State Robert Lansing to come to Washington to work with Joseph C. Grew on problems of prisoners of war and interned enemy aliens. He continued this work until September, 1918, when he left for Bern where he served as assistant commissioner and secretary at the American-German Prisoner-of-War Conference.[3] There were about forty American officers at the conference and only four German, which brought a comment from the Germans that if the Americans could spare that many officers for such a conference, Germany might as well give up. Herter was one of the five Americans working on the joint subcommittee to present a proposal.[4] On the evening of November 11—Armistice Day—the American and German negotiators reached an exchange-of-prisoners agreement which the armistice that day made irrelevant.

Returning to their hotel on the evening of the

armistice, the U.S. negotiators had to pick their way through lines of soldiers who had been called out to maintain order in the midst of widespread strikes in Bern and other Swiss cities. (The seriousness of the Swiss political situation was a factor in the rejection of Switzerland as the seat of the ensuing peace negotiations.) Problems flared elsewhere. Reports that after the armistice many prisoners had broken out of camps along the Rhine and had died caused Herter, along with an American Red Cross official, to visit Rastadt and Karlsruhe—major prisoner concentrations. He talked his way into the camps, past German soldiers wearing "soldiers council" (communist) arm bands, and urged the men to sit tight, assuring them that soon all would be well. Back in Switzerland he cabled Washington about the serious conditions and got quick action. Washington told him to get in touch with his German friend Hahn, then principal assistant to Prince Max of Baden who had taken over the regency of Germany, and to inquire what the United States could do to stop the spread of Bolshevism in Germany. Hahn visited Herter and described German starvation conditions. He said food was the answer to the problem and assisted in organizing quickly a conference with high German officials. This resulted in a German commitment of the country's available gold supply—$350,000,000—for gigantic American food shipments which were a major factor in turning the tide against Bolshevism.

Herter was assigned to the American Peace Commission at Paris, where from January until July, 1919, he served as a secretary and assistant to Henry White.

Unofficially he was aide to Grew, Secretary General of the U.S. Commission, who was becoming increasingly deaf. He worked with a small group on the League of Nations statute, and had an important part in writing into the Covenant the controversial Article 10, "against aggression," which President Woodrow Wilson was to describe as the "heart" of the Covenant.

Returning home, Herter was appointed to the State Department on September 23, 1919, but left six months later, owing partly to discouragement at United States rejection of the League of Nations, partly to assignment to the Personnel Division rather than to a post in China, which he wanted.

Herbert Hoover in 1920 appointed him special assistant and also executive secretary of the European Relief Council, in which capacity he worked on problems of undernourishment in Germany and occupied territory brought on by the Allied blockade during the war.

When Hoover became Secretary of Commerce in 1921, Herter continued as special assistant and also carried responsibilities with the American Relief Association which Hoover set up, and for which Congress voted $25,000,000 in response to desperate appeals for help in Russia. He went to Russia in 1922 with Governor James P. Goodrich of Indiana, and General William N. Haskell, to study conditions there after the 1921 famine. In spite of widespread starvation, the Russians were shipping wheat out of the country to acquire gold for trade purposes. This caused the American group to advise against further relief, but the program continued for another year.

Herter left the government in 1924, largely on advice of Hoover who thought that in his own long-term interest it would be better to get into private enterprise. On leaving, he agreed to join as co-editor with Richard Ely Danielson who was taking over the *Independent*, dedicated according to its masthead, "to the consideration of Politics, Social and Economic Tendencies, History, Literature and the Arts." In an early issue the editors proclaimed themselves "earnest seekers after truth." Herter's job was to write on foreign affairs and to scout articles by outsiders. A Republican, he saw to it that the *Independent* championed the League of Nations and criticized isolationist Senator Henry Cabot Lodge. The publication did not make a wide enough appeal to justify the hopes of the editors, and in 1929 they sold it to the *Outlook*.

After lecturing for a year at Harvard University on international relations and international organization, Herter turned to state politics on advice of State Senator, and a former roommate, Henry Parkman, Jr.,—sometimes called a "gentlemanly" Republican boss. He won a seat in the Massachusetts House of Representatives from the "silk stocking" fifth ward, in succession to another close friend, Henry L. Shattuck, long-time Treasurer of Harvard, who was retiring from politics.

Appointed to the Ways and Means Committee at the behest of its chairman, Albert Bigelow, Herter suddenly found a cause. Though he was neither an orator nor a backslapper, and was rather shy, he took to politics, and proved such a hard worker on the

Ways and Means Committee that he was soon given the most difficult bills to carry to the floor. Besides his conscientious attitude, Herter was gifted with a quick mind and a prodigious memory which distinguished him as one of the House's most outstanding debaters. He became Speaker during his last two terms and enjoyed a reputation of "being scrupulously fair to Democrats as well as to factions of his own party."[5] His tact contributed to compromises generally satisfactory to legislators and the public.

Moderately conservative in economic matters, he could claim distinction of being the father of the Unemployment Compensation Law in 1935.[6] During this period his father painted five historical murals gratis in the chamber of the House.

Herter's interest in the broader national and international scene was immediately demonstrated when the Japanese struck Pearl Harbor. In addition to his legislative duties he accepted a job in Washington as Deputy Director of the Office of Facts and Figures under Archibald MacLeish.

Herter was on the road to a wider field, and it took no persuasion to get him to run for Congress to represent the 10th Massachusetts District, even though it was a "sprawling district with large numbers of Irish, Italians and Germans who might take a dim view of a gentleman from Beacon Hill." Furthermore, he would be opposing George Holden Tinkham, a political fixture and powerful figure in the House, who for twenty-eight years had been able to garner Democratic as well as Republican votes. Tinkham was well known for his world-wide travels and contacts, his skill as a big-game hunter, his almost pathological opposition to President Franklin D. Roosevelt, and his luxuriant beard. He was an "isolationist," and Herter thought it disgraceful that Massachusetts should be represented by an isolationist. With characteristic frankness Herter called on Tinkham and told him that he, Herter, would be a candidate in the coming primaries. During his long incumbency Tinkham had spent little time in his constituency, and his able secretary managed his campaigns. Her unfortunate death at this time was a heavy blow. Furthermore, a number of old friends told him they were supporting Herter. Tinkham then withdrew.

In the November 1942, election Herter defeated his Democratic opponent by a margin of 2,800 votes. He confessed later that Tinkham, if he had stayed in, probably would have won. In succeeding elections his margin increased—up to 67,000 in 1948,[7] though in 1950 this margin fell to 25,000 in a sharp contest with Francis Hurley, State Auditor and a popular Democrat.

Herter entered Congress in 1943 as a critic of the New Deal, but his first concern was to study the needs of the people he represented. He set up monthly "constituents' clinics," of which he gave advance notice, inviting constituents to come in and discuss problems. He found these clinics popular and useful.

His interest in wartime food shortages, whether at home or abroad, carried over from World War I, and in 1945, on request of the Department of Agriculture and UNRRA, he made a trip to Europe. He urged the Congress to grant additional funds to UNRRA.[8]

In domestic matters Herter was a moderate

throughout his ten years of service. His legislative record was a mixture of conservative and liberal tendencies. On the conservative side he voted against the crop insurance bill (1943), supported the President's strike control bill (1946), and backed the gas tax exemptions bill (1949). On the liberal side he voted to abolish the poll tax (1943), discontinue the Committee on Un-American Activities (1943 and 1945), and continue the Office of Price Administration (1946).[9]

In foreign policy Herter was consistently liberal. Indeed his chief interest lay in this field, as appeared from time to time in his support of measures such as the Fulbright resolution (1943) calling for "appropriate international machinery" to maintain a "just and lasting peace," and his endeavors to aid peoples of war-devastated countries. In this latter area he won distinction.

Herter supported foreign aid appropriations after World War II, but thought information was needed on European economic conditions and on methods of administration. He presented a resolution on March 20, 1947 (House Joint Resolution 153), and after Secretary George C. Marshall had aroused public interest by his Harvard Commencement address in June, the House took up the resolution, amended it, and passed it on July 22. It created a Select Committee on Foreign Aid composed of 19 members to study "actual and prospective needs" of European countries "within United States military zones," and provided that aid must not weaken the United States domestic economy.[10] James Reston of the *New York Times* (April 7, 1947) earlier had commented that "at least one member of Congress [Herter] has been thinking about how to look at this whole problem of America's interests in the foreign field instead of viewing it piecemeal." Chairman Charles M. Eaton of the Foreign Affairs Committee, who was named chairman of the Select Committee, was unable to go abroad and Herter took over what became known as the Herter Committee.

In appointing the committee, Speaker Joseph W. Martin acceded to Herter's requests that the members should represent a cross-section of House opinion and that they be hardworking Congressmen.[11] Phillip Watts, appointed executive secretary of the committee, sent out notices to members with the cryptic instruction, "No wives, no dinner coats." It was to be a hardworking committee.

Herter and the committee sailed for Europe on August 27, 1947. There was no time for socializing. He appointed five subcommittees for five geographic areas, and these groups got down to regular work on the ship. Reportedly "Herter worked harder than anyone else."[12] In the field he visited each subcommittee, but allowed each chairman to retain full responsibility for his respective area.

When the committee returned on October 10, Herter commented that American aid could not achieve the desired objective unless each country set its own house in order and cooperated with its neighbors for the fullest use of existing resources.[13] This coincided with the objectives of the Paris Conference of sixteen prospective European relief countries, held the preceding July.

The President transmitted a "Marshall Plan" proposal to Congress in a message of December 19, 1947, providing for an agency known as the Economic Cooperation Administration, headed by an Administrator appointed by the President, who would be under direction of the Secretary of State.[14]

When the House Foreign Affairs Committee opened its hearings on the recovery program on December 17, 1947, Herter presented the unanimous recommendations of the Select Committee in a bill drafted by Allen W. Dulles and Gerald D. Morgan. The bill proposed an independent corporate agency, called the Emergency Foreign Reconstruction Authority (EFRA), composed of a bipartisan board of eight directors appointed by the President and confirmed by the Senate with one of these appointed by the President as chairman. Thus there were two conflicting plans before the Congress for the administration and control of the program.[15]

Secretary of State Marshall objected to the corporate character of the plan. He said that "there could be no separate organization for the plan, apart from the Department of State"; everything had to be done under the control of the President and State Department.[16] A compromise bill eventually evolved in the Senate under direction of Arthur H. Vandenberg, Chairman of the Foreign Relations Committee. Vandenberg and Senator Henry Cabot Lodge, Jr. kept in close touch with Herter who was often referred to as "the Vandenberg of the House."[17] Though the chances of the Herter Bill supplanting the Administration's proposal were slight, it promoted more searching debate in reaching the compromise. The Committee finally rejected the Administration's plan, which would have given control to the State Department, and the bill, as adopted on April 3, 1948, placed the Recovery Act in an Economic Cooperation Administration headed by an Administrator under control of the President, and authorized the latter "to create a corporation with such powers as the Administrator may deem necessary." Any disagreements between the Administrator and the Secretary of State would be settled by the President.[18] Thus the Secretary of State was permitted only an appeal to the President. Herter was pleased. Speaking in the House, March 23, 1948, he said that practically every desirable feature of corporate administration (proposed by him) had been brought into the bill.

Even though his bill had failed of passage, Herter had gained national prominence as an authority in foreign affairs. Eric F. Johnston, Chairman of the Collier's Committee, in presenting an award to Herter (along with one to Senator Alben Barkley) "for distinguished service in 1947," stressed that Herter had chosen a life of "work and self-discipline" rather than "ease and self-indulgence" in spite of his independent financial status. "It was Representative Herter's singular and fruitful work in the field of foreign affairs," he said, "which dictated his selection. . . . This was one of the most influential committee actions in recent years."[19]

Work in promoting this legislation was but one expression of Herter's increasing emphasis on the House of Representatives as an influence in foreign affairs. He believed and stated, e.g., in an address before the American Society of International Law on April 26, 1951, that the House must be well-informed on international affairs, and that, by joint resolution with the Senate, it should participate in approval of any international agreement requiring advice of the Congress as a whole, as in the case of agreements requiring appropriation of funds.

Herter was appointed in 1951 to the Committee on Foreign Affairs, where he continued to support legislation for the European Recovery Act. When the question of aid to Communist-held countries arose he said he favored it if there was starvation and aid could be handled without strengthening the Communist Party; but he would want to be convinced of that.[20]

Herter's career was again about to change. Early in 1952 a "draft Herter" for Governor of Massachusetts campaign started. Leaders were Sinclair Weeks, Republican National Chairman, Joseph Martin, House Minority Leader from Massachusetts, and Senators Leverett Saltonstall and Henry Cabot Lodge, Jr. No Republican candidates for President had carried Massachusetts since 1924, and these leaders wanted the strongest possible state ticket to help elect Eisenhower as well as to oppose the twice-elected Governor Paul A. Dever, a strong Adlai Stevenson man.[21] "For the good of the party," Herter entered the gubernatorial race which was considered a "losing battle."

When he left the House, there was warm praise for his ten years of service. Mr. Auchincloss (N.J.) said Herter had brought to the membership "a wealth of experience and a mind of extraordinary ability. . . . Most of Mr. Herter's life has been devoted to the service of his country,"[22] and Mr. Hale (Maine) expressed both praise and prophecy. "Over the last decade Mr. Herter has been in my opinion one of our ablest and most useful members. . . . No doubt his greatest contribution has been in the realm of foreign affairs." Hale added prophetically that Herter would make "an admirable Secretary of State."[23]

His interest in international affairs during these years was also illustrated by the creation in Washington of the School for Advanced International Studies (SAIS) which owes its existence to him more than to any other person. He was the prime mover. The idea grew out of discussions in 1943 with several friends, including William L. Clayton, Paul Nitze, Joseph Grew and Allen Dulles, who recognized the need for better training at the graduate level for work in the international field, whether government or private. To establish such a school they set up the Foreign Service Educational Foundation to receive donations, and Herter as President assumed responsibility for raising $100,000 annually for the first five years. His success enabled the school—SAIS—to begin operations in 1944. In 1950 it affiliated with Johns Hopkins University, improving its academic status. From its beginning to its growth to maturity, Herter continued to be a mainstay of the School.

Yielding to pressure from Massachusetts Republican leaders in 1952, Herter embarked on his most difficult electoral venture—a campaign against incumbent Governor Dever, whose large victories in the two preceding elections made him appear unbeatable. Herter won in a political upset, by 14,456.[24] Two years later he was reelected by 75,252. This completed his thirteenth electoral gambit—six as state legislator, five as Congressman, and two as Governor, all successful. As Governor, he called for reform in many fields, including government organization, civil service, education, conservation, transportation, taxation, agriculture, public and mental health, crime and corruption, the courts, labor relations, and state and local relations. Even with a preponderantly Democratic legislature over the four years, he could point to approval of 90.2 per cent of his proposals.[25]

His outstanding gubernatorial career brought better organization to the state government, better relations between state and local authorities, improved business and industrial conditions, and a more modern attitude toward disadvantaged social groups. Herter was widely regarded as "one of the best Governors in Massachusetts history."[26] The Republican *Boston Herald* and the Democratic *Boston Post* agreed that his record of useful achievement could scarcely be matched.

Strongly influenced by his interest in international affairs, Herter announced on February 8, 1956, that he would not seek another term, and before his second term ended he was again on the road to wider activity. In the autumn of 1955 he was mentioned increasingly seriously as a possibility for high national office, even for the Presidency if Eisenhower's illness continued. There was no "wave," as the *Springfield Sunday Republican* said, but "he was receiving serious thought." Herter remained silent on the subject, or answered questions discreetly, but by the end of 1956 he was headed in new directions.

# CHAPTER TWO

## THE UNDER SECRETARY

### 1

HERTER BECAME a national political figure during his ten years in Congress and his four years as Governor. His work as Congressman and as Governor revealed a humanitarian concern for the disadvantaged. His arduous labors with the "Herter Committee" in 1947 and its report on dangerous economic conditions in Europe, with proposals for their improvement, contributed notably to the framing and adoption of the Marshall Plan. He was one of a special committee of nineteen that visited General Eisenhower and influenced him to seek the Republican nomination for President in 1952. In the Republican nominating convention Herter played a key role in promoting the "fair play" amendment which prevented the seating of contested delegates until after the convention adopted the report of the credentials committee, thus turning the tide in Eisenhower's favor. His reputation as Governor of Massachusetts enhanced his political standing, and in 1955 it was forecast that he would be one of the dark horses in 1956.[1] After the President's heart attack in 1955 his name was high among those mentioned as possible liberal candidates, and a Herter-for-President boom got under way in Massachusetts, though he disclaimed any interest so long as President Eisenhower was likely to run for another term.[2]

Herter's public appearances increased. Speaking in January 1956 at a dinner of the National Republican Club in New York, he showed interest in the national scene, but refused to commit himself on plans. Several weeks later he announced that he would not run for a third term as Governor and said reasons of health had no bearing on the matter.[3]

Controversy developed on whether Vice President Richard M. Nixon should be on the Eisenhower ticket for reelection, and Herter reportedly said in a television interview that he would consider the Vice Presidency if Nixon were not a candidate.[4] When President Eisenhower said he would be happy with Nixon on the ticket, that seemed to put an end to controversy. The hour was too late for such a change unless the President pulled the rug from under Nixon, which he was not disposed to do. Herter declined to campaign against Nixon and at the National Convention nominated him for reelection. Nixon, he said, was "a great Vice President" who had made that office "more significant, more influential, more useful than ever before in our history."[5]

Herter's place in the Administration seemed assured if the Republicans won. Sherman Adams, the assistant to the President, telephoned to say that Under Secretary of State Herbert Hoover, Jr., was thinking of leaving and that Herter should come down for discussions. When Herter was elected as Governor in 1952, John Foster Dulles had written a congratulatory letter, but added a note of disappointment, saying he would have liked to appoint Herter as Under Secretary. In 1956 the Secretary's attitude was not clear, but Dulles asked Herter whether he would accept the post of Assistant Secretary for European Affairs. Herter demurred. He reminded the Secretary of the letter of 1952 and of his own record thereafter. Further consultation confirmed the correspondence of 1952.[6] The President accepted the resignation of Hoover on December 8, 1956, and announced that Herter would succeed him about February 1. Secretary Dulles, departing for a NATO conference later that day, said at the airport that he was delighted to have Herter—a man of great ability whom he had known for forty years.[7]

Herter received the unanimous endorsement of the Foreign Relations Committee, and on February 21, 1957, the Senate unanimously approved his nomination without debate. Less than two hours afterwards he was sworn in.

Before taking over the new job Herter spent a month in the Department—a useful breaking-in period. He found the departing Under Secretary very cooperative. Hoover was leaving because, as one commentator put it, he was not the best man for the post, as Hoover himself had suggested on entering the Department.[8] The retiring Under Secretary was excellent in matters relating to his own field of interest, as in the Iranian oil controversy, but in others he was difficult, too restrictive in outlook on foreign aid and troops in Europe. He had become known as one of the "three H's," along with Secretary of the Treasury George M. Humphrey and the Director of the International Cooperation Administration, John H. Hollister—a combination noted for extreme conservatism in financial matters.[9]

As for the work of the Department, what would the new Under Secretary do? Secretary Dulles, a dynamic personality, did not easily delegate authority. He expected his subordinates to refer important problems back to him. There was no understanding as to the range of Herter's responsibilities. Assignments were specific, and occasional. One exception was a top-secret committee involving relations with the Central Intelligence Agency. Herter helped take the load off the Secretary by seeing members of Congress and ambassadors, and frequently made recommendations for diplomatic appointments and Department organization. Sometimes he sat in National Security Council meetings. Dulles generally made decisions of which Herter learned afterwards, though sometimes the Secretary called him in for conference. He did see Dulles for about fifteen minutes before staff meetings, and went into meetings with him, though, as one of Dulles' personal staff said, he seldom returned with notes on something to do. When Dulles went away, Herter had full charge with responsibility for decisions; but the Under Secretary was careful to keep in touch.

The new job brought Herter serious misgivings. He wondered whether he should carry on or accept advice of friends and resign. Stewart Alsop likened Herter's situation to having been Number One in a big pond as Governor, and being "reduced to the status of a glorified tadpole."[10] Associates in the Department reported that Herter was kept in "not-so-splendid isolation" and that "a considerable talent was being buried under the weight of one of Washington's most powerful personalities." It was not easy for him to change from the position of Governor where he had all authority to one where he felt he had very little. *The New York Times* observed that "Herter had the misfortune to be Number Two man in a one-man Department."[11]

Herter took occasion to let Dulles know his doubts, but concern with the nation's foreign policy prompted him to carry on. In general Herter fell heir to functions of little interest to Dulles, such as economic and Department operational affairs. When C. Douglas Dillon, a close friend, came into the Department in March 1957 as Under Secretary for economic affairs, Herter still retained his interest in that field.

2

Economic development of less-developed countries was a subject of concern to Herter before he entered the State Department, and as Under Secretary he found that this problem was giving the foreign aid program much trouble. There was growing concern about aid for less-developed countries. The foreign aid bill of 1956 had thirty Senate votes against it, as compared to seven against the Marshall Plan in 1948. The Foreign Relations Committee promoted a Senate resolution in July 1956, ordering an exhaustive study of "the extent to which foreign assistance by the U.S. Government serves, can be made to serve, or does not serve, the national interest.[12] Twenty-two reports came in from various sources, including one by Max Millikan and Walt W. Rostow of the Massachusetts Institute of Technology stressing the desirability of a long-term program based on a long-term capital fund free from political and military commitments. The Policy Planning Staff of the Department was working along the same lines, and in a report of January 1957, emphasized (1) economic aid only to promote economic growth, rather than as a cold war weapon; (2) separating the administration of economic aid from that of military support; (3) a capital fund to be expended over a period of years; and (4) aid on terms more generous than those offered by existing public or private banks. The recommendations of the Senate Special Committee, based on the twenty-two reports, did not go into details but emphasized that the foreign aid programs served the national interest of the United States. They envisaged revolving funds built up over years as the needs became clear. They recognized the need also for soft loans—those permitting repayment sometimes in local currencies.[13]

Herter favored long-term economic planning, backed by Congressional assurance that would make it possible, but his experience made him doubt the possibility of Congressional approval of a long-term development fund instead of regular authorization and appropriation. Objection by Hollister, head of ICA, and the strong opposition of Secretary Humphrey raised doubts about pushing the program. But Secretary Dulles approved the Planning Staff proposals, and Herter strove to secure favorable Congressional action. The Administration bill that finally emerged suffered important alterations. It established the Developmental Loan Fund (DLF) and approved the long-term principle of assistance—an important change of emphasis in the foreign aid program—but without the requested borrowing authority. It cut DLF funds proposed for fiscal 1958 from $500,000,000 to $300,000,000, which was inadequate for the requests for assistance that were piling up. Herter explained the policy in a Seattle speech, pointing out that loans, although on easier terms than commercial credit, would be for sound projects, justifiable on grounds of both humanitarianism and economic self-interest.

Thus he helped launch a program that could contribute to the welfare of less-developed peoples everywhere, and thereby hopefully to peaceful international relations.

Cultural relations were also one of Herter's responsibilities. He was personally interested in the problem and was disturbed over the unhappy state of these relations with other countries. As he had pointed out in an address of November, 1957, "cultural diplomacy" had become important after the Second World War. Technology had transformed the world into a community, he said; proximity had made urgent the need for understanding. It was all the more necessary because of the extensive use of cultural diplomacy by iron-curtain countries, especially the U.S.S.R.[14]

This program of the State Department was running into difficulties because of the proliferation of similar activities in other government agencies. At least ten Departments and nine independent agencies of the government, including thirty-five bureaus, engaged in international cultural relations—interchange of persons, knowledge, skills, in education, science, the arts, or technical training. There was a wide range of activities among agencies, but most important were the International Education Exchange Service (IES) of the Department of State, the ICA, and the U.S. Information Agency (USIA).[15]

The State Department had an immediate problem of coordinating IES (a Department unit) with the semi-autonomous ICA. The House and Senate Appropriations Committees had asked for coordination in 1955, and President D. L. Morrill of the University of Minnesota on request by the Department had made a report in May 1956, calling for more coordination of IES and ICA programs and an "upgrading" of exchange activity by raising the level of the cultural unit.

Herter became impatient with the Department's pace, and in November 1957, wrote a memorandum for the Secretary saying, "we have got to put order into these various programs," and called attention to the fact that Senator Fulbright and Congressman Frank Thompson had introduced bills calling for an Assistant Secretary for International Cultural Affairs. He said someone should be brought in as soon as possible. In the summer of 1958 he authorized grouping all the cultural activities in the Department of State in a Bureau under an assistant to the Secretary.[16] At a meeting in December, Herter as Acting Secretary introduced a new assistant, Robert H. Thayer, and joined with him in explaining tactfully the broad coordinative functions, as he put it, that the Department had in mind. Cultural relations work of the Department thus received new stature, though the rank of Assistant Secretary did not become available until 1961.

Herter's major continuing assignment as Under Secretary was chairmanship of the Operations Coordinating Board (OCB), an organ of the National Security Council that was becoming controversial. The OCB's principal responsibility was "to assist in integrating the execution of those national security policies assigned to it by the President." The Board included the Under Secretary of State, the Deputy Secretary of Defense, Director of Intelligence, Director of the U.S. Information Agency, Director of the International Cooperation Agency, and one or more representatives of the President. By standing invitation of the Board, the Under Secretary of the Treasury and the Chairman of the Atomic Energy Commission regularly attended the meetings.

The job of the OCB was to follow through on policy after recommendations of the National Security Council had received approval by the President. These policies took shape in the Planning Board of the Council composed of representatives of NSC members at the assistant secretary level. The Planning Board's proposals came mostly from participating agencies but sometimes from within the Board. From the Planning Board, proposals went to the NSC where they were thoroughly discussed, the President generally presiding and participating. From there the NSC policy paper went to responsible agencies and the OCB, designated by the President to assist agencies under the policy statement.[17]

The OCB worked primarily through interagency groups or committees. A former assistant to the President, Karl Harr, said there were forty-odd such committees. When the OCB determined the meaning of policy papers (not always easy) it fanned the papers out to the respective committees whose task was to transform them into programs.

There were also special reports on emergency situations, sometimes by regular OCB committees, sometimes by a task force. These special reports might cover any subject, from Antarctica to outer space.

At each weekly meeting the OCB dealt with several reports of the committees. When views differed, as was not unusual, there were efforts to secure further information in the hope of finding later a "practical solution" and "reasonable accommodation." Agreement in the OCB was then reported to the President at the NSC meeting.[18]

The OCB was empowered to inspect action taken by the agencies, prod working committees to action, and call for interim reports. Relations were sometimes strained between the OCB and an agency, e.g., when the OCB thought the agency not sufficiently out-giving. The State Department at times regarded the OCB as a sort of nursemaid looking over its shoulder.[19]

Herter had a warm welcome as chairman of OCB. His good nature and personal diplomacy established an environment for getting work done.[20] This contrasted with the handling of OCB business by his State Department predecessor Herbert Hoover, Jr., who apparently did not like the OCB, and regarded its operations as interference in the Department's affairs. Herter, as chairman, permitted expression of points of view and often appeared, especially in earlier months, to regard discussions as a sort of educational process. There was criticism because of alleged overgenerosity in discussion, and for being "too much of a gentleman." On occasion he knew how to tell a person off, as when a Defense official's proposal, if adopted, would have affected the authority of an ambassador, or when a White House representative tried to infringe on the prerogative of the chairman.[21]

Although Herter regarded the OCB as an expensive exercise in time and personnel, and was not happy about "the damned lot of papers" turned out, he approved unqualifiedly of the weekly Board luncheons which were attended by top representatives of the respective agencies, along with the special assistant to the President for national security affairs, and the executive officer of the OCB. The discussions were informal and Herter found them most useful for keeping in touch with other agencies on matters of common interest, from psychological warfare to moon shots, or whatever.

In a meeting with Senator Henry M. Jackson's subcommittee on National Policy Machinery, Herter as Secretary of State looked back on his chairmanship of the OCB and said his feeling as to the utility of the Board varied a great deal. "At times you felt that you were being very useful. At other times you felt you were fanning the air or spending a lot of time reviewing minutiae." While lauding the weekly luncheons as "extraordinarily useful," he said that "when you get into the formal sessions, you again apply yourself to paper work. Sometimes you get yourself so bogged down in the editing of a word or a sentence that you say, 'My God, why am I spending so much time on this?' Other times pretty important decisions are made and made very quickly." But he added: "If it were not for the OCB, you would have to have something similar. That is always the answer you come up with."

The Kennedy Administration abolished the OCB. Presidential Assistant McGeorge Bundy explained that this act was "not in any sense a downgrading of the tasks of coordination and followup." It was rather, he said, "a move to eliminate an instrument that does not match the style of operation and coordination of the current administration." The decisive difficulty with OCB, he said, was that without unanimity in the Board it had no authority. The new Administration did not conceive of operational coordination as "a task for a large committee in which no one man has authority." By implication there would be more reliance on the Department of State. But an agreed method of coordinating foreign policy among the agencies did not emerge.

3

Herter's activities as Under Secretary included a mission to Southeast Asia, August 23 to September 22, 1957, as U.S. representative to celebrate the independence of the new Malayan Federation. This gave him an opportunity not only to hail that country's new-found freedom, but also to visit and take soundings in other capitals in the Far East—Manila, Saigon, Rangoon, Bangkok, Hong Kong, Taipei, Seoul and Tokyo, thereby enriching his background for future responsibilities.[22] He returned with sobering impressions regarding deteriorating conditions and a feeling that the Far East might require considerable sacrifice on the part of the United States. If Southeast Asia should go, he said, Japan would face an extraordinarily strong adversary.

By Departmental regulations, Herter, as Under Secretary, had responsibility for the Science Adviser's office, created in 1951. That office had not been given much attention until the sensational orbiting of the Soviet sputniks in 1957 sent a shiver through policy makers, causing the President to set up a new office of Assistant to the President for Science and Technology, and spurring activity in the State Department. Herter filled the then vacant post of Science Adviser and announced that the work of that official would be "oriented more closely than before to the objectives of the Department and the Foreign Service," also that Science Attachés would be assigned to leading U.S. embassies in the near future. On a strong budgetary plea he secured additional funds and gave the Science Adviser's function new life. But it was difficult to fill top jobs, as these called scientists away from their normal work and required them to pull into a constructive program varied elements in their respective fields of service. The Science program became indispensable, but appointment problems continued even after the Director gained Assistant Secretary rank, as illustrated by the prolonged vacancy in the Directorship following Ragnar Rollefson's resignation in September 1964.

According to the State Department Manual of 1957, Herter, as Under Secretary, was to serve as Deputy to the Secretary of State and as Acting Secretary during the Secretary's absences, also to advise and assist the Secretary "in the formulation, determination and implementation of U.S. foreign policy." Secretary Dulles, while on duty in the Department, never used Herter's services fully in the formulation, determination and implementation of policy, but after the first year Herter felt increasingly that his relationship approximated that of the Secretary's *alter ego*.

His varied assignments and his experience as Acting Secretary in Dulles' absences greatly strengthened his qualification to take full responsibility. In thirty-eight periods as Acting Secretary he served a total of 244 days, some of them in times of serious crisis. In one of these, during the midsummer Lebanon flareup in 1958, he peremptorily stopped the army from shipping to Lebanon from a U.S. arsenal in Germany guns with "tactical" nuclear warheads, which he regarded as too dangerous a venture. The most important of his "acting" services was the 66-day period preceding Secretary Dulles' resignation on April 15 during his last illness. Thus Herter was thoroughly prepared to take over full responsibility for the arduous duties of Secretary of State.

# CHAPTER THREE

## THE ROAD TO GENEVA, 1959

THE TRANSITION from Under Secretary to Secretary was not easy for Herter. He replaced a man who for six years had played a dominating role in American foreign policy and was viewed by the President as his closest friend and confidant. It was hard for Eisenhower to think of a successor and he waited too long for serious consideration of a replacement. On Dulles' resignation, the President asked Herter for a report on his physical condition, and to inquiring newsmen, who had taken for granted Herter's immediate appointment as Secretary, he said that other qualified persons were also under consideration. Herter's physical difficulty had been previously diagnosed as osteoarthritis, a postural problem at the base of his spine, probably caused by growing too fast. It was not a physical disease but a wear-and-tear problem, and his physical report for the President was favorable. After several days of embarrassing delay, the appointment was made. Unanimous confirmation by the Senate came in short order, the action by Committee and the full Senate taking only four and a half hours. Herter was then ready to tackle pending foreign-policy problems with appropriate authority.

The most difficult and frustrating problem of Herter's secretaryship was the East-West conflict which confronted him when he took over full responsibility for the Department and stayed with him during most of his tenure. He had, of course, been involved in that problem as Acting Secretary since early February, during which time he had kept in touch with ailing Secretary Dulles. It was a period in which American policy appeared hesitating and uncertain owing largely to the absence of firmly established command at the Department. In late April, when Herter became Secretary, events were approaching a crisis.

The problem dated back to Premier Khrushchev's demands of the previous November that the Western Allies get out of Berlin within six months. The Soviet Union had sought a Berlin solution by a variety of proposals, any of which would have strengthened the communist position in Central and Eastern Europe. Lying 110 miles inside the Soviet East German zone, Berlin since the end of the Second World War had been under occupation by the four major victors, each in its agreed sector. Relative calm had prevailed there since the blockade ended in 1949, thanks to the extraordinary work of the Allied airlift. Then Khrushchev in a Moscow speech of November 10, 1958, announced that the time had come for the end of the city's four-power occupation and for a peace treaty with Germany, adding that the U.S.S.R. intended to hand over its powers to the "sovereign German Democratic Republic" (GDR).

The speech was disturbing but left the Western powers guessing as to its significance, since it was vague as to the timing and manner of reaching its objectives.

German Ambassador Wilhelm Grewe expressed his government's deep concern to Acting Secretary Herter who assured him we were watching the situation. Herter advised the President that Soviet unilateral abrogation of specific quadripartite agreements on Berlin was unacceptable, and said the Department was considering tripartite reaffirmation of Western rights, though we ought to avoid overdramatizing the situation. Herter discussed the matter with the President who said humorously he instinctively felt inclined to state that if the Russians wanted war over Berlin they could have it, but the two men agreed that any statement should await developments.

In long notes of November 27 to the three Western powers Khrushchev elaborated and made more specific his demands of November 10. He denounced the occupation as "abnormal" and "dangerous," a threat to the German Democratic Republic. The Western powers, he charged, had violated the Potsdam Agreement (1945), hence the occupation agreements were "null and void" and rights of the Western Allies as "privileged occupiers" had expired. West Berlin, a "dangerous source of international tension," would be transformed into a demilitarized "free city" and be able to choose its way of life, though the "natural solution" would be to join the GDR. At the end of six months the GDR would exercise sovereign rights over all Western access to Berlin. The Soviet Government would negotiate with the other three occupying powers on granting West Berlin the status of a demilitarized "free city," and the unification of Germany should come about by federating the GDR and the Federal Republic of Germany (FRG), which would ensure a gradual merger of the two German states.

Unless the Western powers accepted this proposal in six months the U.S.S.R. would consider itself free of its obligations to them regarding Berlin.[1]

The Soviet challenge came when the Western powers were troubled by internal crises and inter-Allied disagreements such as De Gaulle's nationalistic threats to the North Atlantic Treaty Organization and the conflict between advocates of a wide free-trade area in Europe and signatories of the more exclusive six-nation Common Market. Furthermore, the Western powers were known not to be equally firm in their positions regarding Soviet demands. Khrushchev apparently hoped to find weak spots in the Western lineup through which he could push to his objective.

If the Soviet gambit should succeed, the result would be a sensational triumph for the U.S.S.R. Bringing West Germany into a confederation with Communist East Germany would challenge the entire Western position in Europe. Out of these November 1958, developments flowed a stream of events that led to nine weeks of futile negotiation at a Geneva conference in mid-1959 and ultimately to a spectacularly aborted summit meeting in 1960.

In similar notes of December 31, 1958, to the Soviet Union, the three Allies pointed out the legal and historical fallacies in the Soviet claims, while insisting on their rights and responsibilities in West Berlin. They refused to embark on discussions under menace of an ultimatum, but said they would enter discussions at any time in a framework that included all aspects of the German question, thus tying Berlin in with the reunification of Germany.

The Soviet strategy was to mix hard words with an appearance of sweet reasonableness, combining promises and threats. Typical was Foreign Minister Andrei Gromyko's statement before the Supreme Soviet on December 25, 1958, that his government was "not issuing an ultimatum," but if the Allies insisted on keeping their troops in Berlin "by force if necessary," they would be threatening a "big war."

Another move in Soviet strategy was the January 1959, visit to the United States of Anastas I. Mikoyan, First Deputy Premier of the U.S.S.R. The trip was ostensibly (as per his visa request) to confer with Ambassador Mikhail Menshikov, but he made known his willingness to talk with top government officials. In a 7,000-mile tour across the country the Soviet emissary talked with all and sundry and repeatedly sounded the tocsin of "peace" between our two countries. He brushed off occasional hostile demonstrations with a shrug or a quip, presented himself as a messenger of peace and good will, and generally made a good impression. But discussions with government officials revealed no change in Soviet policy. Nor did an hour with the President before Mikoyan's departure alter this conclusion. The Allies were still on notice to get out of West Berlin by May 27, and if they did not, or were not negotiating to do so, the U.S.S.R. would declare West Berlin a "free city" and turn over control of all access routes to the East German Communist regime.

A Soviet reply of January 10, 1959, to the allied note of December 31 came midway in Mikoyan's visit and underlined heavily the views expressed by him. Annexed to the note was a draft peace treaty with

Germany covering the two Germanys (GDR and FRG): Both would be neutral and practically disarmed "states" united in a "confederation," with West Berlin evacuated by Western troops and converted into a "free city" until the reunification of Germany. The note said the Soviet Union also aimed to convoke within two months a peace conference of all twenty-eight powers engaged in the recent war against Germany, but would be willing to exchange opinions with the Western powers on the treaty before calling the peace conference.[2]

As for German reunification, this was said to be a matter for the two German "states." The note also excluded European security from consideration with the Berlin problem, as the latter presumably required special discussion. The Soviet proposal of a peace conference was clearly a maneuver to force the Western Allies to agree to discussions on Berlin. But the Allies felt they could not discuss the termination of their rights and responsibilities in West Berlin except in terms of a reunified Germany with Berlin as its capital. Although the Allies were united in claiming rights and responsibilities in West Berlin, their views differed as to ways and means, and even as to whether they should go to a conference at all. Therefore Secretary Dulles in early February 1959, made a hasty flying trip to London, Paris and Bonn—his last such effort. It proved impossible in February for the Allies to reach agreement on counterproposals, but they did agree that a conference with the Soviet Union was inevitable, though at first the French objected to a conference before May 27.

In almost identical notes the Allies replied to the

Soviets on February 16, shortly after Herter took over as Acting Secretary. They reaffirmed their right to maintain "their communications with West Berlin." Without going into details, they offered to participate in a conference of foreign ministers to "deal with the problem of Germany in all its aspects and implications" at a time and place to be agreed upon through diplomatic channels.[3]

Prime Minister Harold Macmillan then went on a twelve-day exploratory trip to the U.S.S.R., hoping as he told the House of Commons (February 19) to feel out the situation. The trip caused anxiety in other European quarters, especially in Bonn where Macmillan's motives were under some suspicion. His discussions did not yield what either the guest or host desired. He found, in Khrushchev's own words, that there was no room for maneuver.

After his return from Moscow, Macmillan touched base in Paris and Bonn and then, responding to President Eisenhower's earlier request, flew to the United States, arriving March 19. The Beaverbrook press said he was "assuming the leadership of the West at a moment when no other statesman is available and ready to do so."[4] Macmillan was greatly concerned that the need for a summit be recognized, in order to avoid war. The President remarked that we could not escape war by surrendering on the installment plan. He would not be dragooned into a summit meeting. Herter pointed out that if the foreign ministers meeting broke up we would obviously consider all remaining possibilities, including a summit meeting which might be held in the U.N. Security Council.

Macmillan feelingly observed that a summit meeting was probably the most fateful decision he would ever have to take. Though the President made no formal commitment, there was a general presumption of a summit in the summer. At a tea party given for him by Vice President Nixon, Macmillan again spoke out, saying a summit conference should follow, whether or not the foreign ministers conference was a success. He could not go to the Queen and ask her to approve the evacuation of millions, many of them children, to far places of the Commonwealth, until he had "exhausted every other possibility."[5]

The conference included discussion of the Soviet note of March 2 which reluctantly accepted the Allied proposal for an East-West conference on the foreign ministers level. Herter had a session with Foreign Minister Selwyn Lloyd on a matter of concern to the British—a new international status for the Allied occupation of West Berlin with a view to putting the occupation on a treaty or contract basis rather than conquest. But Herter saw no prospect of getting agreement on a new title that would be as good as the existing one based on conquest and on agreements during and after the war. He thought that any tampering with existing rights, if Soviet consent was involved, could only result in weakening them.

The consummation of the proposals for East-West negotiation came with exchanges agreeing on the time, place and agenda of the conference on the foreign ministers level. In almost identical notes of March 26 the three Western Allies proposed to meet on May 11 at Geneva "to consider questions relating to Germany, including a peace treaty with Germany and the question of Berlin."[6] The Soviet Government approved this on March 30.[7] The four East-West powers agreed also to admit East and West German "advisers," but the Western Allies proposed to limit conference members to the four powers "responsible for Germany," thus rejecting the Soviet proposal to include Poland and Czechoslovakia. The Soviet Government reserved this question for the conference.

The Allied and the Soviet notes differed as to the implications of the foreign ministers conference for the summit meeting. The Allied notes affirmed that the summit meeting hinged on the results of the foreign ministers conference, while the Soviet reply referred to agreement on "a foreign ministers conference and a summit meeting," thus reading the summit meeting into the agreement. The difference did not seem to justify further exchanges. Eisenhower or De Gaulle could still call for a show of "progress" in the foreign ministers conference, and Macmillan could insist on a summit regardless of results.

It remained for the Western allies to coordinate their positions before May 11. The Soviet Union had no such problem, though it did call a formal meeting of bloc members shortly before May 11. Khrushchev continued to make pronouncements regarding the Soviet position, emphasizing that, though there was no ultimatum, if the Allies did not agree to Soviet proposals regarding West Berlin and the peace treaties with the two Germanys, the Soviets would make a peace treaty wtih the GDR which would give it sovereign control of the territory and void Allied rights in West Berlin. On occasion he suggested that circumstances might justify a delay of a month or two in taking such action.

Little time remained for the Allies before May 11. The regular meeting of NATO powers in Washington early in April—the tenth anniversary of NATO—made possible a preliminary meeting of Britain, France, the Federal Republic (FRG), and the United States, and discussion by all NATO members. It was Acting Secretary Herter's responsibility to guide discussions in both these meetings.

There was general agreement among the Four on certain policies: (1) the Berlin problem should be settled within the broader German problem involving reunification of Germany through free elections; (2) rights of occupying Berlin militarily and of access to Berlin should be maintained; and (3) in any settlement Germany should not be neutralized by being denied the right of choosing whether to belong to NATO. The Four were not always in agreement. Herter was willing to face the final alternative of force. He supported a "package" presentation of the Western case at the East-West conference, including disarmament and European security along with German reunification. He also favored having available a draft peace treaty with Germany, either in principles or detail, for the Soviets had presented a draft of such a treaty.

Discussion of East-West problems continued in the NATO Ministerial Council following the quadripartite conferences. The main business was the Berlin crisis, and Lloyd reported on the quadripartite discussions. Herter reported that Soviet policy during the previous year showed surface shifts and fluctuations, with no change of objectives. It followed the familiar communist tactics of probing weaknesses in the free world—witness the Taiwan Straits, Iraq, Iran, Lebanon, Jordan, and then Berlin. NATO's first ten years, he said, had shown that firmness was the safest course. After two days of discussion the Council members agreed on maintenance of Western occupation rights to guarantee freedom of West Berlin, German reunification based on free elections (though these need not be the first step), rejection of neutralization, and the continued presence of United States, United Kingdom and Canadian troops in Europe.

Some differences remained as to strategy and tactics, but none on Allied rights in West Berlin. The outspoken Council chairman, Paul-Henri Spaak, expressed doubt whether the Soviets would ever permit free elections in Germany. Herter was concerned over German reunification. German proposals were rather negative and admittedly influenced by concern that communist forces in East Germany, with left-wing elements in West Germany, might subvert West Germany.

Developments on both sides of the Iron Curtain raised the question whether a basis existed for the upcoming East-West conference in Geneva. Preparations seemed to offer slight chance for the free and communist worlds to agree. How could the Allies avoid a general war without selling West Berliners down the river? How could the Soviet Government yield on its oft-repeated insistence on making West Berlin a demilitarized "free city" or otherwise making a separate treaty with the GDR which would jeopardize the already tenuous communications lifeline with West Berlin? Was there any magic that would produce agreement between communist and Western spokesmen?[8] The question remained whether both sides could make concessions for a peace that would endure until the passage of time worked some miracle.

Herter was not optimistic. He informed the President on April 16 that the chance of agreeing with the Soviets on a German settlement in the near future was practically nil. The most we could hope for was an improvement in our own position. Our proposals must appeal to public opinion and be convincing as to our readiness to negotiate. The proposals should tie into one package progress toward German reunification and measures for European security, with no separable elements except possibly Berlin. He said our Allies generally agreed, though there were some differences. The French and Germans were firm on West Berlin, but the British, rather than face hostilities, might accept arrangements that would weaken our position. The Germans were indecisive about reunification. The French opposed any U.N. participation in the Berlin problem and were dubious about including security and disarmament proposals with those on German reunification.

The United States program, he said, envisaged a phased approach, through four stages, to German reunification and, concomitantly, a four-stage approach to European security, with disarmament provisions dependent on effective inspection. In the fourth stage the all-German government would negotiate a general peace treaty. Berlin would be integrated with Germany through free elections under supervision of the U.N.

Herter did not expect serious negotiations in the May meeting, thinking of it largely as a public relations exercise which would attempt to formulate a summit agenda in terms the Soviets would find difficult to reject. The Western powers should offer their plan as an inseparable package and insist that German reunification was a necessary basis for a peace treaty and for the solution of the Berlin problem.

Herter's pessimism seemed justified by events on the other side of the Iron Curtain. A Soviet note of April 4 denounced the United States, charging it with trying to scuttle the East-West talks by arming Germany with nuclear weapons and by high-level airplane flights to Berlin—above 10,000 feet—which it claimed violated agreed conditions. These charges the United States denied.[9] The Warsaw meeting of the Soviet bloc powers (April 27-29) called for a "free city" in West Berlin and a German peace treaty. It condemned "rearming of Germany" with nuclear weapons (actually these were under United States control), and denounced a package proposal, insisting on limiting talks to Berlin and a peace treaty with Germany. This was the familiar Soviet formula. Relations with the Soviets were further aggravated because the Geneva negotiations on a nuclear test ban had bogged down owing to Soviet refusal to permit inspection and control.

The Allies met once more, in Paris (April 29-May

1). Herter led the American delegation, carrying full responsibility as Secretary of State, a title that had supplanted "Acting Secretary" five days before his departure. As the *Herald Tribune* put it, he was beginning the Paris talks "with the full confidence of the American people."

Before the talks he had a conference with De Gaulle who was skeptical, as was Herter, of accomplishment by the foreign ministers conference. De Gaulle thought Khrushchev's objective was to divide the Allies and that, though the package plan had its public appeal, Khrushchev would not accept it. The Oder-Neisse boundary, he said, should stand; a German settlement was not possible—it was not an urgent matter —and the Allies should deal in generalities. He opposed neutralization of Germany as he thought this would weaken the Atlantic Alliance. When Herter asked about NATO, he said this would be weakened also, but he showed preference for the Atlantic Alliance which he distinguished from NATO. He opposed a summit meeting if the foreign ministers meeting accomplished nothing. Herter said a *modus vivendi* for Berlin was the minimum that could justify a summit meeting.

In formal discussion Herter stressed the need for unanimity along the lines of the American proposals, and was able to report to the President on April 30 that the meeting had been highly successful, that such difficulties as existed were resolved. He added that some difficulties (*e.g.*, with the British) had been swept under the rug but were likely to appear at Geneva.

On his return he reported to the President, met the

Senate Foreign Relations Committee for two hours, consulted his former chief, ex-Secretary Dulles, and others, and then turned to his proximate departure for the Geneva East-West conference to determine the fate of the decisions reached at Paris, especially the so-called package plan. This left little time for other Department problems. Although gratified over Allied unity on the package plan at Paris, he could scarcely hope for acceptance by the Soviets since Khrushchev and other Soviet leaders already had rejected it. But the package provided a good way to present the Western case. There was an informal understanding that the Berlin problem might have to come out of the package for separate treatment. To refuse to discuss it apart from reunification and European security would be hazardous in view of Soviet threats and Berlin's vulnerability. At least a *modus vivendi* for some years seemed necessary.

There was at that stage a conflict of "packages." The Warsaw Pact package called for a "free city" in West Berlin and peace treaties with East and West Germany, but separating the problems of Berlin and the German peace treaties from those of reunification and European security. The Western package called for phased reunification of Germany in freedom, accompanied by phased European security based on limitation of armaments, with Berlin ultimately becoming the capital of reunited Germany. The two programs were incompatible.

In a nationwide television and radio address on May 7—his first report as Secretary of State—Herter warned Americans not to expect quick agreement.

He said he was not going to Geneva with great expectations. The heart of Western policy was a Germany "reunited in freedom, a security system linked with arrangements for arms control, and in the interim a free and secure Berlin." The President and he hoped the Geneva Conference, by some promise of advancing peace, would justify holding a summit conference. We would uphold our rights in Berlin, he said, but would remain willing to negotiate in good faith.

# CHAPTER FOUR

## GENEVA CARROUSEL: I

THE GENEVA CONFERENCE did not immediately get down to business. Skirmishes, pressed by the Soviet delegation for prestige, occupied the first two days and much of the third. They involved tables, chairs, the German language, the status of East and West German delegations, and representation of Poland and Czechoslovakia. Gromyko wanted the GDR and FRG delegates seated on an equal footing at the table with the Big Four ministers, and a round table to accommodate this arrangement (though he would have compromised on a horseshoe table). His motive was to win diplomatic status—in effect, recognition—for the GDR. The Western Allies wanted a square table, one side for each major delegation, and two separate square tables for the East and West German delegations. They rejected any arrangement, as Lloyd told Gromyko, remotely connected with recognition of East Germany.[1] Herter said he would not sit at a table with the East Germans, whatever its shape. The Big Four ministers compromised on a round table and, for the two German delegations, two rectangular tables. The latter were to be placed six pencil-widths from the main table. German advisers were to speak only if there was no objection from regular delegations, though it was informally understood that such objection would be made only to prevent abuse.

But how many chairs for each German delegation? Gromyko insisted on the same number as for the major delegations—ten. Western ministers proposed three or four. The Swiss secretariat chief, Palthey, placed six chairs as a compromise, and when Gromyko objected violently Palthey threatened to take them all away. Gromyko yielded "for the time being."

Playing up to the two German delegations, Gromyko proposed to include German as one of the languages in which conference documents should be issued. This move was blocked by Western opposition.

Following similar tactics, Gromyko put on a two-day propaganda campaign to seat Polish and Czechoslovak delegations in the conference, emphasizing the heavy suffering of these countries during the war. Having made his ploy, he yielded to the West's refusal to give Poland and Czechoslovakia preference over other German neighbors who had also suffered heavily during the war and the West's insistence that the conference, limited to the four major powers responsible for Germany, should get on with its business.

At last Herter made the first speech on substantive business. He said the conference was a continuation of the 1955 foreign ministers meeting which had led to such disappointments. It could be a prelude to the summit meeting if it made progress, and it could go down in history as an exchange of propaganda or a serious attempt to reach a meeting of minds.

It remained for each side to present its plan in detail, and Herter led off next day with the Western peace plan (informally called the Herter Plan). Its aim was to carry out mandates of the 1955 summit conference regarding German reunification and European security. The Western plan rested on conviction, he said, that the Berlin problem could be solved only in the context of a reunified Germany, and that a reunified Germany would be acceptable only in an integrated European security system in which armaments and armed forces were limited. There were three main phases: (1) East and West Berlin would be united by free elections and the city's freedom guaranteed by the Big Four "until Berlin becomes the capital of a reunited Germany." (2) A mixed commission of twenty-five members from West Germany and ten from East Germany would be "set up immediately to draft an electoral law for all-German elections" and facilitate contacts between East and West Germany. A three-fourths vote would be required for action by the commission, thus giving East Germans a veto. (3) Free elections within thirty months would take place for an all-German government capable of negotiating a peace treaty. The plan envisaged step-by-step measures for European security and general limitation of armament, including a mutually-agreed security zone in Europe, prohibition of atomic, biological and chemical warfare in all Germany (West Germany had taken this pledge in 1954) and in certain Eastern European countries, and reduction of over-all ground forces of the four powers. Inspection and control would be required in all cases. The all-German government would be free to decide whether it would belong to NATO or to the Warsaw Pact, or to no alliance at all.

Next day Gromyko tabled the Soviet plan which

was like that of January 10. He rejected the Herter proposals out of hand, saying they lumped together complicated questions. The Western plan would produce a deadlock. Therefore the Soviet plan must be the basis of discussion. Setting up an all-German government would take too long. Peace should be signed with the "two German states" or with the German confederation if it could be formed in time. The Soviet proposal, he said, would facilitate German reunification by promoting rapprochement between the FRG and GDR. All foreign troops would withdraw behind their national frontiers, and both East and West Germany would withdraw from existing alliances and enter no new alliances that did not include all four of the negotiating East-West powers. The peace treaty would solve the Berlin problem, he said, by ending the quadripartite agreements as well as the occupation regime in West Berlin, which would become a demilitarized "free city" pending reunification of Germany.[2]

At the end of the first week, reports from conference circles indicated that few, if any, informed persons expected an agreed solution of the German problem. Attitudes varied from skepticism to cynicism. The "spirit of Geneva" of 1959 was rated as "nine-tenths cynicism and one-tenth hope," a feeling not confined to the horde of newsmen—nearly 1,200 of whom had flocked to the conference—but shared by the Western foreign ministers.[3]

Having gotten past the initial Soviet harassing tactic and presentation of the packages, the parties, during the ensuing week, engaged in a hard-hitting, repetitious and often sharply-spoken give-and-take in justification of their programs. The Western Allies reaffirmed adherence to their package and rejected reports that they would accept an "interim settlement" of the Berlin problem—though they later would have been happy to do so.[4]

The conference room was not the place for speeches to win any concessions, as they were chiefly propaganda exercises. Language in formal sessions sometimes became exasperating, though in general the ministers managed to keep statements within diplomatic bounds. Gromyko's words exceeded the diplomatic niceties on May 21 when he charged NATO with preparing aggressive war and described West Germany as rearming for revenge. Herter warned Gromyko somewhat acidly that he must abandon "accusation and innuendo" lest they lead to "very serious tensions."

It was in bilateral or other discussions at their villas that the delegates sought concessions. Indeed, after dressing Gromyko down on May 21, Herter had him to dinner that evening with Lloyd and Couve de Murville. The dinner was a social success but a diplomatic flop. Herter sat next to Gromyko on a "love seat," but this had no helpful consequences.

Though Herter could not report progress on conference matters, his days were busy, as illustrated by his schedule on that day—May 21, 1959. He had breakfast in bed, read the *Journal de Genève*, and was down at the U.S. Consulate by 8:45. Thereafter:

>     9:00- 9:30—read cables from Washington
>     9:30-10:10—Staff meeting with delegation

10:30-11:00—Conference with David Bruce,
                  Ambassador to Bonn
11:30-12:00—Conference with Loftus Becker,
                  Department Legal Adviser
12:15-12:45—Appointment with Von Brentano
1:00- 2:15—Lunch with Secretary of Defense
                  McElroy, Assistant Secretary of
                  Defense John Irwin, and Assistant
                  Secretary of State Livingston T.
                  Merchant
3:00- 3:15—Conference with Foreign Secretary
                  Lloyd at the Palais des Nations
3:30- 6:38—Tenth session of conference
7:45-11:00—Dinner with the foreign ministers[5]

By the end of the second week the conference had reached a stalemate. Neither side was disposed to compromise. Gromyko held to the position that there could be no German reunification without first a peace treaty, and the Allies insisted that reunification must precede a peace treaty. Herter reported to the President that they had reached a stage where they were likely to sharpen differences rather than narrow them. In plenary sessions it was becoming hard to know what to talk about, but the plenary sessions might have to be kept going because of the German delegations, as these would be left out of restricted sessions. The Secretary thought the conference might last six or eight weeks.

At the end of two weeks there was no agreed basis for negotiation.

The plenary session of May 25 added to the confusion as Gromyko, after paying respects to John Foster Dulles whose death had been announced, engaged in a sharp interchange with Herter in which the latter again had to rebuke him "for resurrecting old fears and bygone hatreds" and trying to confuse their deliberations with charges of motives of another period by depicting the German Federal Government as a revanchist and militaristic regime intent on a third world war.

The time had come for modification of procedure, and the four ministers, before leaving for Washington to attend the obsequies for Mr. Dulles, decided (on Herter's suggestion, later confirmed by Gromyko) that on their return they would meet in secret session.[6] This decision was difficult, as no one wanted responsibility for proposing it.

While they were in Washington the four foreign ministers met with President Eisenhower for half an hour in general discussion, during which the President added his authority to the admonition that progress would be essential to justify a summit meeting. The four ministers traveled together on the return journey, which afforded them an opportunity to initiate a series of private discussions of substantive conference problems. Eisenhower humorously had threatened to instruct them to stay aloft until they reached some decisions. In the relatively relaxed, certainly undisturbed, atmosphere of the flight Herter hosted a unique East-West discussion on West Berlin. On his request Gromyko led off with a review of the Soviet Union's dissatisfaction with the West Berlin situation. There was no meeting of minds, though some of his remarks seemed to indicate a Soviet disposition to compromise. The Western ministers could not agree to surrender rights in West Berlin before Germany was unified, nor could they accept Gromyko's refusal to apply to all Berlin the controls proposed by him. In reporting to the President, Herter noted some satisfaction in the friendly tone of the discussion.

The Washington interlude had marked the passing of a notable personage, and a historical moment. May 27 witnessed the last rites for Dulles, and signaled the end of the six-month "ultimatum" imposed by Khrushchev the previous November. During these weeks Herter was in a difficult position. His style was markedly different from that of his predecessor. As the commentator Drew Middleton put it, he walked warily where Dulles would have plunged ahead. His task was different from that of 1955, before "the French renaissance, Britain's venturesome diplomacy and West Germany's vigorous and constant affirmation of rights." The stakes were much higher than in 1955. But the crucial "ultimatum" date passed without any signs of drastic Soviet action.

The discussions of the three weeks following the return to Geneva went round and round, with no prospect for a firm settlement. Herter's only hope, shared by some of his Western colleagues, was for a temporary arrangement—a *modus vivendi*—to guarantee Western rights in Berlin pending reunification of Germany. Was even this possible? The views of the two sides on the reunification process differed sharply. The West proposed reunification by free elections in two and a half years. The U.S.S.R. insisted on a much faster pace, under Soviet pressure when necessary. In a series of private meetings, Herter and his colleagues, sought a *modus vivendi* to preserve Western rights in West Berlin, whatever the time or method of reunification. In the Soviet view Western rights, if any, were very transient. Gromyko aimed to reduce the Western occupation of West Berlin, even during the interim period, to merely "symbolic" status by a drastic cut in the West's occupying forces and the introduction of Soviet troops. Thus West Berlin (not greater Berlin) would become a "free city" pending reunification. To Herter's inquiry as to the status of Western rights if reunification should take several years, Gromyko would say nothing, positively or negatively. In a private meeting of June 6, Herter and his colleagues concentrated on getting a "yes" or "no" from Gromyko as to rights in West Berlin. This merely led to Gromyko's saying he favored not mentioning rights at all. Herter later said the effort to smoke out Gromyko on "rights" involved one of the strangest catechisms he had seen. There were long pauses between questions and answers. Each of the Allied ministers in turn would say, "well then, the implication of what you say is 'so and so'." Then Gromyko would say "that is your interpretation." Then Herter would say: "Is it a correct interpretation?" and Gromyko would reply: "I won't say yes and I won't say no."[7]

Herter reported on June 8 that the conference was in crisis. The French regarded it as a dead end and wanted to adjourn until mid-July. The British thought the situation made an early summit conference all the more desirable.

The crisis was aggravated on June 9 when Gromyko in a private meeting made the Soviets' most dramatic proposals (repeated in the plenary on the 10th): provisional recognition for one year only of certain Western occupation rights in West Berlin; (2) an all-German committee based on parity between the two Germanys (17,000,000 in the GDR and 45,000,000 in the FRG) to work out problems of reunification to be completed in one year (the West Berlin regime, practically demilitarized, would become a shadow); (3) Western armed forces to be reduced to token contingents, and West Berlin to have the status of a demilitarized free city under 4-power supervision.

Herter said this proposal merely postponed the May 27 deadline one year from the beginning of the all-German committee's work, and he stressed the danger of signing an agreement with the Soviets without reference to rights in Berlin. A two-hour talk with Gromyko by Herter, accompanied by Merchant, got nowhere.

The hope for a *modus vivendi* had vanished, but Herter and his colleagues kept talking, if only to determine "who is going to put the monkey on whose back."[8]

In a final effort the Allies offered limited concessions, including a top limit on Western troops in Berlin. Gromyko offered to extend the one-year "provisional regime"—the *modus vivendi*—to a year and a half. Both gestures were futile, and by common consent the first round of Geneva discussions ended on June 20 with a decision to recess to July 13.[9]

At the final plenary session on June 20, Gromyko,

chairman by rotation, in a ten-minute meeting announced the decision to recess and read a bland communiqué which referred to "a broader exchange of views" and to the belief of the ministers that further negotiations were necessary. On returning to the United States, Herter deplored the lack of progress. He said the conference revealed the Soviets' desire to absorb West Berlin and keep Germany divided until it could be brought under Soviet influence.[10]

Herter had emerged from the first round at Geneva with enhanced diplomatic stature. Slowly at first, but with increasing assurance he showed himself able not only to present the Western case but to counter Gromyko's sallies with finesse and vigor. He was reported to have won the plaudits of his colleagues and to have proved himself an able successor to Dulles.[11]

During the interim between the first and second phases of the conference there were some exchanges between London and Washington, arising out of Prime Minister Macmillan's apprehension of a possible failure of agreement at the resumed conference. One problem was the guarantee of Western rights. Could there be a delay for two and a half or even two years, Macmillan inquired, which Khrushchev probably would accept, rather than demanding that the interim run to reunification? A great deal, he thought, could happen during the interim. The Prime Minister said it was necessary to maintain a public posture in which he could rally the British people to resist a Russian attempt to impose its will by force, as it would not be easy to persuade the British people to go to war in defense of West Berlin. He would have to demonstrate that the Russians would not accept any proposition. President Eisenhower assured the Prime Minister that our government was working on these issues arising out of the conference and that Herter would be in touch with Lloyd. But the issues were so large and the time so short that it might not be possible to reach agreement in advance. It was finally agreed that the Western foreign ministers would work out positions at the conference after probing any possible change in the Soviet position.

There was little in the recess period to justify hope. Soviet First Deputy Premier Frol R. Kozlov arrived on June 28 to open a brilliant Soviet exhibition at the New York Coliseum, but his purpose in his sixteen-day visit obviously was to take a reading of the political and economic climate along the lines of Mikoyan's visit in January. He traveled across the country, lunched and dined with leading businessmen, and talked with political leaders, including the President, Vice President, Secretary Herter, and members of the Foreign Relations Committee.[12] In an extended conference with Herter, staff members, and Ambassador Menshikov, Kozlov followed closely the line taken by Gromyko at Geneva and repeatedly stated by Khrushchev, reaffirming their statements in every detail, including a denial of any Soviet ultimatum, while insisting that the occupation could no longer continue. Herter remarked afterwards that Kozlov's visit had done nothing to ease tensions.[13] The three-week recess likewise offered little promise of compromise in the second round at Geneva.

# CHAPTER FIVE

## GENEVA CARROUSEL: II

HERTER RETURNED to Geneva without much hope. No one believed an overall settlement was possible. The frustrations of the first round seemed to leave the Allies only the alternative of finding a formula referring the issues to the heads of government.[1]

In his opening remarks on July 13, 1959, at the first plenary session after the recess, Herter reviewed previous developments. During the first two weeks, he said, both sides had presented their general plans. Then there was a shift to the narrower question of reducing the "dangers inherent in the Berlin crisis which the Soviets had precipitated." The West had offered to limit troop levels, restrict propaganda and subversive activities in both parts of Berlin, and exclude atomic weapons and missiles from West Berlin, conditional to having free access to West Berlin and arrangements remaining in force until German reunification. The Soviet Union rejected these proposals, the Secretary said, and then on June 10 and 19 presented statements which repeated the previous drastic "free city" demands, along with urgent new proposals for an all-German committee, based on parity between East and West Germany, to prepare for German reunification within a narrow time limit. "It declared that if the conditions were not satisfied it would conclude a peace treaty with the so-called GDR." The

Secretary urged the conference to return to private meetings.[2]

His colleagues, Couve de Murville and Lloyd, followed with supporting statements; but Gromyko came back with the hard line of June 10 and 19, proposing practically to wipe out Western occupation rights (military and political) in West Berlin, even in the interim period, insisting on an all-German committee representing equally the two Germanys, to prepare for reunification. He proposed that "new negotiations be held on the expiry of the time limit" if the all-German committee had not achieved "positive results." He added, menacingly, that the Soviets "preferred to settle the question on an agreed basis." Then followed the masterpiece of Soviet equivocation: "It is obvious that our proposal for subsequent negotiations by no means bears out those who would like to give a false picture of the Soviet Union's position in the Berlin question." The Allies spent many hours trying to find out just what Gromyko's statements meant.

Soviet policy on one point was clear: if the all-German committee achieved "positive results" in a year—meaning German reunification on terms agreeable to the Soviet Union—that would end the interim agreement and Western rights in West Berlin. If positive results were not achieved in that year, what would be the status of Allied occupation rights? Gromyko had talked of "new negotiations" when the interim agreement ended, but how long would the negotiations continue? Could the U.S.S.R. not break them off at its pleasure? What then? On these latter questions Gromyko was studiedly vague. Hence the big questions remained: how and when would the interim agreement end, and what would be the status of Allied rights when it ended?

Allied policy on these situations was clear: the terminal point of the interim agreement (*modus vivendi*) was German reunification by a free-election process. Until that event the Western Allies would maintain their occupation rights. The Soviet-proposed all-German committee seemed incompatible with these aims. Important unclarified questions remained to plague the Allies, who sought clear-cut answers, and got only vague and ambivalent statements, or no answers at all.

In the next plenary session, July 15, they charged that the proposal for an all-German committee revived the German problem as a whole, whereas both sides had abandoned discussion of that subject early in the conference after getting nowhere, and had decided to concentrate on the West Berlin problem. They said Gromyko was jeopardizing the entire negotiation.

Efforts by Herter, Lloyd and Couve de Murville to restore priority to West Berlin problems failed. Gromyko attacked with a restatement of the Soviet position on West Berlin, adding that the U.S.S.R. could never agree to perpetuate the occupation regime in West Berlin. He tied the all-German committee (based on GDR and FRG parity) to the other components of the Soviet West Berlin package, claiming that it would bring reunification by "Germans themselves," ignoring the 17,000,000 to 45,000,000 population disparity and rejecting the Allied proposal for free elections and majority vote.

Private sessions of the Big Four resumed on July 17, after an understanding that such meetings would be linked with luncheons or dinners, because Gromyko, seeking to curry favor with the German delegates, had publicly condemned private meetings which they did not attend. In fact, he was glad to continue private meetings. At this luncheon meeting Gromyko insisted that the Allies agree to the all-German committee for reunification as a condition for an interim agreement on West Berlin. He parried attempts to elicit the reason for linking the two questions. Gromyko was equally difficult on questions of Western rights in West Berlin. It was the old game of "twenty questions"—an ambiguous statement by Gromyko, then about twenty questions by the Allied ministers to clarify its meaning, leading to mystifying "clarification," followed by twenty more questions.[3] When Herter pressed for a clear answer regarding the West's interpretation of Gromyko's June 19 statement, Gromyko aphoristically remarked: "When many statements are made, many questions arise. Perhaps we should make fewer statements." Herter reported to the President that at least a dozen times, in answer to Allied requests for interpretation of his statements on Western rights, Gromyko would say either "now let us discuss the all-German question," or "the Soviet Union has made itself entirely clear on this matter." He was polite and almost genial, but the net impression was close to insulting. The Secretary said they appeared to be approaching the end of the conference.

The Allied ministers met the following morning and decided, as a counter to Gromyko's all-German committee, to propose that the Foreign Ministers Conference continue indefinitely—meeting from time to time—to discuss German problems, including contacts between the two Germanys.

Selwyn Lloyd presented this proposal to the Big Four private session on July 20. Gromyko reserved judgment, though he really rejected the plan, pointing to the difference between the Soviet and Western proposals for reunification and arguing, by inverted logic, that the Soviet plan—the all-German committee—left reunification to the German people, while the Western plan—free elections—did not. As the session was ending Herter asked Gromyko a "leading question": if East and West could not agree on all-German negotiations, and on an interim solution, did this imply that "we go home?" Gromyko's answer was merely "I did not say that."

At the plenary session the same day Herter pointed out that the Soviet all-German committee proposal was "totally unacceptable," as unity in freedom would not be its goal. The Western plan rested on free elections and majority rule but, he said, there was not the slightest hope that the all-German committee, owing to its unrepresentative composition, would call for an all-German government on the basis of free elections. He presented the Western proposals for continuing the Geneva Conference of Foreign Ministers. Gromyko spoke at length, restating the Soviet position, without mentioning Lloyd's remarks and without any new light or fresh hope.[4]

The West faced a serious dilemma: either abandon hope of getting an interim agreement or accept the all-German committee. The latter was "totally unacceptable" to the West, and anathema to the Bonn Government which recognized it as the Soviet design for reunifying the two Germanys, thus bringing intense pressure on the Federal Republic. In the Big Four private session of July 21 the Western Allies bore down on Gromyko with questions to determine whether there was any "give" in his position. Gromyko gave only evasive replies. Herter insisted that he and his colleagues were entitled to know whether the West had to accept the all-German committee in order to get agreement on the West Berlin problem. Had not Gromyko implied that no agreement was possible on Berlin problems without Western agreement on negotiations by the all-German committee? That, Gromyko said, was the Western interpretation for which he could not be responsible. Gromyko did agree to consider Berlin problems "in a parallel manner," but said they would have to return to all-German negotiations. Herter said that if such was Gromyko's position perhaps they should agree to disagree. When Lloyd pressed Gromyko to know whether this was also his position, Gromyko replied that this was the Secretary's comment, not his own.

Herter then reported to Washington that the conference apparently faced an impasse on the all-German committee and on West Berlin negotiations. He recommended that if the Soviets remained adamant the Allies should move rapidly to an orderly conclusion, though he recognized a complication involved in the trip which Vice President Nixon was soon to make to Russia.

In private discussions on the twenty-fourth there was a flicker of hope when Gromyko suddenly proposed to postpone discussion of the all-German committee and take up Berlin problems as cited in a speech by Lloyd on the twentieth. When Herter and Couve de Murville asked for assurance that Gromyko would not link Berlin problems with all-German negotiations, Gromyko without responding to the question, read a list of the Berlin problems posed by Selwyn Lloyd. Discussion of these soon showed the impossibility of agreement on the most crucial ones, especially the level of troops, which Gromyko insisted should be cut to his concept of a symbolic level of three to four thousand, while the West viewed the existing 11,000 to 12,000 as already symbolic. After a discussion punctuated by long silences and efforts at new starts, Herter reminded Gromyko that the purpose of the conference was to narrow differences.

During this period the British became increasingly concerned that the conference might break down and that the Soviets would either sign a peace treaty with the GDR or convoke a peace conference. They were anxious for the Foreign Ministers Conference to end in a summit meeting, because an agreement on Berlin seemed possible only at a summit, and because they thought the summit should come partly on Western initiative, without seeming to be a response to Soviet threats. They regarded the prospects for a satisfactory settlement on Berlin issues as favorable and thought that matters remaining in doubt could be left for the heads of government. Unless the summit meeting preceded the Khrushchev visit, of which Herter had informed the British and French, it was said that suspicions would be aroused among certain allies. Further, it would be impossible to avoid negotiations during the visit, and thus Khrushchev would gain his objective without paying a price. Therefore, the President should couple the Khrushchev visit with a summit meeting, preferably in the latter part of August.

Secretary Herter resented such proposals. He said they were particularly inappropriate in view of the British trip to Moscow the previous winter. He and the President were doing all they could to justify a summit meeting, but they could not detect any progress that would justify one. In fact, there was little prospect that the British hopes for an August summit meeting could be realized. Absence of any precise understanding as to what would justify going to the summit led the President and Secretary, after some consideration in the last week of July, to agree that a Soviet guarantee of Western rights in Berlin, along with a moratorium of at least two and a half years, would satisfy requirements. The thinking of the Western ministers, as well as of Gromyko, was inevitably influenced by knowledge of the anticipated Khrushchev visit to Washington, though there was no discussion of this in the sessions. Knowledge of it did not increase the "give" in the Soviet position, but it did increase the urge to adjourn the conference.

In conference with Gromyko on July 29, Herter spoke of having to leave Geneva the following week, owing to the meeting of the Organization of American States at Santiago, and said there was a question of continuing the conference with deputies or of recessing until the Secretary could return. Gromyko preferred to speed up negotiations but admitted there had been no narrowing of the gap between East and West. Herter was primarily concerned with Soviet insistence on linking the all-German committee to the Berlin interim settlement, and the status of Allied rights at the end of the interim.

In the July 29 meeting Gromyko disclosed to Herter his knowledge of the Khrushchev visit and said he considered an exchange of visits between Khrushchev and the President as settled. Herter urged Washington to release news of the Khrushchev visit before the end of the conference so that the two would not be directly related in the public mind.

A Big Four discussion (July 30) to consider proposals made by each side on the twenty-eighth resulted only in sharpening differences between East and West. Gromyko expressed displeasure that the West continued to seek endorsement of the "indefinite prolongation" of the occupation regime which, he implied, made an interim agreement impossible. He said the Western formula for duration of this agreement—stated in the West's paper of July 28 as five years—was unacceptable, but added that in negotiations following expiration of the interim agreement the status of Berlin should be considered anew. Commitments for the interim settlement would remain in force until the end of the interim, and in following negotiations each party would be free to make proposals. This seemed to say that prior rights would have vanished. The only "promise" Gromyko held out was that the Soviet Union would take no unilateral action during the negotiations. But suppose the U.S.S.R. ended negotiations? Herter and his colleagues realized that the Soviet objective apparently was to trap the West into a vague interim agreement on Berlin which the Soviets later could interpret as they liked. Further discussion of troublesome problems at that meeting was inconclusive and frustrating.

Herter asked the President's advice (July 30) on three problems: (1) the continuation of Allied rights in Berlin after the interim, which the West considered a "practical necessity"; (2) Soviet increasing insistence on drastic reduction in troop levels which, because of its effect on West Berliners, the West could not accept, though it could agree to fixing the troop limit at present levels; and (3) insistence on an all-German committee whose discussions would be restricted to a time limit proposed for the interim agreement. The West, Herter thought, could not go beyond its offer of a four-power East-West committee, working with German advisers, which the Soviets might accept. He also thought the Soviets might drop the linkage of the all-German committee with the interim agreement if they got a concession on the reduction of troops. The President agreed with Herter's views on all three points, though he thought a reduction of troops to somewhere between 8,000 and 10,000 had no military significance, and could be acceptable psychologically in a deal with the Soviets if fully explained to the West Berliners.

Was a deal possible? The Western ministers were indefatigable in efforts to get clear-cut answers from Gromyкo on rights in West Berlin at the end of the interim. But they soon were in the old game of twenty questions, Gromyko making evasive replies such as: "he had already clearly stated the Soviet position," or "a certain situation would exist," or "there should be no mention of rights" in the agreement. The meaning of "a certain situation" could not be clarified, but Gromyko, after evading direct answers to many Allied questions, demonstrated his mental agility, resource, and reserve of somewhat mordant humor by seeking to stem the barrage of questions with the story of an old lady who, after being badgered by people complaining of the bad weather, finally said, "Well, bad weather is better than no weather at all."

In the midst of these events Herter had to deal with anxieties in West Germany. Whereas the British were fearful of an uncompromising attitude on the part of their Western partners, West Germany was becoming fearful that the Allies were about to make damaging concessions to the Soviet Union. Herter, on whom Bonn was counting, was thought to have shown signs of weakening, although he had rejected any compromise on West Berlin's freedom or West Germany's integrity, and had made a special weekend trip to West Berlin (July 25) on invitation of Mayor Willy Brandt to reassure that city of United States and Western support, and to participate in the ceremony renaming a street "John Foster Dulles Allee." He was not deterred from going by Gromyko's warning (when Herter told him of his intention to make it) that the Soviet Union would regard the trip as "provocative."

A few days later von Brentano expressed to Herter deep concern over what he feared was a tendency toward the erosion of the Western position in the conference, and he emphasized the responsibility of the United States. Herter explained in detail that the latest Soviet proposals were unacceptable and that the only other concession which he would consider would be on troop levels—this contingent on the Soviets dropping their link between the all-German committee and Berlin interim arrangements, which latter, as proposed, would reduce Allied forces to shell-like tokens and introduce Soviet forces into West Berlin. He also informed von Brentano of the coming Khrushchev visit and the President's desire for a Western Big Four conference to precede it.

Von Brentano urged Herter to assume the role of leader in the conference. It was impossible, he said, to have three equal negotiators. It was a challenge to Herter, and his answer threw a revealing light. He said he understood von Brentano's meaning but the suggested role was not an easy one for him. It was contrary to his nature to be a "boss." There were other ways in which he could be effective, *e.g.*, by the substantive positions he was taking. Nor could he overlook the *amour-propre* of others.

The Secretary's lunch with Gromyko on August 1 was a climactic event in Herter's thinking on the conference. The Secretary spent a long time trying to get from Gromyko a statement that the juridical situation of Allied rights would be the same at the end of any interim agreement as at its beginning. Gromyko was difficult. He wondered why the Secretary was dissatisfied with previous statements on the Soviet position. Herter said it was because previous Soviet statements implied that each side would interpret differently the effect of an interim settlement on Allied rights. Gromyko summed up the situation, saying: "at the end of an interim agreement the obligation under it would lapse." New negotiations would then begin for the purpose of reaching another understanding. The Soviet position was that the occupation regime should end. Thus, at the end of the interim period the allies would have only the unpromising alternative of "negotiation," with no legal basis for claims.

Because of the delicacy of the negotiations Herter stayed with the dialogue to the point of frustration and disillusion. He finally withdrew from it with the remark that he had come to understand the Soviet point of view, but that what troubled him was the sinister implication of his understanding of the Soviet position.

Meantime, on August 1, the news of the Khrushchev visit had leaked to the public. It was reported in Geneva that Eisenhower had received the unanimous approval of Western heads of government for an invitation to Khrushchev to visit the United States, and that Khrushchev had told Vice President Nixon on the latter's departure that he hoped to visit the United States when the time was ripe.[5] The decision on the visit soon became known and it was correctly reported that the conference impasse had lost its critical aspect, and that the only problem remaining was how to end the discussions.

The question was whether the four East-West ministers could agree on a communiqué for the Wednesday final plenary. They worked strenuously on Monday (August 3), struggling for language that would set forth areas of agreement and disagreement. The West would have liked to mention rights, which Gromyko opposed. Gromyko wanted the communiqué to call for a summit meeting, but the West could not agree. Gromyko also wanted it to say the discussions were in an atmosphere of "complete candor," but this encountered Herter's objection on grounds that Gromyko's refusal to answer directly Western inquiries regarding Western rights at the end of an interim agreement was anything but candor. The Ministers finally agreed to say "frank and comprehensive" negotiations.

In the final plenary session (August 5) each of the Big Four ministers and the two German "advisers" made closing remarks. Secretary Herter in one of his best speeches outlined the main developments of the conference, pointing up Allied efforts first to secure an all-German settlement, including reunification, and then, when these efforts failed, an interim arrangement for West Berlin that would maintain the freedom of that city pending reunification of Germany. Herter thought the conference had contributed to isolating the issues which could lead to a Berlin settlement. He exuded no optimism.[6]

Thus the conference ended in deadlock without setting a date for another meeting. Its communiqué gave slight indication of the verbal battles that had rocked it. The results were variously assessed but, as

Herter told American newsmen before departure, tensions had eased somewhat. The outstanding fact was that the projected Khrushchev visit had eased the ending of the conference. It threw a "protective shade" over the Berlin crisis.[7]

Herter's own role at the conference was very important. While in touch with the President he had exercised, with the President's approval, a wide range of authority, and played a leading part in holding the Western team together. As one observer put it, he showed himself "keen, persevering and calm."[8] Mrs. Herter and Mrs. Gromyko also maintained good relations which led to an exchange of gifts before the delegations departed. Mrs. Gromyko gave Mrs. Herter champagne, caviar and some guides to Moscow. Mrs. Herter gave Mrs. Gromyko a polaroid camera. On seeing Mrs. Gromyko again before departure, Mrs. Herter asked her whether she had taken any good pictures, to which Mrs. Gromyko replied that her son, an engineer, had taken the camera apart and had not put the pieces back together, so she had been unable to try it out.

Good personal relations, on whatever level, were not decisive in the outcome of the conference. Neither Herter nor the Western team could dissipate the cloud of political realities that enveloped West Berlin and doomed it to remain a political island in a hostile sea, with its inhabitants hoping against hope for the miracle of German reunification in freedom, or for some other healing miracle that the efflux of time might bring about.

# CHAPTER SIX

## THE U-2
## AND THE ABORTED SUMMIT MEETING

THOUGHTS OF A SUMMIT MEETING as a means of easing East-West tensions had found frequent expression for several years before 1960. Only brief reference to these can be made in these pages. Even though the 1955 summit meeting was a fiasco, the idea lingered on in some quarters that summit meetings offered the best hope of escape from the threatening disaster of an East-West conflict, and the Swiss Federal Council in November 1956, called for a heads of government meeting to avoid a third world war. Soviet leaders regarded summits as important propaganda platforms and sounded off for a summit shortly after the Swiss appeal and repeatedly thereafter. The Kremlin's "Barkis is willin'" sign was always out. The U.S. Government, having been burned in 1955, was persistently shy regarding summit proposals unless there was a good prospect of definite achievement, based on advance preparation at the foreign minister level. The U.S.S.R. regarded the Foreign Ministers Conference of Geneva, May to August, 1959, as just a step toward a summit meeting, regardless of the Geneva meeting's outcome. The United States position was that a summit meeting would follow only if progress at the Geneva meeting was promising. Britain strongly favored the summit in any

77

case, France was highly skeptical, and West German leaders regarded it as inevitable, but forecast a failure.

The Geneva Conference did nothing to justify a summit meeting on U.S. terms, but Khrushchev's visit in September 1959 about which Herter had grave doubts, glossed over the conference's failure and brought heavy pressure on Eisenhower for a summit meeting. After a spectacular cross-country tour, full of flamboyant displays of mercurial moods, Khrushchev joined President Eisenhower and Herter at Camp David where for two days they (chiefly the President and the Soviet Chairman) battled over burning issues without getting anywhere.

Yet Khrushchev, anxious for a summit meeting, realized that Eisenhower had to have a plausible justification for U.S. participation, and therefore agreed to remove the time limit from the Soviet "ultimatum" on the evacuation of West Berlin, though on condition that negotiations would not be prolonged. It was a very tenuous and unsubstantial commitment, but Eisenhower accepted it as the open sesame to the summit. Circumstances seemed to leave him no alternative. The British were delighted with the commitment, but the French were skeptical, De Gaulle having grave doubts as to what could be gained. Finally in December 1959, the Western heads agreed to invite Krushchev to a summit, and agreement was reached after several diplomatic exchanges, that the meeting would convene on May 16. Diplomatic sparring filled the intervening months as the summit date approached. Then suddenly an untoward event of fateful import happened on the road to the summit.

1

While Secretary Herter was attending the opening session of the NATO Ministerial Conference at Istanbul, May 2, 1960, Livingston Merchant, Under Secretary for Political Affairs, handed him a note with information just received from a CIA representative. It stated that a U-2 plane was apparently down and the agreed cover story was being issued. The issuance of this story had been checked with Acting Secretary Dillon. The message did not go into details, but Herter and Merchant were aware of the plane's mission and assumed that it was down in Russia. They were disturbed, but not seriously. They thought, as did everyone in Washington, that the plane and any evidence as to the nature of its mission would have been destroyed, and that the pilot would probably have been killed. The next day the Air Force announced in Adana, Turkey, that a NASA U-2 weather research plane apparently went down in the Lake Van area of Turkey on May 1, and said among other things that the pilot had been experiencing oxygen difficulties. This statement was given out orally to newsmen in Washington the same day.[1]

During his stop at Athens, Herter got word on May 5 of Khrushchev's speech of that day before the Supreme Soviet. During the speech Ambassador Llewellyn Thompson, innocent of any knowledge of the events, was sitting in a front box. Khrushchev told of shooting the plane down and asked whether the plane had been sent by the President or by "Pentagon militarists," but he said nothing about the fate of the pilot. These facts gave more reason for concern.

When Herter got to Washington the next day, Friday, about 5:00 p.m., he learned of other developments. After Khrushchev's speech of the fifth, further statements were deemed necessary, under pressures especially by newsmen. Top officials, on a civil defense exercise away from Washington, had met hastily. Acting more or less in the dark without full information on the facts, particularly about the fate of the pilot, they had agreed that the State Department should handle all publicity relating to the incident and that the President should not be involved. Meanwhile, State Department and CIA officials in Washington prepared a statement approved by Under Secretary Dillon on his return from the civil defense exercises. Press Officer Lincoln White read it to the newsmen at 12:45 p.m. The statement followed the general line of the May 3 cover story: an unarmed U-2 weather research plane based at Adana, piloted by a civilian, was missing since May 1. It could be the plane referred to by Khrushchev. The pilot had reported difficulty with the oxygen equipment and might have lost consciousness. The NASA U-2 aircraft could have continued on automatic pilot and accidentally violated Soviet airspace. The State Department was asking Moscow for information, particularly on the fate of the pilot.[2]

NASA officials, who had not been informed as to the nature of the U-2's mission, and had not received word that the State Department was to handle further statements on this subject, put out another statement at 1:30 p.m. on the same day, going into considerable detail. The Defense Department followed suit with a statement reaffirming the announcement of May 3.[3]

Confusion was further confounded the next day when Lincoln White, who unhappily also was not on the inside of the U-2 story, relying on the detailed NASA statement of the fifth, assured newsmen that "there was absolutely no—N-O—no deliberate attempt to violate Soviet airspace, and there never has been."

On his arrival Herter found that the credibility of the U.S. Government was being put in jeopardy by stories quite ill-fitted to the actual shape of events. About this time word came from Ambassador Thompson of information gleaned at a diplomatic reception (May 6) that a Russian official had gleefully explained Soviet confidence in their spy story by saying "we've got the pilot." This "gossip" was confirmed the next morning when Khrushchev, before the Supreme Soviet, exuberantly said, "Comrades, I must tell you a secret. When I was making my report on the fifth I deliberately did not say that the pilot was alive and in good health and that we had parts of the plane . . . had we told everything at once the Americans would have invented another version." He poured scorn and ridicule on American assertions, discussed the details of Francis Gary Powers' mission and the pilot's equipment, and threatened serious consequences to "countries that make their territory available for the take-off" of such planes. He laid the blame on the "American military," thus leaving the way clear for President Eisenhower to disclaim responsibility.[4]

The problem facing Herter was unprecedented in diplomatic embarrassment, and possibly in ominous portent. A major intelligence operation, traditionally a hush-hush matter, had gone wrong. What to do in this case where the evidence was made public and the captured pilot had admitted incriminating facts? The State Department had primary responsibility for handling the problem.

Herter was unhappy about the cover stories of the third and fifth. It would have been better, he thought, if none had been issued. But in view of these and Khrushchev's statement of the seventh, he agreed that the State Department could not remain silent with the press "hounding everybody" to know what answer would be made to Khrushchev.[5]

On the seventh, therefore, top-level State Department, CIA and White House officials engaged in prolonged discussions to find an appropriate reply. There were differences of opinion on positions to be taken with regard to the flight itself and as to responsibilities—whether to admit nothing or to admit everything including responsibility at the top, or, as Herter thought, to admit the flight without involving the President. CIA Director Allen Dulles' offer to take full responsibility was rejected as not feasible. Herter's opinion prevailed and the statement issued late that day said that insofar as the "authorities" were concerned, "there was no authorization for any such flight . . ." But "an unarmed civilian U-2 plane" probably had made a flight over Soviet territory "to obtain information now concealed behind the iron curtain." The United States, it said, did engage in "intelligence collection activities . . . practiced by all countries . . . as measures of legitimate self defense," made necessary "by the excessive secrecy practiced by the Soviet Union. . . ." President Eisenhower was inclined to feel (as did his Press Secretary, James Hagerty) that he should assume responsibility, but after telephone conversations with Herter he agreed to the wording of the statement as proposed.[6]

The situation changed over the weekend. The news of pilot Powers' confession and the cumulative evidence of facts clearly belied cover story statements. Furthermore, the President was faced with the alternatives of admitting the facts or admitting the charge, to which he was so sensitive, that his government was being run by the military and the CIA. The dilemma was emphasized by Khrushchev in his remarks at the Czechoslovak diplomatic reception on the ninth, where in a bitter attack on the State Department he said the U.S. Government could not admit and could not deny. "The statement that nothing was known about it [the flight] by the State Department . . . is too thin . . . And what about Allen Dulles?" Khrushchev still did not place direct responsibility on the President, but he presented him with the ugly alternative of not being in command of the ship of state."[7]

The moment of truth had arrived and a full confession was in order. As Herter put it officially, "In a case of this kind telling the truth was better than getting deeper into fabricating excuses or disavowing responsibilities."[8] Privately he said, "we just couldn't go on lying." It seemed better to come out fighting with a vigorous attack on the conditions which made this espionage necessary, and that is what Herter decided to do.

The Secretary's statement of the ninth reminded the Soviet leaders of their rejection in 1955 of the President's "open skies" proposal, and that they had almost complete access to the open societies of the free world, supplemented by vast espionage networks, while keeping their own society tightly closed and rigorously controlled. It emphasized the danger of surprise attack, which their closed society made possible, and which could face the free world with the choice of abject surrender or nuclear destruction. The Government, it said, had a responsibiility to the American people and free peoples everywhere to take measures to lessen and overcome that danger. "In fact, the United States has not and does not shirk this responsibility." The President had put into effect "directives to gather by every possible means the information required to protect the United States and the free world against surprise attack. . . ." The U-2 incident should not damage the scheduled summit meeting, it said, but should underline the importance of achieving effective safeguards against surprise attack and aggression.[9]

The President, in his news conference two days later, reaffirmed Herter's statement regarding Presidential directives to gather intelligence in every feasible way to protect against surprise attack. This was "distasteful but a vital necessity." But "we must not be distracted from the real issues of the day by what is an incident or a symptom of the world situation today." Thus Herter and the President treated the U-2 affair as an unfortunate and unpleasant incident in Soviet-American relations, however embarrassing when exposed. This incident, they argued, should not interfere with larger concerns and current efforts to ease tensions and seek agreements that would make such espionage unnecessary.

Not surprisingly, Khrushchev in his news conference on the same day (but held before that of the President) took a different view. This incident was so important, he said, that it would be taken to the United Nations. He poured out his wrath on Herter, who, he said, had made "an outrageous statement." He charged the Secretary with justifying "aggressive actions" and with saying "they would continue." Herter had made the Kremlin doubt the correctness of its "earlier conclusions that the President . . . did not know about the flights," and had admitted that the President had issued the intelligence-collecting directives. He had "removed all wrappers."

For the first time Khrushchev attacked Eisenhower directly, though with less apparent animus than shown against Herter. How would it affect Soviet public opinion? "I would not like to be in Eisenhower's place," he remarked. As to whether Eisenhower should visit the Soviet Union, Khrushchev said hopes had been "somewhat disappointed." "The people will say: 'Are you nuts? What kind of a dear guest is he who allows a plane to fly to us to spy?'" The "militarists" had put him, Khrushchev, "in a very difficult position." But he did not rule out Eisenhower's visit. As to the incident's effect on the summit meeting, he said, "Let those who sent this spy plane think over this question . . . they should have thought about the consequences beforehand." He did not rule out the summit and even spoke of exchanging views with Eisenhower in Paris about postponing his visit.

Herter's phrase that "the United States had not and does not shirk this responsibility" (of intelligence collecting) was generally interpreted by the press and public to mean that U-2 operations would continue. W. J. Jorden, reporting for the *New York Times*, expressed the prevailing view in saying in his lead sentence that "Christian A. Herter indicated today that the United States would continue intelligence-gathering flights unless there was a marked change in Moscow's attitude toward measures guaranteeing the world against Communist aggression."[10]

The drafters of Herter's phrase, weighing every word, were undoubtedly aware of its ambiguity. Perhaps no reference to the subject was necessary at that time. Newsmen could have been kept guessing as to future surveillance-flight policy. But any reference to it on May 9 had to be ambiguous as no policy decision had then been definitely reached and there were those, including the Vice President, who opposed renunciation of such flights.

The ambiguous wording left a free field for interpretation and speculation. Press Officer White underwent a grilling at the hands of newsmen seeking amplification and explanation. But White said he could not amplify the statement which he had just read. When a newsman said, "you realize that a normal interpretation of this would be that we intend to continue," White could only say, "Well, I leave it to your interpretation." So it was left in that state of ambiguity, denounced by Communists and deplored by allies.

2

The cumulative events connected with the U-2 affair contributed to a general feeling at home and abroad, even in the most friendly countries, that Khrushchev had won an important propaganda victory on the eve of the summit. Press reactions throughout the world were either strongly condemnatory or, in friendly countries, expressive of sad disillusionment. In Britain there were widespread shock and annoyance. Occasional compliments for frankly admitting the facts were drowned out by complaints such as: "shocking," "fantastic," "incredibly stupid timing," and "humiliation for the West."

Expressing a widely held opinion, the London *Times* (May 9, 1960) said the public admission of spying handed Khrushchev his "propaganda triumph on a plate." Although *The Times* did observe that however "foolish" the flight, it should not "obscure the fact that the Russians do their full share of spying too." The *Observer* (May 8) commented: "It is hard to say which is more irresponsible, the American order for such a flight ten days before the summit or the Russian exploitation of this folly."[11]

In nonaligned Sweden the press, from left to right, deplored the timing of the flight and the handling of the incident, and it regretted the propaganda victory which the press said it gave the U.S.S.R. Leading news organs viewed the American handling of the incident as "unbelievably clumsy," "careless, even naive," showing "gross lack of judgment" that would "shake the authority and prestige of the United States," and probably cause "serious military and political consequences." There were some qualifying statements, for instance, that democracies needed information on Russian military capabilities and that Herter's "disarming frankness" would neutralize some of the harmful effect on American prestige and reputation. The semi-official *Stockholm Tidningen,* under an "Honest Herter" heading, said the initial American flat denial had "turned into an eagerness to confess which knows no limit." Honesty is certainly a virtue, it wrote, "but it should be applied with judgment and at the right time."[12]

At home the *New York Times* reported that there was unanimous agreement in the Congress that the timing of the flight was "deplorably bad"—an opinion which it and much of the American press shared. Nevertheless the domestic press and much of that in friendly countries recognized the dilemma faced by the American Government: the closed Soviet society, and the risks of surprise attack. The *Washington Post* voiced prevailing opinion in saying Herter was right "in acknowledging what Mr. Khrushchev . . . had made evident that he already knew."[13] In view of the damage done by cover statements issued before Herter returned from Istanbul, the Secretary had no acceptable alternative.

Even if the Government had "stonewalled" it for

some days after the plane was known to be down it is difficult to see how admission of the grim facts, possibly without admitting Presidential responsibility, could have been long delayed. Traditionalists everywhere were surprised at the American confession. Even Khrushchev expressed surprise that top officials had accepted responsibility. British officials believed their government would simply have refused to discuss intelligence matters. But there had never been a parallel case displaying the damning evidence while the U.N. forum was hearing the case and passing judgment.

The statement that the government would not shirk its intelligence-collecting responsibilities, as the *Washington Post* said, tended to put everyone on the spot, particularly the allies whose bases had been used in connection with the U-2 flights.[14] Repercussions in certain countries were serious, though the presumption that the flights would continue made the situation more difficult. In his speech of May 7, Khrushchev had warned those countries with bases on their territories that "if they allow others to fly from their bases" to Russian territory, "we shall hit at those bases." In reply the U.S. Government immediately gave assurances that it would defend such countries from Soviet attack.[15]

Norway, Pakistan, Turkey and Japan were specially concerned. Afghanistan was involved because of overflights. The U.S.S.R. brought pressure to bear on all of them, especially on Norway and Pakistan which were immediately involved. In response to urgent messages from these countries the United States gave requested disavowals of past or future use of their territory as bases for intelligence flights. It assured them that U-2 flights had been discontinued.

During these U-2 developments the question came up frequently whether there would be a summit meeting. On May 6, Press Secretary Hagerty told inquiring newsmen that he knew of no change in the President's plans to go, but on that day the President was overheard to drop an "if I go" in a casual talk with AFL-CIO President George Meany, which stimulated newsmen's interest.[16] When reminded of this "if" at his May 11 news conference, the President said he had not changed his plans, "but you never can tell from one day to the other what is happening in this world . . ." He said, "I expect to go." Preparations for his departure proceeded.

There were indications that the Soviet Government was taking a hard look at its relations with the United States. The Soviet Embassy in Washington, May 6, ordered the Cuneo Press in Milwaukee to remove all references to President Eisenhower from the June issue of *U.S.S.R.*, the English-language Soviet monthly published in the United States. In it were pictures and stories that bore upon the President's anticipated visit to Russia.[17] Soviet Air Marshal K. A. Vershinin on May 2 postponed a scheduled visit to the United States, returning General Nathan Twining's recent visit to Russia. On May 4 he confirmed the visit, then on May 12 cancelled it.[18] These were straws in the wind which suggested trouble.

3

The real character and dimensions of the trouble did not become apparent until May 15, when in Paris the Khrushchev strategy began to unfold. In a news conference of May 11 in Moscow he had said, "I am an incorrigible optimist. I regard the provocative flight of the American intelligence plane . . . not as a preparation for war but as probing." There was no change in this position before his arrival in Paris on the fourteenth, a day earlier than that of other heads of government—a matter of some surprise. On arriving he gave no clue to his intentions, though there was an ominous overtone in his remarks. After effusively thanking "the French people and Government" for their "warm and friendly reception" on his April visit, he said the summit meeting to be held there was "of great significance in international affairs," and expressed hope for its success. He then observed that "influential quarters" seeking "to revive the cold war" had noticeably intensified their activities in certain countries. The reference, with vague implications of trouble, was obvious.[19]

Secretary Herter also arrived in Paris on the fourteenth with the advance guard of the American delegation. The frosty state of American-Russian relations was reflected in his tight-lipped no-statement departure from Washington and arrival in Paris. He was not forecasting regarding progress at the summit. Later that day he told American newsmen that on

May 9 he had not said surveillance flights over Russia would continue. He said his statement meant that if there was a question of survival we would take such measures as we felt necessary.

He had arrived early in Paris to coordinate policy with Foreign Ministers Lloyd, Couve de Murville and von Brentano. One major task was to consider new Soviet proposals on Berlin and Germany. He found little new in them. The Soviet objectives were still to get the West out of Berlin and to break West German ties with the West by demilitarizing and neutralizing the GDR and drawing it closer to the Soviet orbit. These objectives were obviously unacceptable. Herter said the essential conditions of a Berlin settlement were those previously presented by the West. The Western Foreign Ministers also reached agreement in nuclear test ban negotiations, then stalemated in Geneva.

Early the next day, May 15, the four Western heads of government met with their foreign ministers and agreed on positions to be taken at the summit on major subjects. But Western preparations for the summit were already being overtaken by events.

President Eisenhower arrived early on the fifteenth, as did Macmillan and West German Chancellor, Konrad Adenauer. At Orly Airport the President said the hopes of humanity called on "the Four" to purge their minds of prejudice, and their hearts of rancor. Too much was at stake "to indulge in profitless bickering." The West would meet Khrushchev halfway and America would "go every foot that safety and honor permit."[20]

But Khrushchev made appointments with President de Gaulle and Prime Minister Macmillan, not with President Eisenhower. In individual conferences he informed them that the conditions on which he would participate in the summit were that President Eisenhower must: (1) condemn the overflights; (2) indicate that they would not occur in the future; and (3) punish those responsible for past overflights.

Marshal Malinowsky and Foreign Minister Gromyko accompanied Khrushchev to these and all his conferences, and he looked frequently at them as though seeking support for his statements. Khrushchev talked of being threatened with overflights, referring to the Secretary's statement of May 9 and the President's confirmation of it. He admitted that they all carried on espionage, but felt that when they were caught they ought not to admit it or say that it is right. He told each of them the story of his boyhood when he had been caught trapping sparrows, the upshot of which seemed to be that "when you're caught don't admit it." He said governments should not say they were doing this sort of thing and he wanted some expression on the subject from the President.

The dimensions of the summit crisis were becoming apparent. Conference prospects looked very dim. "The Three"—the Western heads, with foreign ministers— conferred late on the fifteenth. They discussed the Herter statement of May 9 and agreed that Herter had not said the flights would continue, but that the United States would protect itself; and this was conditional on "the absence of Soviet cooperation." What about Khrushchev's conditions for attending the summit conference? As to the overflights, the President had never said they were right. They were not legal or right; but he was not going to be the only one to raise his hand and promise never to do again something everybody was doing. In any case U-2's were almost obsolete. Should the President see Khrushchev alone? The President was inclined to feel that the four of them should settle the matter, but he could still offer to see Khrushchev in the afternoon.[21]

Events of the next day precluded such a meeting. On Khrushchev's insistence the first East-West meeting of the Heads (ten o'clock on the sixteenth) was not a formal summit meeting but a "preliminary meeting." While Chairman de Gaulle was granting Eisenhower's preceding request to speak, Khrushchev, who had also asked to speak, seized the initiative and released his verbal torrent against President Eisenhower. His government could not negotiate, he said, under the threat that American aircraft would continue to fly over the Soviet Union's territory. His tirade climaxed with the demands previously stated to De Gaulle and Macmillan—condemnation of the flights, cessation of such forays and punishment of the guilty. He added that there should also be an expression of regret. These were the conditions on which he would participate in the summit meeting. In addition, he cancelled the scheduled June 10 visit of Eisenhower to Russia and postponed Soviet participation in a summit conference six to eight months.[22] Khrushchev's position had hardened since he left Moscow.

President Eisenhower's reply was restrained and conciliatory. He made no apology for the overflight and justified it under the circumstances, but said such flights had been discontinued, not to be renewed. (He later added that he could guarantee a cessation only for his administration.) The United States favored United Nations aerial surveillance to detect preparations for attack. He would propose this to the U.N. and would be willing to enter bilateral negotiations with the U.S.S.R. on the subject at the conference. But Khrushchev's ultimatum would never be acceptable. Khrushchev, he said, had apparently come to Paris with the sole intention of sabotaging the meeting.[23]

Macmillan urged Khrushchev to get on with the business in hand, since Eisenhower had discontinued the overflights. De Gaulle asked why Khrushchev had not raised his questions before the conference, emphasized the importance of the problems and suggested a one-day recess. Khrushchev remained unmoved. "As God is my witness," he said, "I come with clean hands and pure soul." He insisted on United States condemnation or regret for the "public insult to the Soviet Union," and said he would publish his statement. When Herter asked whether he intended to include in his published statement his withdrawal of the invitation to the President, he said he would as he "couldn't explain even to a small grandson an invitation as honored guest to one who sends planes to overfly. Efforts by Macmillan and De Gaulle to dissuade him were futile. Adjournment was the only alternative. Khrushchev said he would not participate in a summit conference until the United States had publicly removed "the threat it had imposed."

The Americans and French regarded the summit conference as dead, particularly after Khrushchev had published his statement. For them there remained only a problem of its obsequies. The British thought disaster might threaten if the summit died a-borning and urged that a major effort be made to save it. They objected to becoming involved in a war that might arise out of the disputes over the question who should sign travel permits controlling access to West Berlin—a problem that would arise if a Soviet treaty gave East Germany control over this traffic. When Selwyn Lloyd asked why the President could not say he was sorry about the U-2 incident and try to remove this obstacle to the summit meeting, Herter replied that the President could not say he was sorry, for the very good reason that he was not sorry.

Some circles, especially French and German, viewed with satisfaction the prospect of a sabotaged summit, since presumably at least six to eight months would be gained by Khrushchev's postponement for that length of time of Soviet participation in a summit. It was assumed that the Soviets would maintain the *status quo* during this period. (This presumption was confirmed privately by Gromyko in Paris, and by Khrushchev in a speech in Berlin after leaving Paris.)

But how should the Allies proceed in view of Khrushchev's charges and demands? Herter ruled out the possibility of a bilateral Eisenhower-Khrushchev meeting, as Khrushchev had crossed the Rubicon and could not retract his ultimatum. The Secretary thought there was no purpose in any further quadripartite meeting. The exigencies seemed to call for another effort to clarify East and West positions. Next morning, therefore (the seventeenth), the three Western heads, later joined by the foreign ministers, canvassed the situation and agreed that President de Gaulle should send an invitation to the heads for a meeting that afternoon. Herter raised a point, emphasized by President Eisenhower, that the invitation should make it clear that there had been no behind-the-scenes changes of position since the day before. De Gaulle thought his note did this by stating his desire "to ascertain whether the summit conference can begin the examination of those questions we had agreed to discuss."[24] The meeting was set for 3:00 p.m.

When the Western three—heads and foreign ministers—met, Khrushchev, as anticipated, was not present. He had not replied to De Gaulle's invitation, but he had told the press that he would not attend any meeting unless there were apologies. Telephone calls from the Soviet Embassy frequently interrupted the Western discussions. The sum and substance of the different messages was that if the meeting were called to discuss the preliminary conditions for holding the summit meeting the Soviet leader would come. Otherwise not.

Answers to the inquiries were obvious and it seemed equally obvious, as De Gaulle said, that under Khrushchev's conditions there would be no summit. The British urgently wanted another try for a meeting, feeling that De Gaulle might persuade Khrushchev to come. Khrushchev might have misunderstood De Gaulle's invitation. Telephone exchanges, they thought, were insufficient. There should be a written record. Perhaps, by the grace of God, Khrushchev might change his mind.

Uncertainties were cleared away by a Khrushchev press statement that afternoon. It said that if the United States had really decided "to condemn the treacherous incursion of American aircraft into the air space of the Soviet Union, publicly express regret over these incursions, punish those who are guilty and give assurance that such incursions will not be repeated," the Soviet delegation would be ready to participate in the summit conference. This statement, with its impossible demands, convinced everyone that the summit was dead.

There were inevitable repercussions and post mortems, including adverse criticism of United States handling of the U-2 crisis, especially for "telling all" in admitting responsibliity for the U-2 flight. Even Khrushchev expressed surprise to De Gaulle at this. The President reported to the nation on TV and radio, and Herter testified before House and Senate committees. There was general agreement that the U-2 cover stories were a big error. Herter felt that they and other facts foreclosed the possibility of silence on responsibility for the U-2 flight. He said the situation was unique. He had not known of the precise day of the flight. (President Eisenhower did know of it.) But Herter thought the risk was worth taking in view of the urgency of the information sought. In Communist thinking the U-2 disaster justified Khrushchev in aborting the summit. Herter thought other reasons were decisive, *e.g.*, Khrushchev's fear of failure and loss of face in the Paris meeting, and growing opposition to his policies among members of the Soviet hierarchy as well as sharp criticisms coming from Communist China. The *New York Times* (June 6, 1960) pointed to "egregious errors at the outset" of the U-2 problem, but it commended Herter's statement that "we would have dug ourselves in deeper and deeper in a denial of something that was perfectly self-evident."

The U-2 summit debacle had an important bearing on subsequent events. It contributed to an indefinite postponement of another major East-West confrontation, though it did not prevent Khrushchev, in the following months, from renewing threats of a separate peace treaty with East Germany.

It sparked Khrushchev's efforts to induce the U.N. Security Council to brand the United States an aggressor in the U-2 affair. After heated argument, the Council on May 27, 1960, by a 9 to 0 vote (the U.S.S.R. and Poland abstaining), expressed regret for the failure of the summit meeting and appealed to the major governments to avoid provocative acts and to resume discussions as soon as possible.[25]

The cancellation of Eisenhower's visit to the U.S.S.R., on which Khrushchev and Eisenhower had agreed at Camp David, was more unfortunate as the tour was regarded by its American advocates as an opportunity for the "Eisenhower personality" to make a favorable impression on the Russian people and to improve relations with the U.S.S.R. Herter thought

Khrushchev was never enthusiastic for this visit as he had favored postponing it to the spring of 1960 rather than having it in the autumn of 1959, as first contemplated by Eisenhower.

Next came the "postponement" by the Japanese Government of the President's long-planned visit in June 1960, to celebrate the 100th anniversary of American-Japanese relations, and to solemnize agreement on the revised American-Japanese treaty of cooperation and mutual assistance. Opposition by neutralists and leftists was fanned by the U-2 incident and Soviet threats to retaliate if U-2 planes flew over Russia from Japanese territory. Khrushchev's rough treatment contributed to the fury of riots protesting Eisenhower's visit, riots which caused the Japanese Government to cancel the trip after the President's arrival at Manila. Secretary Herter, who during the preceding weeks had relied on Japanese assurances and reports from Ambassador Douglas MacArthur II regarding the trip, informed a Senate committee on June 21 that in anticipation the size and violence of the demonstrations in Tokyo had been misjudged. He accepted responsibility, though he said "it was a joint decision."[26] He later wrote Senator Alexander Wiley that the President, after accepting the invitation, had no choice but to go, unless the Japanese Government itself cancelled or postponed the visit. In this "communist victory," as the President put it, the U-2 incident and the summit debacle played leading roles.[27]

In spite of the breakoff at the Paris non-summit meeting, and Khrushchev's postponement for six or eight months of Soviet participation in an East-West summit, hope remained among neutrals and some allies of healing the breach sooner than Khrushchev had indicated. The presence of Khrushchev at the General Assembly that same year, ostensibly to promote a General Assembly summit meeting on disarmament, offered hope of beginning the healing process by bringing President Eisenhower and Chairman Khrushchev together to discuss urgent international problems. Five neutralist leaders sought to bring this about by a resolution in the General Assembly and a letter to the two parties on September 29, 1960, calling attention to the deterioration in international relations and urging that these leaders meet to begin seeking solutions for outstanding problems.

The President replied on October 2. He expressed sympathy with the motives behind their letter, but called attention to Khrushchev's refusal in May to participate in the "long-awaited summit conference" on these subjects. Nothing in Soviet words or actions, he said, promised productive results, but if the U.S.S.R. did wish to discuss concrete measures to reduce tensions, U.S. representatives, including the Secretary of State, would be available for that purpose; and if exploratory discussions revealed that the U.S.S.R. was prepared to return to peaceful negotiation with some prospect of fruitful results, he personally would be willing to meet with Soviet and other heads of governments, whose interests were involved.

The British were inclined to regard the President's reply as an acceptance of the idea of meeting with

Khrushchev in New York, subject to the "reasonable conditions" stated. But Herter informed them that there was no such intention. He emphasized that essential pre-conditions were (1) the release of two members of the U.S. RB-47 crew, shot down on July 1 and held incommunicado since then, and (2) Soviet willingness to resume disarmament discussions which it had broken off in the 10-power commission. The United States, he said, did not favor the resolution in its existing form and, for reasons stated in the letter, was not keen for a bilateral meeting. The RB-47 incident had become a definite symbol to American public opinion.

Khrushchev, after shrewdly waiting for the President to decline, responded on October 4, saying he could not meet the President in any case unless the President was ready to condemn the overflights. Thus the gambit of the neutralists fell apart, to their annoyance chiefly with the United States, and they withdrew their resolution.[28] East-West relations continued in deep freeze.

Secretary Herter had not expected much from the projected summit meeting—probably only a beginning of a series of meetings which ultimately might solve some of the East-West problems. But the abrupt and brutal disruption of the conference left State Department officials stymied on East-West relations and caused much thought in top echelons regarding action that might be taken.

Before the month of May 1960, the United States was leading its allies in a major effort to engage the U.S.S.R. in negotiations. The collapse of summit and disarmament negotiations ended that effort. During the ensuing six months the administration faced the possibility of marking time in foreign affairs. Responsible officials felt the need for a "fresh start after Paris"—some dramatic new initiative to revitalize United States leadership in the free world. Election-year paralysis was unacceptable.

Dangers lay ahead. Communist China might take more aggressive action. Soviet policy was already hardening—witness Khrushchev's announced visit to Cuba. The North Atlantic Community needed bolstering, though De Gaulle was reported to be waiting for the new administration to work out existing difficulties. U.S. defenses should be studied and strengthened to convince the Soviet bloc of U.S. readiness to risk nuclear war. A high-level review of hazardous and sensitive intelligence programs was needed to make sure that in each case the advantages warranted the risks.

Herter assured the President that the Department was working on these problems. Summitry received special attention. On the basis of careful studies made in the Department, Herter advised the President that while the Administration, under the pressure of world public opinion, might go to a summit again to avoid appearing unwilling to take a chance for peace, the problem would be to avoid being maneuvered into going on disadvantageous terms. Such meetings, he said, tend to cultivate wishful thinking and a deceptive euphoria, and failures become all the more serious as there is no higher court of appeal. Normal diplomatic procedures, including informal diplomatic

conversations and friendly visits of heads of government, avoid the dangers to which a summit is exposed,
such as unwise hasty decisions, misunderstandings
arising out of summit language expressed in broad
generalities, and grave public disillusionment over
failures. He thought summits appropriate only when
prospect of agreement was very great or under
gravest emergencies such as a brink-of-war situation.

Although East-West negotiations were definitely
stalled by Khrushchev's action, other critical situations, strongly affected by political radiations from
Moscow, claimed Herter's attention. Disarmament,
Cuba and Latin America generally, Southeast Asia,
Africa, the United Nations and NATO were among
the continuing or developing challenges to our diplomacy. Limited initiatives could be taken in some
cases; in others it was more a problem of containing
or beating back dangerous threats to peace and security. But a national election was in the offing, and soon
thereafter a new Administration would take over,
leaving little time to Herter for problem solving. In
these terminal months, for the first time during his
Secretaryship, Herter was at least free from concern
with preparations for or participation in an East-West
conference, and could give more time to other problems.

# CHAPTER SEVEN

## TURMOIL IN EAST ASIA

THE LATE 1950's were a period of developing or exploding crises in the Far East, Middle East and Africa. All these troubled areas reflected spreading nationalism and the impact of advanced industrial economies, as well as the worldwide clash of ideologies.

1

Communist China in August 1958, set off a train of events in Asia by renewing the bombardment of the offshore islands, Quemoy and Matsu, in its campaign to extend control over Taiwan (Formosa). The bombardment created an awkward situation for the United States which, on the basis of a Congressional resolution of January 29, 1955, had guaranteed the security of Taiwan and the Pescadores Islands. The immediate question was whether an attack on Quemoy and Matsu was essentially an attack on Taiwan or the Pescadores, and therefore called for action under the resolution. This ultimately would involve a decision, probably highly subjective, by the President.

Secretary Dulles was specially concerned with this case, but Herter kept closely in touch with developments. As Acting Secretary in late August 1958, he

105

expressed concern to an interagency group that Taiwan was endeavoring to involve the United States in
hostilities before making all possible efforts on its
own to cope with the situation. He thought we should
maintain our commitment to defend the offshore islands. Happily, the President was not called upon
to decide whether to intervene, as the Chinese Communists refrained from pressing the test of American
firmness. Herter summed up the situation in a letter
of July 20, 1960, to Congressman Chester Bowles. He
said the United States maintained its commitment to
support Taiwan and the Pescadores and continued
to promote a peaceful resolution of the Taiwan problem. No formal cease-fire had been achieved in the
Warsaw talks (carried on intermittently), and the
Chinese Communists had refused offers of a mutual
renunciation of force, but had abated their bombardment in the autumn of 1958. The United States was
reluctant to put pressure on Chiang Kai-shek to evacuate the offshore islands in spite of their admitted
vulnerability. Herter believed that no inducements
which could reasonably be offered would persuade
Chiang to evacuate them. He thought the risks of
failing to persuade Chiang were so great, the chances
of success so slight, as to make the risk not worth
taking.

The perennial question of recognizing Communist
China was discussed during this period, especially
in liberal and business circles. The United States in
1933 had recognized Communist Russia; why not
recognize the communist regime which undoubtedly
controlled mainland China? Secretary Dulles, in his

San Francisco speech of June 28, 1957, had mentioned "certain customary tests," but had added that "always . . . recognition is admitted to be an instrument of national policy, to serve enlightened self-interest."[1] On this subject Herter pointed to practical reasons for not recognizing the Chinese Communist Government. Spelling these out to an inquirer in October 1958, he said that recognizing Communist China would greatly enhance its prestige and influence around the world, decrease resistance to communism among free Asian nations, and make more difficult our effort to maintain security in the Pacific. Further, our recognition of the Republic of China "helps keep alive the symbol of a China which is not Communist" and "enables it to challenge the claim of the Chinese Communists to represent the Chinese people."

Herter likewise opposed Communist China's entrance into the United Nations. He told visiting Japanese Foreign Minister Kosaka in September, 1960, that Chinese Communist behavior during the preceding year had not indicated that the Peking regime was prepared to fulfill the obligations of a United Nations member. It remained condemned as an aggressor by the United Nations and had continued its expansionist pressures. The Secretary said United States policy on Communist China had not changed.

Herter was also concerned about Tibet, where early in 1959 the "suzerain," Communist China, set up direct military rule in clear violation of guarantees in 1951 of that country's political and religious autonomy. This action caused the Dalai Lama to take refuge in India, to Nehru's embarrassment, and be replaced by the Panchen Lama, a Chinese puppet. Acting Secretary Herter expressed "deep shock" in March 1959, at reports of "ruthless suppression of human liberties in Tibet."[2] He welcomed the "initiative of the Dalai Lama" in bringing the problem before the U.N.[3] In his General Assembly speech of September 17 he called attention to "the revolting spectacle of brutal Chinese Communist repression of the fundamental human rights of the Tibetans," and said: "Certainly this organization must speak out in clear terms in the face of such events."[4] But it was difficult to get even a mild protest from the General Assembly.

2

Even more disturbing situations were developing in Southeast Asia. The peoples of that area were struggling with the consequences of many years of colonialism, complicated by World War II and the patched-up Geneva settlement of 1954. The latter had sought to find a workable compromise between communist and anticommunist forces dominating the scene in Indochina after French military efforts had failed, although massively aided since 1950 by American war material and other assistance. Most exposed and involved were Laos and South Vietnam, (the latter known as "the Republic of Vietnam"). Both Laos and South Vietnam had a recognized status by virtue of the Geneva Conference agreements, and both had undertaken to grant equality of citizenship to all nationals and impose restrictions on foreign troops and foreign military bases.⁵ The United States was not party to the agreements and therefore was not bound by them, but had stated that it would "refrain from the threat or use of force to disturb them" and would "view any renewal of the aggression in violation" of them "with grave concern."⁶

During the late 1950's, Vietnam was on the back burner of American diplomacy, and the heat on the Vietnam regime was temporarily reduced, but signs indicated that it would be turned up again. General J. Lawton Collins, on special mission to Vietnam, had reported pessimistically in January 1955, that United States support would be essential to help that country retain its independence. He said independence could not be guaranteed, even with such aid, but without it Vietnam would surely be lost to communism. These were prophetic words.

President Eisenhower in October 1954, had announced that the United States purpose was to assist Vietnam "in developing and maintaining a strong, viable state, capable of resisting subversion or aggression."⁷ When President Ngo Dinh Diem conferred in Washington in May 1957, Eisenhower renewed the offer to continue "effective assistance within the constitutional processes of the United States." Both Presidents agreed that aggression or subversion threatening the independence of the Republic of Vietnam would endanger peace and stability.⁸

The situation worsened with the increase of Viet Cong (South Vietnam Communists) activities from 1957 to 1959. This caused Eisenhower on April 4, 1959, to sound an alarm regarding South Vietnam's need for assistance in meeting the dual threat of aggression and subversion. He warned that capture of the new republic by the Communists would threaten the remaining Southeast Asia countries and start a crumbling that could have grave consequences for American freedom. He said the national interest required the United States to help sustain South Vietnam's morale, economic progress, and military strength necessary to its continued existence in freedom.[9]

At that time the President's statement was not taken very seriously. During 1959 roving journalists and others were commenting, generally favorably, on conditions in South Vietnam and on Diem's achievements. A year later observers saw a different picture—the increase of sabotage and terrorism accompanied by more dictatorial government policies, arbitrary arrests and denials of civil liberties, with rising discontent among intellectuals and the peasantry.[10] Communist guerilla activities were reviving, the political atmosphere worsening.

The meaning of this situation for American policy in 1959 was not clear. The hands of the terrorists and guerillas were presumably the hands of the Viet Cong. Was the voice directing these hands the voice of President Ho Chi Minh of the Hanoi Government? Secretary Herter was not rushing to conclusions. When asked at a press conference on July 9 whether the killing of two Americans in South Vietnam in a reportedly communist terrorist attack was related to the spread of communism in South Vietnam, Herter said terrorist organizations had been operating there for some time.[11] In the late 1950's the North Vietnam Communist party—the Lao Dong (Workers' party)—decided to step up communist activities and terrorism in South Vietnam. The Party Congress of September 1960, called for a communist National Liberation Front there. In December the N.L.F. was set up.[12] No one could foresee developments in South Vietnam, but the Administration thought it wise to continue increasing the number of military advisers, first introduced in 1950, hoping their aid would enable South Vietnam to suppress terrorism and withstand guerillas. By the end of 1960 these advisers had increased to nearly 900.[13]

3

Crisis in Laos was more evident and urgent than in Vietnam, and remained so to the end of Herter's tenure as Secretary. There were presumptions of internal stability in South Vietnam which did not exist in Laos, and the clash of international policies in Laos was more acute. The Geneva settlement of 1954 gave Laos independent status along with Vietnam and Cambodia. All three were "protocol" states under the SEATO compact which gave each the same assurances against external attack and internal subversion—which assurances, to be sure, were not crystal clear or airtight.[14]

Well before the Geneva agreements Laos was in serious trouble. The Pathet Lao, pro-Communist rebels, in 1953 and 1954 had established themselves in two northern provinces—Phong Saly and Sam Neua—

with strong assistance from the Communist Viet Minh of North Vietnam. The Geneva accords provided for regrouping the "fighting units of Pathet Lao" in the two provinces "pending a political settlement." The Lao Government separately "resolved to take the necessary measures to integrate all citizens without discrimination." The neutralist Premier, Souvanna Phouma, in 1957 reached a compromise with the Pathet Lao which appeared to do this. The Pathet Lao leader, Prince Souphanouvong, half brother of the Premier, was taken into the cabinet. This compromise arrangement came apart after the elections of May 1958 which increased the electoral strength of the Neo Lao Hak Xat, the party of the Pathet Lao. Tensions increased between the extreme left and the rightists. Souvanna Phouma resigned in July, 1958. His successor, pro-Western Phoui Sananikone, took over in August on a program of internal reform and strong resistance to subversion.[15]

A special problem was the administration of foreign aid which had become so riddled with bribery, profiteering and general mismanagement that the Pathet Lao was able to make political capital of it.[16] In August 1957, Under Secretary Herter had complained of the program's deficiencies and called for administrative reform. In early 1958 the abuses reached scandalous proportions. Disclosures in the *Wall Street Journal* and in other papers led to temporary suspension of aid on June 20. After agreement with the Phoui government on major reforms, including exchange rates and the sale of import licenses, aid was renewed in October on a reduced scale.[17] It dropped from $43,400,000 for 1957 to $25,100,000 for 1959.

Meanwhile Phoui's efforts to free his government of communist influence sharpened the internal conflict with the Pathet Lao and worsened relations with North Vietnam, the primary source of Pathet Lao support. The military situation also was deteriorating. In December 1958, and again in February 1959, Phoui in messages to the United Nations charged North Vietnam with making incursions into Laotian territory.[18] In July 1959, widespread guerrilla warfare expanded into open fighting, in some of which Phoui claimed the North Vietnamese were involved. In August he proclaimed a state of emergency in five provinces and requested Secretary Hammarskjold to inform U.N. members that North Vietnam was giving aid to the Pathet Lao forces.[19] The U.S.S.R. and Communist China vigorously espoused the Pathet Lao demands for restoration of the Geneva accords and reactivation of the International Control Commission (ICC) set up in 1954, composed of India, Poland and Canada. This commission had adjourned *sine die* in July 1958, "at Prime Minister Souvanna's request," when presumably its mission had been accomplished.[20] The Pathet Lao had excluded the ICC from territory under its control.

The State Department expressed alarm on August 11, 1959, accusing the communists of creating "a dangerous situation." It suggested that "the Soviet Union might be promoting the fighting," and asked whether the Laotian conflict was "part of a broader communist design."[21] Meeting with members of the Senate Foreign Relations Committee on August 24, Herter said he considered the Laotian situation "very dangerous." He thought a U.N. team of observers should be sent there, as desired by the Lao Government.[22]

The State Department emphasized that "contrary to repetitious allegations from Hanoi, Peking, and Moscow, the United States . . . had no military bases, airstrips, or other military installations in Laos." It announced also that, owing to the communist military threat to Laos, the United States in response to specific Laotian requests was authorizing additional aid to permit an increase of the Lao army from 25,000 to 29,000 and of the village militia from 16,000 to 20,000.[23]

In a talk with French Ambassador Hervé Alphand on August 25, 1959, Herter said it was very difficult to obtain accurate information on Laos, though he added there had been incursions either by North Vietnam Viet Minh or by old Lao Communists re-trained in North Vietnam.

The Lao Government on September 4, without con-sulting the United States, Britain or France, appealed to the U.N. for assistance against attacks from across the northeastern border, which, it said, foreign troops had been crossing since July 16.[24] The State Depart-ment immediately indicated that the United States would support the appeal of Laos for a United Na-tions emergency force, charging that the Communists clearly intended to direct a rebellion in Laos.

The Lao Government had considered appealing to SEATO as well as the United Nations, but on State Department advice it abstained, awaiting results of its appeal to the United Nations. SEATO members were nevertheless interested, owing to commitments to Laos, Cambodia and South Vietnam. Representatives met on September 4 with Acting Secretary Dillon.[25] Hoping to avoid involvement, they agreed to press for action either in the Security Council or the General Assembly. Their concern not to become involved was relieved temporarily by the action of the Security Council on September 7 in voting, ten to one (U.S.S.R.), to send a subcommittee to Laos to make an "inquiry" (not an investigation) without drawing conclusions.

The task of the Subcommittee proved extremely difficult, owing to bad communications, bad weather, the subtleties of evaluating testimony, and communist evasive tactics. The fighting subsided, but Laos claimed the communists were lying low.[26]

After four weeks in Laos the Subcommittee reported that "the ensemble" of its information "did not clearly establish whether there were crossings of the frontier by regular North Vietnam troops," but "varying degrees and kinds of support" had been supplied to hostile forces from the North Vietnamese side. Also, "practically all witnesses (40 out of 41) stated that support for rebel forces did come from North Vietnam in the form of equipment, arms, ammunition, supplies and help of political cadres."[27] The U.S.S.R. commented gloatingly that Laotian charges had "collapsed like a house of cards." Herter's view was that, taking into account the facilities of the Subcommittee, it was "a very objective and good report," which did not say or imply that the Subcommittee had got to the truth of the matter.[28] He thought it had "a tranquilizing effect on the dangerous situation."

The report of the U.N. Subcommittee on Laos was a blow to Premier Phoui Sananikone who resigned in December 1959. King Savang Vatthana authorized a caretaker government under the elderly Khou Abhay, President of the King's Council.[29] The April 1960, elections were an overwhelming victory for the government. Owing largely to physical confinement of some eligible Pathet Lao candidates, including Prince Souphanouvong, it won 56 out of 59 places in the National Assembly. The rigged election caused strong opposition protests, stiffer attitudes in Hanoi and Peking, and increased guerilla activities.

The repercussions led to the coup of August 9, 1960, which reflected dissatisfaction with the government, nominally headed by Tiao Somsanith, on the grounds of corruption, neglect of the troops, and subservience to the United States. The active agent of the coup, a theretofore unknown young captain named Kong Le, at a stadium rally said he aimed to stop the campaign against the Pathet Lao, and to end corruption in the army, the bureaucracy and the National Assembly.[30] The coup brought back Souvanna Phouma and emphasized the three-way split among neutralists, pro-Western forces, and pro-Communists. It sharpened East-West tensions as well as policy differences among the Western allies.

Souvanna Phouma was the key figure throughout the negotiations which followed. He had declared his intention to end the fighting with the Pathet Lao and solve problems with the "brothers in the jungle."[31] His intentions regarding the relation of the Neo Lao Hak Xat (NLHX—the party of the Pathet Lao) to the government were not clear, as his statements were sometimes equivocal. But *The Times* of London said there was "little ground for anxiety about his personal views."[32] On going to Luang Prabang in late August 1960, for royal confirmation as Premier, the prince proposed a new government with Phoumi Nosavan, leader of the pro-Western forces, as Deputy Prime Minister. The King approved the proposed government, which did not include any recognized communists, although one leftist, Quinim Pholsena, was in it.[33]

Ambassador Winthrop Brown immediately recommended that the United States indicate approval of the government, believing it the best to be hoped for; but the State Department made no move, though it recognized the regime a month later. The situation changed when Kong Le denounced the appointment of Phoumi, who, with Prince Boun Oum, flew at once to his headquarters at Savannakhet. On grounds of "personal insecurity" Phoumi refused Souvanna's urgent request, supported by a strong plea from the American Embassy, to join Souvanna's government in Vientiane, except on conditions impossible of acceptance. In the name of Boun Oum on September 10, 1960, he declared the existing government and constitution "abolished," and said his group would take over.[34]

During this period Souvanna was trying to conciliate the Pathet Lao and give them a larger role in the

National Assembly without bringing them into the government, but the Pathet Lao laid down unacceptable conditions, including the dismissal of all pro-Western Cabinet members.[35] They also stepped up their military activities with important successes. In this three-cornered struggle Souvanna was caught between left and right extremes, without major military resources. He told Ambassador Brown that his object was to unite rightists and neutral forces to be able to negotiate from strength with the Pathet Lao. He informed the diplomatic corps on September 10 that because of the rebellion of Phoumi and Boun Oum he would have to stop all conversations with the Pathet Lao.

The position of the United States was difficult. Souvanna had come into office under a cloud, from the U.S. viewpoint. He had become Premier under the auspices of a leftist whose coup had driven a pro-Western government out of office, and whose declared purpose was to establish close relations with the Pathet Lao as well as with the U.S.S.R. Souvanna's record of collaboration with the Pathet Lao in 1958, though in a broadly representative neutral government, was not pleasing to United States policy makers. At the same time he was not himself a communist, and in his cabinet appointments of late August 1960, he made clear his desire to include rightists, even Phoumi Novasan. He assured Ambassador Brown that he did not want communists in the cabinet, though he sought better relations with the Pathet Lao.

Souvanna's position was equally difficult. The denunciation of his government by the Phoumi rightist forces made impossible a strong line with the Pathet Lao.[36] Souvanna was further embarrassed by an un-acknowledged Thai blockade. Help was not available from the United States, though the State Department tried unsuccssfully to get Thailand to raise the block-ade. On September 30, 1960, Souvanna announced his intention to establish diplomatic relations with the U.S.S.R.[37]

4

September 1960 was a crucial month in Laotian developments. The American Embassy in Vientiane was not always in agreement with Washington. Am-bassador Brown was convinced that Souvanna Phou-ma was the only person capable of finding a peaceful noncommunist solution and that the best course for the United States was to throw full support behind him in hope of unifying the anticommunist forces, including Phoumi, enabling Souvanna to set up a viable neutral state. The members of Brown's country team shared these views.

Washington was not convinced. It was skeptical of Souvanna, who had apparently lost control of the military situation (caused largely by Phoumi's defec-tion and buildup) and was making approaches to the U.S.S.R. and the Pathet Lao. The Department decided early in October 1960, to suspend cash-grant aid to Souvanna as long as part of it might fall into Kong Le's hands.[38] It decided also to step up military assis-tance to Phoumi's units fighting the Pathet Lao, and to make a last effort with Souvanna.

Accordingly, it sent J. Graham Parsons, Assistant Secretary for Far Eastern Affairs, posthaste to Laos, accompanied by John N. Irwin, II, of Defense, and Vice Admiral Herbert Riley. Parsons' mission was to induce Souvanna to break relations with Kong Le, defer negotiations with the Pathet Lao, and transfer the machinery of government at least temporarily to Luang Prabang, the royal capital, under the conservative influence of King Savang Vatthana.[39] Parsons arrived at an awkward time—the day after Souvanna reopened negotiations with the Pathet Lao and the day before the arrival of Soviet Ambassador Abramov. Parsons and Ambassador Brown had two conferences with Souvanna. Irwin and Riley talked with Phoumi in Savannakhet, apparently without well-coordinated instructions.

Souvanna refused to break with Kong Le or postpone negotiations with the Pathet Lao, though he seemed to acquiesce in moving the government to Luang Prabang. As for Phoumi, Souvanna thought it was up to him to recognize the government's authority. Souvanna denied leftist aims, but said, as he had announced earlier, that if the United States refused aid he would have to go elsewhere. Parsons was reported as telling him he would find that the communists did not play a neutral game. The day after his conferences in Vientiane, Parsons, a former Ambassador to Laos, flew to Luang Prabang to consult the King. Reportedly Souvanna was highly displeased. After consulting with Parsons, Brown secured Souvanna's agreement for the United States to supply military aid directly to Phoumi, since Phoumi was actively fighting the Pathet Lao, on condition that the military equipment not be used against Souvanna. In return, supplies as well as financial aid would be renewed to Souvanna.[40] The United States was thus in the admittedly anomalous position of supporting a rebel regime against a government with which it had diplomatic relations, and doing this with the consent of that government. On October 17, 1960, the State Department announcd the resumption of cash-grant aid to the Souvanna Government.

Souvanna's relations with Washington did not improve. His weakening position, which he blamed on the United States, made him more responsive to Soviet advances, which were backed by propaganda accusing the United States of planning to crush his neutralist government by armed intervention. Souvanna's announcement on October 27, 1960, that he had accepted in principle an offer of Soviet aid, added to American skepticism.[41]

Discussing the "confused Vientiane situation" with the French Ambassador in mid-November 1960, Herter said we still hoped for some constitutional adjustment, but Kong Le was cooperating with the Pathet Lao and Souvanna had called for communist assistance. What the United States had in mind, he said, was a genuinely neutral Laos, not leaning toward the communists.

Faced with numerous defections, and the resulting Phoumi buildup, Souvanna speeded his negotiations on the left. He announced his intention to send good-will missions to Peking and Hanoi and to form a coalition government, including the NLHX party. He flew to Sam Neua in Pathet Lao territory on November 18 for two days with his half-brother, Souphanouvong, and secured agreement in principle on a coalition government to include both Pathet Lao and Phoumi members, but not Phoumi.[42] On November 22, Souvanna said his government would ask the Soviet Union for all aid it was willing to give—economic, military, or other—adding that "we are short of everything." Ambassador Abramov said the U.S.S.R. would be "only too happy to oblige."[43]

In conversation with the British Ambassador on November 25, Herter was asked about including two Pathet Lao in Souvanna's cabinet, which the British favored. The Secretary said that would be the beginning of a slippery slope. Before long there would be four, then six, and in the end a Communist takeover. He thought it a mistake to assume the possibility of working with the Pathet Lao, and expressed loss of confidence in Souvanna. He said the King was the key to the situation and that he too apparently had lost confidence in Souvanna. Would the King take a strong stand? The Secretary regarded the situation as grave and said that "if Laos goes, the rest of Indo-China goes very rapidly." He recognized with regret that British and American policies differed over Laos.

Meantime, crisis loomed in Vientiane. Souvanna, on November 26, 1960, told a cheering crowd that foreigners were interfering with his efforts to restore political peace. He said his only desire was "to bring peace to all our people," adding that "we must not let our country become a battleground between East and West." He denied being either communist or pro-communist—a statement which most British, French, and other observers apparently believed. Many in the diplomatic community reportedly thought American coolness toward Souvanna might drive him toward the Communists.[44]

Souvanna's efforts to bring Phoumi into a left-neutralist-right government, and to stave off his campaign against Vientiane, ended in his own flight to Cambodia on December 9, 1960, after delegating his powers to the senior army officer in Vientiane, General Sounthone. Pro and anti factions juggled power for several days, but Phoumi forces arrived on the fourteenth and took over from Kong Le, who with Soviet artillery reinforcements temporarily had gained the upper hand. Kong Le withdrew on the sixteenth, taking with him much American military material. A majority of the National Assembly, meanwhile, had met in Savannakhet and voted to censure the Souvanna Government, and shortly thereafter the King, who had little regard for Souvanna, entrusted "temporary conduct" of the Kingdom's affairs to the Revolutionary Committee headed by Boun Oum. The United States immediately promised full support to the new anticommunist government to thwart any threat of external aggression.[45]

The flight of Souvanna and the takeover of Vientiane by Phoumi and Boun Oum, followed by immediate recognition of the new regime by the United States, put a new face on the Laotian complex. By not resigning, Souvanna raised a constitutional question as to the status of the Boun Oum Government. The Soviet Union, surprised by Souvanna's departure, sent a sharp note to Washington (December 13) charging the United States with becoming "a direct participant" in rebel military operations "against the legal government of Laos" in violation of the Geneva agreements of 1954 and placed on it "all responsibility for the consequences" of its "aggressive actions." The United States reciprocated by placing "responsibility for the current strife in Laos . . . squarely upon the U.S.S.R. and its agents," condemning the U.S.S.R. for violating "every standard of legal conduct" in "airlifting weapons and ammunition in Soviet planes to rebel military forces fighting the loyal armed forces of the Royal Government." It said the United States policy of supporting Laos in its determination to maintain independence and integrity would continue, and warned "against efforts to gain control of or to subvert that free nation."[46]

Herter worked for a common policy among the Western allies. In Paris on December 15, 1960, he explained American policy to his British and French colleagues: he said it didn't pay off to put Communists in the government. Souvanna had gotten himself into a noose that way. A neutral buffer, "yes", a communist-infiltrated state, "no". The question was: were we going to let these small countries go down the drain? "If we could pull out of Asia, it would be lovely, but we don't relish the consequences": friendly countries falling into the Communist orbit.

Herter said we would intervene directly only if required under the SEATO treaty. Was it to our interest to let Southeast Asia go down the drain? If the North Vietnamese acted openly in support of the

Pathet Lao the obligations under the SEATO treaty would be clear. Couve de Murville thought such Vietnamese intervention should be prevented, but Herter asked whether we would say to the North Vietnamese: "Sweethearts, if you stop bringing arms in we will play ball with you." Herter asked the three governments whether they would deal with the new Lao government. The British thought this would be necessary, though they wanted Boun Oum to broaden the government. The French held off, regarding Boun Oum as incompetent.

Herter reported that the French as well as the British were extremely skittish about the situation in Laos—as to whether the Boun Oum government was constitutional. He said the British, harassed by questions in Parliament, lacked "a staunch stomach" regarding Laos, and the French were equally wobbly. In the NATO Ministerial Council on December 16, Herter said the American objective was a united Laos, with a government embracing all anti and non-communist elements, a defensive internal security army, a policy of neutrality friendly toward the West, with means, willingness, and desire to maintain independence against assault from without or from within. He said we could not ignore the results of Pathet Lao intrigue and insurgency during recent years.

At year's end, 1960, the Western allies had no common policy on Laos. Livingston Merchant, Under Secretary for Political Affairs, said the United States was virtually isolated on the issue of the legality of the Boun Oum government. Americans, he thought, could count on support of Thailand, South Vietnam, probably the Philippines and Pakistan, but not on other allies, let alone uncommitted countries. Herter bore down on his SEATO colleagues, warning of their responsibilities in Laos. They were in no mood for action, and in conferences of December 18 and 19 expressed concern regarding a report that the Lao government was about to request SEATO assistance. Foreign Minister Lord Home said the British people did not want SEATO to become too active. Herter therefore took steps to warn the Lao and Thai governments against making any unwise appeals to SEATO and to make none without consultation.

Charges by Boun Oum on December 30, of large infiltrations of troops from North Vietnam, though widely regarded as exaggerated, brought Herter back from vacation to confer with the President.[47] The State Department notified the communists, December 31, that it was following closely the grave situation in Laos and was consulting with allied governments. It said it would "take the most serious view of any intervention in Laos by the Chinese Communists or Viet Minh armed forces, or others" supporting the rebel Communist Pathet Lao.

The Department then called for the earliest possible meeting of the SEATO Council.[48] Permanent representatives, meeting in Bangkok on January 2, 1961, found "ample evidence" of weapons given to the Pathet Lao and of Soviet planes dropping arms to rebels. Pote Sarasin, the Secretary General, said there was nothing definite on charges that communist troops had intervened from North Vietnam. He said bravely that "it is always SEATO's aim to find peaceful means and we hope they can be found." The communiqué reflected the indecisive character of the meeting.

At year's end, 1960, the military situation had worsened. The Communists had captured Laos' strategic central plain and made important gains elsewhere. A Department press release on January 3, 1961, charged the Soviet Union and North Vietnam with widespread "participation in the Communist military operations against the Royal Lao government" and people, involving an extensive airlift of war material and North Vietnamese personnel. It gave "hard evidence" of at least 180 sorties, indicating dates, locations and the identification numbers of some planes.[49]

Drastic action was necessary to establish what all would call a neutral state. Britain and France had counted themselves out, except as negotiators or mediators.

Time was running out on the Eisenhower Administration and little could be done to point the way out of the diplomatic-military tangle. Herter's last three weeks were occupied largely with efforts to check the drift toward an East-West confrontation. What to do? Troublesome questions were: Should there be fresh terms of reference for the I.C.C.? Should a preparatory commission, representing the Indian, Polish and Canadian governments, pay a preliminary visit to Laos to agree on terms of reference? Should the Commission deal only with the King, the Boun Oum government, or whom? Could phraseology enable the Commission to work ostensibly with the King though actually with the Boun Oum government, thus saving face for the U.S.S.R. which did not recognize Boun Oum? Time ran out before Herter could find answers.

Secretary-designate Dean Rusk sat in on a review of the Lao situation on January 17, 1961. Herter said he would not want to make any move limiting Rusk's freedom of action. Rusk commented that the I.C.C. should not be reactivated unless free to operate throughout Laos.

Herter made his final official contribution to the problem in a meeting on the nineteenth with President Eisenhower and President-elect Kennedy. When Kennedy asked what the retiring Administration recommended on Laos, Herter said that if a political settlement were possible without setting up a new government including communists, that would be most desirable. Experience of the past fifteen years had indicated clearly that governments which included communists always led either to elimination of the communists or to takeover by them. A political solution, he said, depended largely on the military situation. The legal government of Laos had the right at any time to request SEATO for aid against aggression, and the Russian airlift, in the U.S. Government's view, was an aggression. The administration, he said, had felt there was no choice but to honor that obligation, though the British and French hoped such a request would never be made, and it was doubtful whether the French felt they had any obligation.[50]

American policy in Laos was in trouble. Speaking of the turbulent months of 1960, a high-level officer in the Foreign Service said, "our policy was difficult to define because of conflicting points of view in the

Government. CIA and JCS favored supporting the right-wing elements, whereas the State Department favored getting agreement among the various groups, though excluding communists." Laos, he said, "was a good example of no solution." Herter passed the problem along to the new Administration when the tide of events was at the flood.

# CHAPTER EIGHT

## THE SIMMERING MIDDLE EAST

THE MIDDLE EAST was not a major preoccupation of Secretary Herter, though it was inevitably a matter of concern because of its geographic location, its resources, its cultural heritage, and the conflicting forces at work in that area. The favored Western position in the Middle East, built up during the nineteenth century, had long been threatened by the Russian push to the south, which became more serious during and after World War II. The U.S.S.R. had a handy propaganda weapon in the developing nationalism of the area, which gained strength after 1945, exacerbated by the cry of "Western imperialism." The postwar clash of peoples, cultures, economic interests and political objectives made the Middle East a disorderly part of the world tottering constantly on the edge of crisis and occasionally going over the edge.

1

Britain, France and the United States sought to stabilize the situation in May 1950, by declaring "their unalterable opposition to the use of force . . . between any of the states in that area," and pledging to limit to defense needs the supply of arms to Israel and the Arab states. A further effort to contain the Soviet push took shape in the Baghdad Pact of 1955, consisting of the "northern tier" of states, including one Arab state, Iraq. But the U.S.S.R. denounced the pact as an "imperialist device" and Egypt rejected it, which stimulated Arab opposition. Western diplomatic moves sharpened the clash of policies, as illustrated by a Soviet arms deal with Egypt in September 1955, and later Soviet denunciation of the Tripartite Pact of 1950.[1] Erosion of Western strength in the Middle East resulted from the Suez crisis of 1956. Soviet influence increased in that area, especially in Syria. A feeling developed in Arab circles that the United States was not interested in their problems.[2]

The Eisenhower Doctrine of January 5, 1957 (approved by Congress on March 9), sought to stabilize the peace by promising economic aid and armed support to any Middle East nation desiring protection against "overt armed aggression *from any nation controlled by international communism*" (italics added). Thus the policy was restricted in range and could cause difficulties of interpretation. Only Lebanon openly accepted it. Other states either rejected it, *e.g.*, Egypt and Syria, or feared the imperialist tag placed on it by its enemies. Reviewing Middle East developments with Eric F. Johnston on April 6, 1957, Herter, then Acting Secretary, agreed that the situation was getting worse and that time alone would not cure it. Johnston and Herter both regarded the Arabs as politically incapable of doing many things that they, the Arabs, realized should be done. In a memorandum of March 15, 1958 to Secretary Dulles, Herter said he thought Iraq, Jordan, Lebanon and Saudi Arabia would soon need United States help. Herter's appraisal was verified by Assistant Secretary William Rountree who toured the major Middle East centers.

Events soon caught up with forecasts. In Iraq the coup of July 14, 1958, against King Faisal and Premier Nuri-al-Said, brought about by nationalist officers, put a bloody end to the pro-Western government after Nasserite nationalism and communism had undermined it. These events also stimulated the struggle between international communism and Nasser's Arab nationalism for control of Iraq. In Lebanon border incidents and hostile activities against the government built up fears. President Camille Chamoun requested military aid of the United States in mid-May, 1958, but there was doubt in Washington that the Eisenhower Doctrine would be applicable. Herter told James Reston that if the Lebanese troubles turned out to be only a civil war without major outside assistance, that would be another thing—but aid would be given only on request of Chamoun and his government. There was disagreement as to the seriousness of the communist threat from outside, but the Lebanese Government, under heavy pressure from rebel forces, officially requested military assistance in July, at a time when events in Iraq were in crisis and the Jordanian government was also threatened. American marines landed near Beirut on July 15, 1958, the day following the dramatic Iraqi coup. British paratroopers flew (in American planes) into Amman, Jordan. The Marines were not welcomed by the commander of Lebanese armed forces, General Fuad Chehab, and armed resistance was narrowly averted. Differences were later papered over when Robert D.

Murphy, on a special mission for the President, assisted in effecting transition of presidential power from Chamoun to General Chehab.[3]

In a speech of September 1958, Herter defended the United States action, saying that Lebanon faced a threat to its independence and integrity, and that the "urgency of the situation made it necessary to respond as it did," rather than through the U.N., though the United States immediately went to the U.N. to find an international solution so that American troops could be withdrawn.[4] Herter later remarked that his most satisfying contribution to the Lebanon episode came when, as Acting Secretary for a short period, he learned that "Honest John" nuclear delivery systems were about to be sent from Western Europe to the Lebanon area. Realizing the impression such action might give, he took up the matter at once with Defense Secretary Neil McElroy who stopped it.

After Soviet proposals for a summit meeting and conciliatory efforts of the Security Council failed, an "international solution" was found in an emergency session of the General Assembly, which on August 21, 1958, adopted a 10-power Arab resolution calling for mutual respect for territorial integrity, nonaggression and noninterference in each other's internal affairs, as well as for appropriate action by the Secretary General. Withdrawals, in stages, were completed by United States forces on October 24, and the British from Jordan on November 2.[5]

Prospects for stabilizing Arab relations appeared brighter after the Lebanon-Jordan crisis. Herter expressed cautious optimism in a news conference of

July 9, 1959, saying that the outlook for "normalizing" the situation in that area was encouraging, adding that the United States was maintaining a friendly attitude toward the United Arab Republic (U.A.R.-Egypt) and Iraq in hope of improving relations. The position of the West in the Arab world seemed less difficult than it had threatened to become after the revolution in Iraq. Speaking to the U.N. General Assembly in September, the Secretary contrasted the "relative quiet" then prevailing with the crisis of the previous year. The trends, he hazarded, were "a hopeful portent."[6]

Though it did not reach the explosive stage, the Arab power struggle, after July 1958, continued unabated. Iraq's Premier Abdel Karim al-Kassim, competed with Egypt's Nasser for leadership in the Arab world, and played the U.S.S.R. against the U.A.R. Kassim sought to weaken Nasser's control over Syria which country, in February 1958, had joined with Egypt in forming the U.A.R. (then withdrew in 1961). Nasser struck back in anti-Kassim demonstrations in March 1959, accusing the Iraqi Premier of trying to subject the Arab peoples to a "communist reign of terror" and of working with agents of a foreign power (the U.S.S.R.) to break up the U.A.R.[7] He exchanged verbal blows with Khrushchev, but their feuding over Iraq and Syria did not interfere with their unity of purpose in denouncing Western imperialism.

Anti-imperialism propaganda was a potent stimulant of Arab nationalism and anti-Western feeling, but it was not strong enough to unite Arab peoples under one political framework as desired by Nasser. Divisive political, economic, and sectarian forces, and mutual distrust were too powerful. The anti-imperialism charges of the U.A.R. and the U.S.S.R. had a damaging effect, as intended, on United States relations with the Arab Middle East, though they were useful only as a flag to raise in connection with other, more serious, issues.

2

The major Middle East perplexity facing Herter at the end of the 1950's was the deepening rift between Israel and the Arab states. Assistant Secretary Rountree after a Middle East tour in December 1958, reported that the main obstacle to better American relations with the Arabs was Israel. This was made clear when Nasser, meeting with Eisenhower and Herter on September 26, 1960, during the 15th General Assembly session, said the creation of Israel, for which he held the United States primarily responsible, was the "first barrier" to come between the United States and the Arab people. Sir John Troutbeck, former British Ambassador to Iraq, had written early in 1959: "The creation of Israel . . . was neither forgiven nor forgotten" by the Arab middle class, which had become an important factor in the Arab world.[8] The difficulty of the situation was accentuated by the absence of direct negotiations between the parties, owing to Arab refusal to admit that the belligerency had ended, to recognize the existence of Israel, or carry on diplomatic relations with it.

The United States desired to support Israel's independence and improve relations with the Arab peoples. The delicacy of the situation was illustrated by an inquiry from the House Foreign Affairs Committee regarding a proposed Congressional concurrent resolution to extend greetings of the United States on the tenth anniversary of Israel's indpendence (May 15, 1958). Acting Secretary Herter replied that of course the Government intended to send appropriate felicitations, but he observed that this function was one exercised by the President and the Executive Branch. He cautioned that a concurrent resolution would establish a precedent that might be embarrassing in the future. In existing Middle East tensions such a resolution might be interpreted as partisanship in the bitter Arab-Israeli dispute, hence it was necessary to be extremely circumspect. No concurrent resolution was sent, but each House sent a resolution for itself, toned down from the originals, but still expressed largely in superlative terms.[9]

Israeli political sensibilities were severely pricked by international reactions to plans for a parade in Jerusalem to celebrate Israel's tenth anniversary. These plans anticipated bringing in more troops and heavier military equipment than permitted by the terms of the 1949 armistice agreement with Jordan.[10] Reports from Jerusalem and a warning from Secretary General Hammarskjold indicated danger of border trouble with Jordan and possible shooting. Acting Secretary Herter considered warning American citizens in Israel of the danger, but the Israeli Government reacted with surprise and shock to his projected press release which, it said, would create an atmosphere of crisis and would be viewed as an unfriendly act. Israel and Jordan subsequently accepted the presence of U.N. military observers along the parade route. Herter decided not to issue the release, but the purpose had been served and the celebration went off without incident.[11]

Behind these sensibilities lay difficult Arab-Israeli problems. Some 900,000 Arab refugees from Israeli territory were sheltered in neighboring Arab countries, supported by funds provided in large part—up to seventy per cent—by the United States and administered by the U.N. Relief and Works Agency (U.N.R.W.A.). The problem had been on the U.N. agenda since 1948 when the General Assembly adopted Resolution 194 (III) providing that refugees wishing to return to their homes should be allowed to do so as soon as practicable, and that compensation should be paid for loss or damage to property to those not desiring to return. The Palestine Conciliation Commission (P.C.C.) was established to "facilitate the repatriation, resettlement and the economic and social rehabilitation of the refugees and the payment of compensation." This principle, though not acceptable to Israel, was frequently reaffirmed by the General Assembly. In December 1959—in Resolution 1456 (XIV)—it directed the Palestine Conciliation Commission by an 80 to 0 vote to make further efforts to carry out the instructions of 1948.[12]

The refugee program of 1948, repeatedly invoked by the General Assembly and calling for repatriation or compensation of refugees, lacked somewhat in realism. Offhand it seemed to be the obvious answer to the puzzling problem of the refugees, and the Arab nations clung steadfastly to that proposed solution. But it ran up against the realities of Israel's do-or-die relations with the Arab world. Repatriation on a large scale would have intolerable effects on Israel's plans for a Jewish state, and compensation on the proposed scale would be far beyond Israel's financial capacity.

Was there a possible compromise acceptable to both parties? Herter was hopeful that during the General Assembly session of 1959 discussions on Palestine refugees would light the way to an eventual solution. He thought he saw an improvement in Arab attitudes. Israeli Ambassador Harman told him that Israel was ready to negotiate on the refugee issue, but the two sides came no closer together. In June 1960, Herter proposed to the President a new approach, the key element of which would be acceptance by all parties of a program offering to the refugees the options of repatriation, resettlement, or compensation. Only a small portion, presumably, would elect to live permanently in Israel, and the repatriation would be phased over a period of years so that no mass influx of refugees would pose a security threat to Israel. The plan could satisfy the Arab countries that the repatriation principle was being upheld. It could also improve Israel's standing in world opinion and offer the best prospects for progress on the long-standing problem.

The President approved the plan, but it failed to gain the support of either side. In a conference with the President and Herter at the General Assembly session of 1960, Nasser confirmed the U.A.R. view that Israel should take back all Arab refugees, noting that it would then no longer be an all-Jewish state. Discussing the subject with Secretary Herter in September, Israel's Foreign Minister, Golda Meir, said her government considered the "free choice" concept (the right of refugees to choose) out of the question. Over ten per cent of the population of Israel was made up of Arabs, and she could not see adding 300,000 to 350,000 Arabs to a population of something over two million. It would, she said, be bringing an atomic bomb into the country. Many well-meaning people talked of the desirability of an Israeli gesture of taking back 100,000 Arabs. Her government, she said, was willing to participate in gestures, but wanted to stay alive after the gesture was completed. Even the notion of "family reunion" raised grave problems, since no one knew where a family started and stopped. In her view, resettlement was the only answer.

Herter commented that the Congress was extremely discouraged because no progress had been made in solving the refugee problem. The government renewed pressure on Israel and the Arab states to end their 12-year dispute on refugees, but nothing came of it, and Herter's hopes for a compromise settlement failed of realization during his term, as also in the successor administration.[13]

3

Arab-Israeli relations were further complicated by the U.A.R. blockade of the Suez Canal to Israeli shipping following the armistice of 1949. The U.A.R.

claimed the blockade was legal. There had been no peace treaty since the armistice; therefore Nasser said there was still a state of war. The U.N. Security Council had rejected Egyptian arguments in August 1951, but to no avail. In March 1959, Nasser extended the blockade to include vessels of other nationalities carrying Israeli cargoes.[14]

In his General Assembly address of September, 1959, Herter said: "The United States continues to support the principle of freedom of passage, as endorsed by the United Nations." He discussed the Suez problem with Hammarskjold who after a conference with Nasser thought he had secured a satisfactory compromise, but the understanding did not hold. Nasser ignored it, as was indicated early in 1960 by the forced unloading and confiscation of Israeli cargoes on two freighters, the Greek *Astypalae* and the Danish *Inge Toft*.[15] In discussing this problem with the President and Herter during the New York General Assembly meeting, Nasser said there had been a sharp reaction in Egypt to American statements, *e.g.*, by Vice President Nixon and Senator John F. Kennedy, then running for election to the presidency, who "unfairly said open the Suez Canal to Israeli shipping." If the United States wanted the canal open to Israeli shipping, he said, the United States should try just as hard to get Israel to implement U.N. resolutions on which it was in default.

There was some question as to who should carry the ball in the canal controversy. Herter had no yen to do so. When questioned on the subject on February 8, 1960, he said the Secretary General had undertaken "to try to adjust this matter as between Israel and Egypt." Hammarskjold's efforts were continuing, though the outcome was still uncertain. Herter felt that working through Hammarskjold was the best way to handle the problem. When the question was raised again on March 25, Herter said the United States was not considering taking the initiative on Suez. The Secretary General's efforts had not ended, and the U.S. Government was supporting him.[16] Hammarskjold, who had no luck on this, was reported to have remarked on a tendency in some unnamed quarters "to expect from the Secretary General some action which rightly belongs in the Security Council."[17] This issue awaited a more explosive turn of events.

There were other troublesome problems. Israel was at odds with Lebanon, Syria, and Jordan over Jordan River water rights. Eric Johnston in 1955, with the advice of Arab technicians from the countries involved, proposed a proportional allocation of the Jordan waters to bordering states; but this proposal was rejected by the Arab League, reportedly because of Syrian objections. Israel went ahead with its land development according to the Johnston water-diversionary provisions, which led to threats, incidents and other water-diversionary plans.

The United States, in an even-handed role, supported Jordan's proposal in 1958 to tap the Yarmuk River. Ambassador Harman questioned whether this was in line with the Johnston plan, and he complained to Herter that the United States was giving stronger support to Jordan than to Israel. Herter expressed great regret over the miscarriage of the Johnston plan, but assured Harman as to the propriety of the Jordan plan and said that both plans could be carried out.[18] In the early 1960's Jordan completed an irrigation project, diverting part of the Yarmuk waters, and Israel utilized Jordan and Tiberias waters. Neither reached agreement on the Johnston plan.

The issues in Arab-Israeli relations, aggravated by Arab nonrecognition of Israel as a state, inevitably reflected feelings of insecurity on both sides and a concern for military preparedness. The United States sought to avoid an arms race, but Herter encountered increasing pressures from Israel as tensions mounted in 1959 and 1960, stimulated—as mentioned—by the formation of the U.A.R. by Egypt and Syria in February 1958. Ambassador Harman expressed great concern in November 1959, over "continued massive rearmament" of the U.A.R. by the Soviet bloc, which he said had heavily upset the arms balance in all areas, giving Egypt and Syria both a tactical and strategic advantage. He reminded the Secretary of a statement by former Secretary Dulles that Israel should be in a position to turn back aggression from neighboring countries, and he called for more military and economic aid. Herter said his government would gladly study Israel's list of arms requirements, but reminded the Ambassador that the United States, while glad to help Israel with small defensive items, preferred that for larger items Israel look to traditional sources of supply, the U.K. and France. He called attention to severe Congressional curtailment of foreign aid appropriations. But border raids by Arabs in February 1960, caused Foreign Minister Meir and Ambassador Harman to express alarm to Herter and to stress the need for Israel to acquire arms to preserve a relative balance of strength.

The American position was delicate, as emphasized by the visit of Israeli Prime Minister David Ben-Gurion in early March. Heads of ten Arab missions conferred with Herter on March 7 and expressed great concern over the visit. They cited Israeli statements and activities which, they said, indicated that the purpose of the visit was not so much to accept an honorary degree at Brandeis University as to damage Arab-American relations, which had improved. Herter assured them that the United States did not anticipate any change in its relations with the Arab states as a result of Ben-Gurion's visit, and pointed out that earlier Israeli pressures to prevent the United States from supporting a World Bank loan to the U.A.R. for improving the Suez Canal were not successful.[19]

Herter advised the President that Ben-Gurion's real purpose was to have a private conversation with him, and the Secretary noted that the United States interest in Israel since 1948 was expressed in government aid totalling $715,000,000 and in private contributions of one billion dollars. He said normal and friendly relations between the United States and all Middle Eastern countries were in the interest of both the United States and Israel. Undue political and economic pressures on Arab nations, unilaterally applied, could only inflame anti-Western emotions and create exploitable opportunities for international communism and make solutions of problems more difficult. He reminded the President—in view of an expected request by Ben-Gurion for extensive military support—that traditionally the United States had refrained from becoming a major supplier of arms to the Near East.

As Herter forecast, the Prime Minister presented a large "shopping list" for arms, totalling $600,000,000, which the United States might either give directly or make available elsewhere by providing economic assistance. Ben-Gurion made an impressive case, emphasizing the threats to Israel's existence, detailing Israel's military inferiority to the U.A.R., recalling commitments by the President and Secretary Dulles in 1958. He urged that at the prospective summit conference in Paris the West should endeavor to secure a declaration in favor of maintaining the *status quo* in the Middle East. If Israel did not remain free, he said, it would be exterminated as the Jews had been exterminated by Hitler in Germany. The items most needed from the United States were anti-aircraft missiles and aviation electronic equipment. Major arms supplies had come from Britain and France, and hopefully these would continue. The answer to the Prime Minister was much the same as that previously given by Herter to Ambassador Harman and Foreign Minister Meir: the United States viewed Israel's defense needs sympathetically, but had endeavored to avoid becoming a principal supplier of arms to the Middle East in order to be in a position of arbitrator. Israel's best source of arms was Western Europe. The United States would study Israeli requests for anti-aircraft missiles and electronic equipment and see what could be done.[20]

In a conference with British Foreign Secretary Lloyd, Herter said that a summit agreement on the territorial *status quo* in the Middle East, desired by Ben-Gurion, was not credible, as Russia scarcely would agree to a territorial guarantee. He doubted that it would be appropriate at a summit meeting for the four powers to appear to "control the world." Lloyd agreed. Herter notified Harman in May 1960, of willingness to accept Israel's request for electronic warning and detection equipment, but demurred on offensive weapons or large quantities of military equipment, though he thought an extension of credit repayable in dollars would be possible. Ben-Gurion expressed disappointment at not getting the anti-aircraft missiles. He pointed to Israeli airfields without missile defenses, and did not abandon hope of finding a way to solve that problem. Foreign Minister Meir followed up with Herter in late June, stressing huge acquisitions of military supplies by the U.A.R. and Nasser's unrelenting bellicosity. Her government, she said, was grateful for the early warning equipment but was deeply troubled by the outstanding questions of Hawk missiles and of financing the large additional expenditures required for "necessary" arms. Herter pointed to special Congressional difficulties that year in foreign aid appropriations, and said the Department fully appreciated Israel's difficult defense problem and would keep the matter under review.

The Israeli Government thought it had a good case, arguing that the Hawk missiles were defensive weapons incapable of being used offensively. But Herter stated the United States position conclusively in a careful letter to Ben-Gurion in August, explaining that American policy in the "Near East" was to assist in preserving territorial integrity and reducing the danger of hostilities. We would continue the policy of not becoming a major supplier of arms to that area. To depart from it would tend to intensify an arms race to the detriment of the states concerned. While the Hawk system was purely defensive, it was easy to imagine that some outside power, anxious to exacerbate tensions, would yield to the importunities of Israel's apprehensive neighbors and equip them with missile weaponry, including, perhaps, missiles with surface-to-surface capability, against which the Hawks would not be a defense. He said we were gratified that Israel had been able to obtain heavy military equipment elsewhere. As to the large financial burdens, the United States had not contributed directly to Israel's defense budget, but the substantial economic aid since Israel's birth—$700,000,000—had made that burden easier.

Eisenhower and Herter, in conference with Nasser at the U.N. General Assembly session of 1960, sought to improve relations and reach agreement on stabilization of armaments in the Middle East, but did not succeed. Nasser said Israel could get arms from the West and the U.A.R. could not. But the U.A.R. could get them elsewhere. The arms race was on, and Anglo-American officials could see no means of breaking the spiral.[21] Arms competition colored other Arab-Israeli relations and contributed to the "Six-Day War" of 1967 and to further exacerbation of tensions in the Middle East.

# CHAPTER NINE

## EMERGING AFRICA

THE MOVEMENT of African peoples from colonialism to independence reached flood tide during Herter's secretaryship. The process was a historical phenomenon. Before World War II there were four independent states in Africa: Liberia, Ethiopia, South Africa and Egypt (a British Protectorate until 1949). Six more were added during the 1950's—Libya, Morocco, Tunisia, Sudan, Ghana and Guinea. In the climactic year, 1960, "The year of African independence," seventeen newly independent African states emerged. Sixteen of these were added to the drama of an already dramatic 15th session of the U.N. General Assembly (1960) by becoming active participants immediately in that international forum.

The rapidly accelerated thrust of African peoples to the fore, after four hundred years of relative quiescence under Western influence, was a startling revelation to the West. Persons in the early 1950's, thinking of Africa's future, generally regarded independence for its peoples as lying decades in the future, though the British began to consider the problem seriously after riots in the Gold Coast (later Ghana) in 1948.[1] African Freedom Day, April 15, 1959, highlighted what the *New York Times* called "sudden, thrilling, agonizing upheaval of the African races, after countless centuries of primitiveness, subjection and isolation

147

from the civilized world."[2] By that time the wave of nationalism sweeping over Black Africa had left no area untouched.

Herter was not without misgivings—discreetly expressed. Speaking to the General Assembly on September 17, 1959, he noted that "four new African states" were to achieve independence in the coming year (even then he was not fully aware of the sweep of the tide.) He said that the United States welcomed them "in accordance with its historic policy that all peoples should have independence who desire it and are able to undertake its responsibilities."[3] In the General Assembly the following year, September 1960, welcoming thirteen African nations to U.N. membership, he said their achievement represented "a dramatic expansion of freedom." Then he gently admonished them, saying that "with freedom comes responsibility, responsibility for national development as well as participation in the international development of the world community."[4] To the UPI Conference of Editors and Publishers in September 1960, the Secretary explained that "the United States wishes to help Africa channel her energies into nation building rather than conflict. But while we are interested in stability, we know our approach cannot be merely tranquilizing and conservative. New forces are on the march. There is an atmosphere of change." Our role, he said, was to help channel the changes in the direction of economic, social and political progress.[5]

The American people were not prepared for the epochal changes that Africa was undergoing in the 1950's. They were not "Africa conscious" and had

generally regarded that continent as of special concern to European powers. That area therefore received relatively little attention at top levels of government. George C. McGhee, Assistant Secretary for
Near Eastern, South Asian, and African affairs (an
enormous area), sounded the first policy alert in an
address at Oklahoma City on May 8, 1950, saying that
though Africa was not a crisis area at the time, and
communism had made no significant inroads, "we
Americans cannot neglect it." He urged that the
study of Africa be strengthened in the United States.[6]

The State Department became aware in the mid-
1950's that Africa was undergoing a transformation
tending to make it a continent mostly of independent
states rather than a grouping of imperial appendages.
In 1956, by organizational adjustment, the Department gave greater recognition to African problems,
and in 1958 with Congressional approval it established
the Bureau of African Affairs.

Owing to the independence movement in Africa,
the United States found itself on the horns of a dilemma caused by the conflict between its traditional anti-
colonialism and its close ties with major European
powers which had important African colonies.[7]

In its relations with France, the United States faced
this dilemma during Herter's secretaryship. Insurgency had been spreading throughout Algeria since November 1954. Some 30,000 insurgents were pinning
down 400,000 or more French troops. The Algerian
problem had been brought before the United Nations
annually since 1955, though France regularly insisted
that the matter was strictly within its domestic juris-

diction. The United States pursued a cautious course, trying to protect French interests without abandoning its traditional principles of freedom of peoples. To do this became increasingly difficult. The problem gradually worsened, and by 1958 terrorism and bloodshed reached crisis proportions. Neither side seemed to be winning. The United States still sought to protect French interests, and in the Political Committee of the U.N. it voted against a relatively drastic 17-nation Afro-Asian resolution favoring Algeria, which nevertheless was carried by a simple majority. In the plenary session the resolution was watered down, but still was offensive to France, as it recognized the right of the Algerian people to independence, called the situation a threat to international peace, and urged negotiations between the parties. The resolution fell short of the necessary two-thirds, by one vote, the tally being 35 to 18, with 28 abstentions. The United States was among the abstainers and thereby incurred the displeasure of each side, particularly of France.

The United States was already suspect by De Gaulle. French Ambassador Alphand, in a long talk with Acting Secretary Herter on April 18, 1958, inquired whether reports were correct that the United States had changed its policy on French relations with Algeria. Herter said such reports were unfounded, as the United States attached the highest importance to the need for a peaceful, democratic, and just solution of the problem, and hoped that France itself would achieve such a solution. Alphand told newsmen he was satisfied with Herter's assurances.[8] But the French Government was far from satisfied with American abstention from voting on the December 1958, resolution on Algeria. De Gaulle registered sharp displeasure.[9]

The Algerian problem was a major issue in the 14th session of the U.N. General Assembly, 1959. Twenty-five African and Asian nations, on July 14, asked that "the question of Algeria" be inscribed on the agenda. Meantime, the French began discussions with Herter to make sure of strong American support. Herter noted in a talk with Couve de Murville that the French had abstained from participation in the debates in 1958 and had asked the United States to take a tougher stand in the U.N. than France itself was willing to take. Would the French participate in the debate on Algeria in 1959? The French thought it would be impossible to participate, as they did not regard the U.N. as competent in the Algerian affair. Herter said such a French position would make the United States situation much more difficult. He thought the French could reserve all their rights as to the competence of the U.N., while at least defending themselves in the debate. He hoped Couve de Murville would give further thought to the United States standpoint.

In late August 1959 it appeared that De Gaulle had something "cooking" for the Algerian problem. Ambassador Alphand told Herter that De Gaulle had a plan which was very liberal and which showed great imagination. He thought it would justify full United States support in the U.N. General Assembly debate. Herter expressed pleasure that the French would have a fixed plan for Algeria. Premier Michel Debré, in view of the prospective policy declaration, thought France's allies should take the pledge. He said France's Algerian policy "must not be contested or contradicted by anyone who wants France as an ally." He accused France's allies of not understanding what France was trying to do in Algeria.[10]

The mystery was revealed by De Gaulle on September 16, 1959, when he proposed to permit Algerians to choose their own future four years after a cease-fire. They could decide on "secession"—so-called independence—which, he said, would be "incredible and disastrous," or out-and-out identification with France—that is, integration—or "government of Algeria by Algerians, backed by French help." He said it was an offer of "the peace of the brave."[11]

State Department officials, favorably impressed, hoped the Arabs would not reject the plan out of hand. Press opinion saw lack of clarity and precision in its terms.[12] President Eisenhower, in a news conference on September 17, expressed approval, calling the statement "a courageous and statesmanlike declaration."

But the President's statement did not satisfy De Gaulle, who wanted an early and forthright public statement that the United States would vote for France on the Algerian item. Couve de Murville on September 21 emphasized to Herter the great responsibility of the United States and its influence in the United Nations. He "appreciated" the President's statement, but said it left open what precisely the United States position would be in the U.N. Herter said the President's position was clear and forthcoming. The Arabs might change their tactics as a result of De Gaulle's speech. The United States could not say in advance that whatever the Arabs might do would be wrong. Couve de Murville replied that the crucial question was how the United States would vote, and it was important to state immediately that it would support the French position in the U.N. Herter said he wanted to think further about it, but he could not give a blank check in advance.

In a speech on September 22, 1959, in New York at a luncheon of the U.N. Correspondents Association, Herter said that although many details of De Gaulle's speech remained obscure, "a great stride had been taken," and he hoped that no action in the General Assembly "would prejudice the realization of General de Gaulle's far-reaching declaration."[13] Herter's statement pleased the French but irked the Arabs, especially the Algerian insurgents. Herter remarked privately on September 22 that he had not formed a judgment on the fuzzy parts of De Gaulle's proposals, but in a news conference of October 6 he said, "we are tremendously heartened by General de Gaulle's proposal," and noted that President Habib Bourguiba of Tunisia, had taken a "constructive and courageous attitude."[14]

Relations with France meanwhile were exacerbated by permission given to three representatives of the Algerian Provisional Government (FLN) to come to the United States. Herter pointed out that legally there was no basis for rejecting the passports issued in Tunis since it could not be proven in court that admitting the representatives was contrary to American interests, as distinct from French interests.[15]

The United States strongly supported France in voting against a 22-nation Afro-Asian resolution opposing French nuclear testing in the Sahara.[16]

The final vote on the Afro-Asian resolution on Algeria came on November 2, 1959. The French remained adamant in rejecting any resolution of the U.N. on a settlement of the war in Algeria. Such a resolution, said Ambassador Berard, "would be illegal and harmful," and his delegation stayed out of the debate.[17] The United States opposed the resolution in committee, but abstained from voting on a watered-down draft in the plenary session, which still recognized the "right of the Algerian people to self-determination," and urged "pourparlers" to implement this right. The vote of 39-22-20 fell short of the necessary two-thirds.[18]

At the NATO Ministerial meeting in mid-December, Foreign Minister Couve de Murville took Herter to task for criticisms made off the record by General Nathan Twining, American representative, in the NATO Military Committee, regarding French nationalistic military policies involving its fleet, atomic stockpiling, and military integration with NATO forces. The criticisms unfortunately leaked to the press. The Foreign Minister also deplored U.S. abstention in the U.N. Assembly on the Algerian resolution and emphasized the damaging public effects. Herter explained the difficult decision involved in U.S. abstention. He said he had wanted no resolution at all, but could not take exception to the operative paragraphs as finally presented. As to the Twining statement, Herter said it was made by a military man in military company and was quite proper. He regretted that the statement had become public knowledge and said a thorough search indicated that no leak came from American sources. Of the latter, Couve de Murville was unconvinced.

The war in Algeria remained stalemated during 1960 on both military and political fronts. The Algerian Provisional Government in Cairo, discouraged over prospects for a negotiated peace, sent Premier Ferhat Abbas to Moscow and Peking where he got immediate support. The U.S.S.R. granted the FLN *de facto* recognition with promise of material and political support.[19] Having already recognized the FLN, Communist China promised Abbas "unlimited help." Abbas said this promise created a "completely new situation," and he was no longer interested in negotiations with De Gaulle.[20]

De Gaulle spoke on November 4, 1960, and gave assurances that his program aimed at self-determination, which he said meant "an emancipated Algeria" in which the Algerians themselves would decide their destiny. He continued to insist on a preliminary cease-fire and said France could not deliver Algeria unconditionally to the FLN, though its leaders could take part in talks. Nor could France accept U.N. supervision of the referendum.[21]

Herter advised Couve de Murville that De Gaulle's speech, while meaningful to the United States, would be less so to those not knowing French intentions.

The timing of the program was especially vague, and he emphasized that a precise definition of French intentions might make possible the adoption of a moderate resolution. If the French Community of African states would sponsor a resolution, which Herter thought essential, the United States would work hard to recruit additional sponsors.

The French Community states were unwilling to submit a resolution to the 1960 General Assembly, hence a 24-nation Afro-Asian resolution was the only one before the General Assembly plenary session. Most items in the resolution passed by a vote of 63-8-27. They recognized the Algerian people's right to self-determination, the imperative need for effective guarantees to insure its implementation, and the responsibility of the U.N. to assist in carrying it out. For the first time the Assembly affirmed that the U.N. had a role to play in Algeria. The United States abstained, as Herter had made clear to the French that the United States could not vote against the principles stated in the resolution.

The outcome of the General Assembly action left some Algerian questions still unanswered; but plebiscites of January 1, 1961, in France and Algeria gave a loud and clear answer with strong majorities in both areas in favor of provisional Algerian autonomy and ultimate free choice as to the political future. On Herter's departure from office, Franco-Algerian relations were apparently moving toward peaceful adjustment which, after months of tortuous negotiations, eventually removed the Algerian problem from serious U.N. and American concern.[22]

2

The Belgian Congo became a problem of special concern to Herter during the latter half of 1960. The Congo was catapulted into independence after three generations of very little preparation for such status. The Belgian Government had taken control of the Congo in 1908 after King Leopold II's personal rule of twenty-three years, but the training and experience given Congolese in education, military or other profession was far from adequate to enable them to assume the responsibility of power. It was generally thought that at least a generation would be necessary to prepare this colony for independence.[23]

Not until 1958 did the urgency of the problem become clear to Belgium. The Congo had been largely isolated from the rest of Africa and had remained relatively calm, but in 1958 events contributed to changing the situation: (1) Congolese leaders mingled with other African leaders and exchanged ideas at the Brussels World Fair; (2) De Gaulle visited Brazzaville, across the river from Leopoldville and, in launching the French Community, announced self-government for the French Congo; and (3) the first All-African People's Conference, which Patrice Lumumba, a Congolese nationalist, attended, met in Accra, and pledged assistance for the liberation of other African peoples. The wave of nationalism sweeping Africa, aided by an economic slump, hit the Belgian Congo hard. As a result of bloody riots in Leopoldville in January 1959, the Belgian Govern-

ment in a Brussels conference of January 1960, prom-
ised full independence as of the following June 30.
This precipitate action led to the first major East-
West clash of policies in the heart of Africa.

Elections in May 1960, in preparation for independence on June 30, set the stage for the play of
conflicting forces. As a political compromise between
incompatible individuals, Patrice Lumumba became
Prime Minister, and Joseph Kasavubu, a more moderate nationalist, became President.

Internal disorder followed. It began on July 5 with
a mutiny among the troops of the *Force Publique*,
disaffected by low pay and the continuance of Belgian officers in command after the political side of
the government had been "Africanized." Widespread
terrorism for some weeks led to mass evacuation of
Belgians and the return of Belgian troops to protect
Europeans. Personal enmities, inter-tribal rivalries
and special mining interests complicated the situation, and on July 11, Moise Tshombe, an opponent of
Lumumba and centralized government, declared the
independence of Katanga, the richest Congo province
in mineral wealth. Repercussions of this event exacerbated personal and tribal relations within the Congo,
as well as between East and West, and, most damag-
ingly, between U.N. Secretary General Hammarskjold
and the U.S.S.R.

The reappearance of Belgian troops gave Lumumba an opportunity to request outside help. On July 11,
Herter said a request from Lumumba for technical
assistance to help restore discipline in the Congolese
army had "undoubted merit." He felt differently

about a request for United States troops to cooperate with loyal Congolese troops to restore order. He discussed this latter proposition with the President, saying that he was averse to sending in troops, and the President agreed.[24] In view of cold war overtones, already audible, Herter and the Secretary General agreed that unless a new formula could be found for American action, the United States would do nothing unilaterally, except provide food.

In the early hours of July 14, 1960, after seven hours of debate, the Security Council adopted a resolution calling on the Belgian Government to withdraw its troops and authorizing the Secretary General to provide necessary military assistance "until the national security forces are able to meet fully their tasks."[25]

The timing of withdrawing Belgian troops immediately became a vexing problem. What, in fact, did the resolution of July 14 mean? According to Ambassador Alphand, the French Government was extremely concerned. It thought Belgian troops should remain, as the U.N. forces would be inadequate. Herter reminded Alphand that the Soviet amendment calling for "immediate withdrawal" had been defeated, as had two other Soviet amendments, and that the United States interpreted the resolution to require Belgian troop withdrawal only when the U.N. forces had the situation under complete control.

Herter gave the same assurance to Belgian Ambassador Scheyven, who recalled the Soviet threat to act if the Belgians did not cease their activities in the Congo. Herter said he would think it over. An understanding between Lumumba and the U.S.S.R. became evident when, on the arrival of a U.N. force of 4,000, Lumumba demanded that the U.N. clear out all Belgian troops within three days, saying that otherwise his government would call in "Soviet Russian troops."[26] The American reply through Ambassador Lodge at the U.N. was that the United States would do what was necessary "to prevent the intrusion of military forces not requested by the U.N."[27] While not asking for immediate action, the United States wanted Belgian withdrawal to begin as soon as possible. Belgium was already committed to withdraw as soon as order was restored, and Herter advised Camille Gutt, Belgian Minister of State, that his government should state more fully its intentions to phase withdrawals with the takeover by the U.N. forces. The Minister assured him that his government would reaffirm its willingness to withdraw in stages as U.N. troops came into the Congo.

Herter explained to his news conference on July 21, 1960, that the United States, on request of the U.N., was providing transportation for U.N. troops, but that "our own troops are not involved in United Nations action." He expressed shock at the attitude and statements of Soviet spokesmen alleging the contrary. The U.S.S.R., he said, had voted for the same resolution as the United States, but almost immediately afterwards Khrushchev publicly had assured Congo leaders that he was prepared to intervene militarily if U.N. action did not proceed to his satisfaction. "The threat to take unilateral action could only increase tensions in the area and make more likely the continuation of hostilities." The United States regarded the demand of the Soviet Government for immediate withdrawal of American "military personnel"—actually 20 members of service personnel required by the airlift for the U.N.—"as a deliberate, unilateral attempt to obstruct the U.N. efforts in the Congo."[28]

The United States was caught between demands by the Congo and U.S.S.R. governments for immediate Belgian withdrawal and the Belgian policy of "deliberate speed" which aimed at phasing withdrawal with the restoration of law and order. Soviet spokesmen bitterly attacked Belgium and the West, while Ambassador Scheyven complained to Herter of lack of American support for his government, as expressed in the warm welcome given in Washington for Congolese Premier Lumumba in July, and also the United States vote in the U.N. on July 14 for the anti-Belgian resolution on the Congo. Herter expressed regret that the events had caused trouble in Belgium, but explained that any other reception for Lumumba would have been a refusal of normal courtesies. He added that he had advised the U.N. Secretary General to go slowly in sending troops into Katanga where Belgium had special interests.[29]

By the end of July 1960, the U.N. troops in the Congo numbered 11,155, deployed in all provinces except Katanga. Belgium on July 28 announced withdrawal of 1,500 troops; the State Department expressed gratification, but absence of precise further commitments was disturbing.[30]

Hammarskjold then explored the situation in Leopoldville and Brussels, and Herter consulted with the

British and French Foreign Offices. The Secretary of State thought the Congolese were punishing the Secretary General for not sending U.N. troops into Katanga, trying to make a case that he had failed to get the troops out. Herter feared they would charge the U.N. with failing, and then invite in Soviet troops. The Secretary General was meanwhile trying to get a commitment from Brussels to withdraw all Belgian troops from the Congo, including Katanga, but another Security Council resolution was necessary (August 9) to hasten evacuation of Katanga province where many Belgian nationals lived.

Katanga became a center of controversy. Hammarskjold wanted to send in U.N. troops to relieve the Belgian forces, while remaining neutral as to domestic conflicts. Lumumba wanted the U.N. troops to wipe out opposition to the central government, including Tshombe's forces in Katanga. But the Security Council on August 9 voted 9-0-2 in support of Hammarskjold's position of political neutrality in the Congo's domestic politics.[31]

Tshombe, who at first opposed the U.N. forces, allowed Hammarskjold to enter Katanga with the first U.N. troops on August 12, and Belgium evacuated the bulk of its troops before the end of August, though some Belgians remained in key positions. Lumumba, supported by the U.S.S.R., from which he had received military equipment, broke with Hammarskjold over his "neutral" attitude and his refusal to use U.N. troops to bring Katanga back under the Central Government.[32]

The State Department was much concerned regarding Soviet intentions in the Congo, because of indications that the U.S.S.R. was pouring in expert civil and military personnel and materiel, also arms and transport. In an address of September 1, 1960, Herter said the U.N. efforts in the Congo pointed up "the central obstacle to the establishment of a world order." The Soviet Union had "sought to complicate rather than assist U.N. efforts to aid the Congo Republic to get on its feet." Khrushchev had set himself up as a court of last resort.[33]

Strong Soviet support of Lumumba's extreme nationalism helped to widen the rift between President Kasavubu and Premier Lumumba and, on September 5, Kasavubu suddenly dismissed Lumumba and replaced him with Joseph Ileo, a moderate as Premier. But Lumumba refused to accept dismissal, and the U.S.S.R. and many other states, especially African and Asian, did not regard him as dismissed. The result was two rival governments and two rival delegations before the General Assembly.

Herter was concerned regarding Hammarskjold, who had exercised great firmness in carrying out Security Council resolutions. He told Ambassador Alphand that the U.S.S.R. would not be able to secure a vote to reverse the Secretary General's powers already granted by the Security Council. Herter also told Hammarskjold that he, Herter, was with him 100%, and said he did not want the impression to get out that the U.N. was vacillating. As to Soviet charges regarding Hammarskjold's closing Congolese radio stations and air fields, Hammarskjold himself suggested that the whole issue be put before a special session of the General Assembly where he (the Secretary General) believed he would be able to get 60 to 70 percent of the votes.

Hammarskjold's forecast was borne out by action in the Emergency Special Session beginning September 17, 1960, which, by a vote of 70-0-11, approved a 17-nation Afro-Asian resolution supporting the Secretary General's position and calling on all states to refrain from military assistance to the Congo during the temporary period, except through the U.N. on request of the Secretary General.[34] Hammarskjold's triumph cost him good working relations with the U.S.S.R.

Soviet feelings were doubtless exacerbated by the the action of Colonel Joseph Mobutu, Chief of Staff in the Congo, who on September 14, 1960, took military control of the government without disturbing Kasavubu, with whom he was on good terms, but permitting attacks on the Soviet and Czech missions. The Soviet flag was "ignominiously hauled down," and the Soviet Ambassador was ousted to the accompaniment of Congolese jeers.[35]

The Congo had become a field of maneuver for parties to the cold war, and its future was unpredictable. Herter remarked to Japanese Foreign Minister Kosaka on September 12 that while there was instability in many areas of the world, Africa posed the most difficult problems, the worst of which was the Congo where there were only sixteen men with university degrees, and no lawyers, doctors, or judges, and few technicians. When asked in a news conference on September 14 to give a current assessment of the situation in the Congo, Herter said, "I wouldn't dare do that. Hour by hour the situation changes." It was clear, he said, that the power struggle between Kasavubu and Lumumba was continuing. "One day one seemed to be on top, the next day the other."[36]

The U.N. faced the delicate problem of deciding between the conflicting claims of Kasavubu and Lumumba. The constitutional President, Kasavubu, had exercised his legal authority in dismissing Lumumba and appointing Ileo, but the parliament disapproved the dismissal and apparently supported Lumumba. The President thereupon suspended the parliament on September 14, and the government became essentially a Kasavubu-Mobutu regime.[37] The Security Council could not give the answer to the recognition question, so deeply divided were East and West. The Assembly finally acted two months later. That body voted the Congo into the U.N. on September 20, but left to the Credentials Committee the question of seating its representatives. A few days later Herter assured Belgian Foreign Minister Pierre Wigny that the United States viewed Kasavubu as head of the only legal government, and that it would support this position in the Credentials Committee. It was a period of maneuvering, with pro-Lumumba forces on the offensive, fortified by reports by Rajeswar Dayal, of India, who became Special Congo Representative of the Secretary General on September 8.[38] His disparaging comments on Mobutu policies and on Belgian activities led to setting up a conciliation committee to visit the Congo to seek "a speedy solution" of the internal conflict."[89]

Herter and Hammarskjold were disturbed by the ominous prospect. The Secretary General had been careful to preserve a neutral stance by avoiding taking sides in the controversy, but he agreed with Herter that it would be disastrous for Lumumba to regain power, even though existing leadership left much to be desired. Kasavubu brought the crisis to a head by arriving suddenly at the U.N. and appearing before the General Assembly on November 8. He asserted his claims for recognition of his government, named its representatives, and demanded that they be seated. The Credentials Committee by a 6-1 (U.S.S.R.) vote on November 10 approved the United States motion to recommend Kasavubu's delegation, and on November 22 the Assembly, after a long and bitter debate, approved the recommendation by a 53-24-19 vote.[40]

Following the recognition given the Kasavubu-Mobutu Government, implied in the seating of its delegates, a series of events increased the political deterioration and instability in the Congo. Among these were the arrest on December 1 and imprisonment of Lumumba; the establishment of a rival Stanleyville regime by Lumumba's followers, with control over much of the eastern Congo; bitter attacks by the U.S.S.R. on "colonialist NATO powers led by the United States"; violent protests in other African states; and disruption of the Congo's economic system. The murder of Lumumba in January 1961, under mysterious circumstances, produced a fury of repercussions and further weakened the Kasavubu-Mobutu Government.[41]

Viewing the Congo as his Secretaryship approached an end, Herter regarded its situation as precarious. No leadership was developing. The prospect of a united Congo seemed doubtful. In briefing the President for his meeting with President-elect Kennedy on January 19, Herter noted that pro-Lumumbist, Antoine Gizenga, controlled Orientale and Kivu provinces and threatened further expansion; Tshombe was still a standout in Katanga, having refused to attend a conference to promote unity; U.N. contingents had clashed with Congo National troops, but were not an effective counterforce to the expansion of the pro-Lumumbist Stanleyville regime. This could forecast the permanent division of the Congo, which might become another source of protracted East-West conflict and of serious division among African states. The British had little new to offer on the Congo problem and the French had not taken a position. A U.N. solution, Herter told Eisenhower, was still the best remedy, and adherence to the U.S. policy of support for the U.N. outweighed possible advantages in unilateral action. Superficially there seemed to be hopeful factors in the outlook as Herter's term ended, e.g., the reduction of Soviet influence by the ouster of the Soviet mission (and the Czech mission) in September 1960; the physical presence of the U.N. with a military force of 19,400 as a restraint on big-power and cold-war operations; and a Congolese central government under the moderate, if non-charismatic, leadership of Kasavubu, Ileo and Mobutu. But underlying currents, internal and external, were strong. The sins of political neglect were visited heavily on the Congo, making impossible any short-term solution. Herter could only deplore having to pass the Congo problem along to his successor.

## 3

In South Africa, Herter encountered a problem of special racial character. It appeared to be a matter of strictly domestic politics, but became a matter of concern to the United Nations as a problem of human rights and fundamental freedoms.[42]

The General Assembly in November 1959, approved a resolution which chided South Africa for violating the terms of the Charter, and appealed to all member states to use their best efforts to achieve the resolution's objectives.[43] The United States voted for it, while France, Portugal and Britain voted against it. Ambassador Lodge noted that South Africa's discrimination was not just a matter of custom but was sanctioned by law.[44]

Demonstrations in March 1960, against a law requiring all Africans to carry "pass" books led to fighting with South African police in which some 70 demonstrating Africans were killed and about 200 wounded. The State Department immediately deplored violence in all forms and expressed hope "that the African people of South Africa" would be able to "obtain redress for legitimate grievances by peaceful means." It regretted the "tragic loss of life resulting from the measures taken against the demonstrators."[45] Herter did not see the statement before it was issued and was not happy with its language. He told the President that we had jumped awfully fast on that one and had made a mistake by taking sides. He thought we might be accused of inciting revolution. Meanwhile the Afro-Asian group met and voted unanimous thanks to the United States for the statement and requested an immediate meeting of the Security Council. Ambassador Lodge told Herter he should be pleased by the tremendous credit and good will which had come out of this from African peoples.

Responding to a question in a news conference on March 25, 1960, Herter had said he favored putting the South African item on the U.N. agenda. Such procedure had been the U.S. government's policy regarding *apartheid* for the last five years, he said. When asked whether, in reverse circumstances involving the United States, he would favor putting the item on the agenda, he said the situation would be entirely different. "In the United States we are doing everything we can to defend the rights of minorities . . . I think the other nations of the world are convinced that this is our attitude and that we are trying to do this." Under apartheid, he said, "a very different situation prevails."[46]

South Africa protested to the United States against the U.N. Security Council meeting to discuss South African race riots, claiming that riots were a domestic matter that could be aggravated by U.N. discussion. The Republic's Ambassador, du Plessis, noted with diplomatic finesse that such discussions could be a precedent for discussions of "racial and other disturbances in any other country."[47]

Herter managed to soften the draft resolution, but not enough to satisfy the British, and on April 1, 1960, the Council by vote of 9 (including the United States) to 0, with 2 abstentions (U.K. and France), approved a resolution recognizing that the situation in the Union, if continued, "might endanger international security." It called on the Union "to initiate measures aimed at bringing about racial harmony based on equality," and requested the Secretary General, in consultation with the Union, to make arrangements that would uphold the principles of the Charter.[48] In a news conference on April 8, Herter said he thought the test must always be whether there was a clear case of racial discrimination that involved a deliberate violation of human rights or threatened the peace of the world.[49]

Herter also faced the problem of "taking sides" on colonialism as a broad issue. The U.S.S.R. raised this point in the General Assembly for propaganda purposes in a "Declaration" of September 23, 1960, calling for "complete independence" forthwith of all colonial and non-self-governing territories and elimination of all manifestations of colonialism or any other special rights detrimental to other states. After long and often bitter debate, marked by tumultuous and table-thumping tactics by Soviet and satellite delegations (involving one peremptory adjournment of a session by the President owing to the offensive character of remarks), a more moderate, though still rather drastic resolution emerged, sponsored by 43 Asian and African delegations. It proclaimed "the necessity of speedily and unconditionally ending colonialism in all its forms and manifestations." "All peoples have the right to self-determination," and "immediate steps shall be taken . . . to transfer all powers to the peoples of dependent territories."[50]

Western powers with residual colonial holdings were not happy with the resolution, but its wide sponsorship assured overwhelming approval. Outright opposition might make matters worse, but abstention could be defended. For Herter it was the old dilemma: whom to offend? Would loyalty to NATO allies justify fracturing an anti-colonial principle and antagonizing Afro-Asian states? Portugal, a NATO ally, was hit worst of all, with colonies in East and West Africa. Its Ambassador, Esteves Fernandes, complained to Herter on December 7, 1960, that United States abstention and some allied negative votes in committee had shocked his government and disturbed public opinion. This, he said, would strengthen the left neutralists who wanted to get Portgual out of NATO and would weaken Portugal's position in Africa. He bluntly commented that Portugal expected its friends to stand by its side and it expected United States support and not abstention on the upcoming vote. Herter promised earnest consideration of the matter, but could not say that the United States would shift its position. He pointed out that despite strong pressures to vote for the resolution in committee, the United States had shown its sympathy for Portugal by abstaining.

After much consideration of the problem within the Department, Herter with the support of his staff was for the resolution, and so informed the President. But British opposition and Macmillan's persuasiveness prevailed with Eisenhower, who cast the die for abstention in the final Assembly vote on December 14, 1960. Thus Herter could seize neither horn of the dilemma, and could satisfy neither Portuguese nor Afro-Asian hopes. The United States remained in an enigmatic position on this problem which Herter had to pass along with other unfinished business to his successor.

# CHAPTER TEN

## INTER-AMERICAN RELATIONS: I

WHEN CHRISTIAN HERTER became Under Secretary of State in February 1957, relations with Latin America were not of serious concern to the United States Government or public. There were no crises calling for immediate attention. Events caused no alarm. This was evidenced by general lack of concern in thoughtful nonofficial circles. *Foreign Affairs* quarterly carried not a single article on Latin America during 1957, and in 1958 it carried only one, this limited to Mexico.

Inter-American relations, which had suffered severely during several decades of United States expansionist policies, had improved markedly after the 1920's because of commitments in the 1930's to the good neighbor policy and nonintervention, and increasingly close trade relations.[1] President Eisenhower, in his State of the Union message of 1957, assured Latin American nations that their security and prosperity were "inexorably bound to our own."

In spite of commitments and high-level assurances, the word was spreading in Latin America that good deeds were lagging well behind fine words. Fears developed that the United States was more concerned with political security and economic exploitation than with Latin American prosperity.[2] Desperate economic conditions widely prevalent among the masses, and high concentration of wealth in ruling oligarchies, created a field for maneuver by advocates of extreme doctrines.[3]

Left-wing forces with strong communist leanings took over in Guatemala in 1950 under Arbenz Guzman, but succumbed in 1954, thanks largely to United States policies. Communist influence had become a factor in Latin American politics, but Secretary Dulles did not take a grave view of the situation. He said, "we see no likelihood at the present time of communism getting control of the political institutions of the American Republics."[4] There was no sense of urgency, or of growing crisis. The successor to Assistant Secretary for American Republics Affairs (ARA), Henry Holland, who retired in August 1956, was not nominated until April 1957, and confirmation of Roy R. Rubottom for that post waited until July. Nor, during the "Acting" period, did Rubottom have a deputy.

1

The stirrings of discontent with conditions in Latin America found most dramatic expression in Cuba where decisive events were getting under way when Herter became Under Secretary. Fidel Castro, a 30-year-old firebrand, was then holed up in the mountain fastness of the Sierra Maestra in eastern Cuba, with a small band of followers. He had a turbulent background, tremendous drive, and an intense hatred of the autocratic Batista regime and the concept of "capitalist imperialism," with which he associated the United States.

Castro soon became a hero in Cuba and, to an extent, in the United States, thanks largely to Herbert L. Matthews of the *New York Times*, who in February 1957 visited the rebel leader in his mountain hideout and wrote glowing accounts of his "genuinely idealistic and democratic motivations," "determination to succeed," and "overpowering and charismatic personality."[5]

During 1957, Castro's hit-and-run attacks, bombings, and other terroristic tactics began to threaten the position of Batista, who fought back with counter terrorism and martial law. In January 1958, through Ambassador Earl E. T. Smith, the State Department urged Batista to eliminate violence and create conditions for free elections.[6] Batista restored constitutional liberties for a time, but could not eliminate violence while Castro's guerrillas were increasingly active.

Under Secretary Herter informed an inquirer in January 1958, that it was Department policy to maintain friendly relations with the Batista government and with the entire Cuban populace. The existing unrest there, he said, and the measures taken by the Cuban government to quiet it, were regarded as internal matters. Diplomatic relations did not imply approval or disapproval of that government's policies. He further explained to a friend on May 21 that the United States was committed to a policy of nonintervention in the affairs of the other American Republics and that intervention by the Organization of

American States (OAS) to supervise elections in Cuba would be contrary to that Organization's basic principles.

During March,1958, Batista's position weakened on all fronts, the worst blow being United States action embargoing arms shipments to Cuba and cancelling a shipment of twenty armored cars, contracted for eleven months previously. The State Department said arms shipments were embargoed because Batista had used for domestic purposes arms that had been made available under the 1952 Mutual Defense Assistance Agreement which limited use to Hemisphere defense purposes. The action was psychologically devastating and militarily damaging.[7]

Events forecast the end of the Batista regime. The Department of State concluded toward the end of 1958 that pressure should be used to bring this about, but it was puzzled as to the succession. Castro loomed as the dominant revolutionary figure and appealed strongly to opponents of Batista and to many Americans. Matthews of the *New York Times*, Jules Dubois of the *Chicago Tribune*, and others joined in adulation of the popular hero. Castro promised return to the constitution of 1940 with its guarantees of political and civil rights, social reform, "truly honest" elections at the end of one year, and a provisional government that would lead the country back to full constitutional and democratic procedures. These promises assured him support of all moderates.[8] His 1957 program, promising "a total transformation of Cuban life," profound modifications of the property system, and a change of institutions to a "democratic, na-

ionalist, and socialist" state, opened doors to all anti-
Batistianos of the left.[9]

The State Department was in a dilemma. The alternatives were unpromising. The Department thought
Batista and his corruption-ridden regime ought to go,
and it sought informally, though unsuccessfully, to
persuade him to step down.[10] But the alternative of
Castro with his anti-United States prejudices, his op-
portunism, his bands of terroristic followers, and his
extreme left-wing associates offered little, if any,
hope. A State Department request for advice from
Latin American sources, leading possibly to media-
tion, got nowhere. The bugbear of nonintervention
blocked action.[11]

Time was running out, but the State Department
believed that maneuvers were still possible. As late
as December 28, 1958, Under Secretary Herter sent
a memorandum to the President outlining developments in Cuba and pointing to the harshly repressive
measures of both government and rebels. He explained that the communists were using the Castro movement, as would be expected, but that there was insufficient evidence that the rebels were communist
dominated. He said Batista would have to relinquish
power, whether as Chief of State or as the force behind a puppet. The Department did not want to see
Castro succeed to the leadership, and was doing all it
could, without violating our nonintervention commitments, to help create a situation in which a third force
could move into the vacuum between Batista and
Castro.

For several weeks in December 1958 certain Latin

nations worked with the State Department to find a
solution for the crisis.[12] But no third force could be
conjured up before Castro forces seized power on the
morning of January 1, 1959. Batista, seeing the blow
coming, took plane with his entourage to the Dominican Republic late in the night of December 31.

The first official acts of Castro after seizing power
relieved some anxieties in the State Department. The
"Supreme Leader" appointed Urrutia Lleo President
and Miro Cardona Premier in the Provisional Government. Both were war heroes and moderates. The
Provisional Government announced the restoration of
constitutional guarantees suspended by Batista, dis-
solved the Congress, removed from office all Governors, Congressmen and aldermen who had served
under Batista, and proclaimed that the Provisional
Government would rule by decree for at least eighteen months, after which there would be free elections.[13]

In Washington there were the questions of recognition and diplomatic representation. The State Department thought Ambassador Smith should be replaced because he was suspect in revolutionary circles, owing to his close relations with Batista. Under
Secretary Herter regarded him as a "playboy extraordinary" and said that if he were not replaced he
would be declared *persona non grata*. President Eisenhower, a personal friend of Smith, preferred to
delay the change to avoid embarrassment; but he accepted Herter's warm recommendation of Philip Bonsal, a career Ambassador serving in Colombia; and
Bonsal took over on January 19, 1959.

After receiving from the Cuban Ministry of State
n January 6 appropriate assurances regarding the
ew regime's control of power and the Republic's
tention to fulfill international commitments and
greements, the Havana Embassy notified Foreign
Minister Daniel Agramonte of United States recogni-
on. It expressed "the sincere good will of the Gov-
nment and people of the United States toward the
ew government and the people of Cuba."[14]

The new Cuban regime received the benefit of the
oubt from the American public generally. The *New
ork Times* led the way in paying tribute to "the
oung man of thirty-two who, armed with little more
an the biblical slingshot, has felled a seasoned and
thless dictator." Castro was understood to favor
oderate progressivism and to have "explicitly re-
udiated a program he once endorsed calling for
tensive nationalization."[15]

Hope and optimism soon began turning to con-
rn and shock. The spirit of the Provisional Govern-
ent's pronunciamentos did not prevail in Castro's
thless pursuit of persons charged with "war crimes"
nder Batista. Many of those accused were hastily
nvicted and executed by summary and sometimes
umhead methods. On January 22, 1959, three offi-
rs of the Batista regime were brought in prison
rb before a frenzied crowd in the Havana Sports
ena for a summary court-martial. Castro addressed
e meeting, denounced crimes of the Batista regime,
d called the accused "war criminals." The crowd
outed "kill them, kill them."[16] The revolutionary
nzy caused widespread criticism. The *New York*

*Times*, often an apologist for Castro and his presumed objectives, expressed shock at the "mob howling for blood" and the violation of normal civilized canons of justice.[17] During the first three weeks after Castro's takeover the *Times* estimated that more than 250 Batista adherents were executed by firing squads. Many more executions followed.

Angry reactions in the United States led to tensions with Castro's entourage, which was very sensitive to any adverse criticism. Castro flayed his critics and blasted the United States. To a large crowd on January 21, 1959, he said there was no reason to "offer explanations to the United States" for the execution of war criminals.[18] In a televised program for "Meet the Press" on February 20, he charged the United States with interfering in Cuban affairs for more than fifty years. He said its entrance into the Spanish War of 1898 was a useless gesture, and accused the United States of continually threatening Cuba with reduction of its sugar quota.[19]

Castro decided to visit the United States in April 1959, and came on invitation of the American Society of Newspaper Editors, thanks to the good offices of Jules Dubois of the *Chicago Tribune*. The U.S. Government would not have invited him. In fact, Eisenhower would have liked to refuse him a visa.[20] In an early mellow mood, Castro viewed United States public opinion as friendly. Later, in a less mellow mood, he said he would demand that the United States increase Cuba's sugar quota, seek financial aid, and endeavor to counteract the "defamatory campaign" against his regime.[21]

While in this country, from April 15 to 26, the "Supreme Leader" was the center of tumultuous public interest, much more favorable than unfavorable. President Eisenhower absented himself from Washington during the visit, hence it fell to Acting Secretary Herter's lot to put on a luncheon for Castro and several top advisers. This Herter did, along with twenty-five high level national personalities whom Herter, with difficulty, managed to round up. It was a bizarre diplomatic luncheon. Castro brought eight "goons" with him, each armed with a gun. They insisted on being in the dining room. After some brandy was given each of them they consented to stack their arms in a neighboring room, but they sat around the room along the wall.

Having in mind previous statements of Castro, Herter sought to ascertain his wishes. But the Secretary's efforts to promote serious discussion failed. Subjects such as cigars and sugar were touched on lightly. Top Castro aides, Lopez Fresquet, Felipe Pazos and Regino Boti later met, on invitation, with Assistant Secretary Rubottom, who made clear United States willingness to be helpful on the financial side. But Castro, on arrival, had forbidden them to request or to accept any offers.[22]

Later Herter told of his luncheon conversation with the Finance Minister who explained the inexperienced character of the new Cuban government. The Minister said that in the previous week he had attended the first cabinet meeting of the Castro government and had a slip of paper with figures showing how much each cabinet member could spend during the next thirty days. There was no discussion, no dissent, though the Minister had expected some. The next morning a member of the Cabinet appeared at his door rather early, and the Finance Minister thought he had come to protest. But the other Minister had not come to protest. He said he had come to get the money, and he had brought his suitcase to carry it away.

In numerous other appearances Castro sought to create a favorable impression of his motives, and of the character of his government. Speaking to the American Society of Newspaper Editors, he said there was no communist influence in his government; his revolution was a "humanistic one"; his regime had executed only persons guilty of war crimes; he had no intention of abrogating the agreement with the United States regarding the naval base at Guantanamo Bay; Cuba would not confiscate foreign private industry; Cuba was not a beggar, and he had not come to this country for money. Ninety-five percent of the Cuban people supported the revolution, and he favored the principle of nonintervention in the internal affairs of other nations. He said also that there might not be any elections for three or four years. When he finished speaking there was, reportedly, prolonged applause.

He conferred with Vice President Nixon, who talked to him like a Dutch uncle. He met privately with a group from the Senate Foreign Relations Committee and the House Foreign Affairs Committee on April 17, and received a generally favorable response, though Senator J. William Fulbright was impressed by the thug-like character of Castro and his three husky guards.[23] At a National Press Club luncheon, and elsewhere later, Castro repeated assurances against communist infiltration of government; land confiscation or nationalization; and dictatorships of any kind. He even promised that "when we finish our job we will cut our beards off."[24] The *New York Times* glowingly concluded that Cuba would support the West, favor free enterprise, welcome American investment, and would not knowingly become a base for foreign invasions. Most of all it would want the friendship of the United States.[25]

Castro felt that his trip was a success, and reactions in the United States indicated hope for peaceful relations.[26] These hopes began to fade with Castro's return to Cuba and the adoption of the agrarian legislation, signed on May 17 and promulgated on June 4. It was the first major step in the transformation of Cuba's social structure and marked an important development in United States relations with Cuba. In Washington, Castro had given assurances that the program would be carried out "legally," with compensation for expropriated property, but the legislation did not carry out his commitments. The program aimed at breaking up large estates (latifundia) and forbade sugar mill operators to own cane plantations. The law applied to foreigners and Cubans alike. The expropriated properties were to be paid for by 20-year 4½ percent bonds, and the value of the properties would be determined by assessed value for tax purposes. The proceeds were to be reinvested in Cuba and could not be converted into dollars.

The land reform law, though expected, was regarded in the United States as excessively drastic. American owners of sugar mills in Cuba lodged a strong protest with the Department of State, arguing that breakup of the large estates would be uneconomic and that payment in 20-year 4½ percent bonds not convertible into dollars was not expropriation but confiscation. They suggested broader authority for the U.S. Government to change the Cuban sugar import quotas at any time as a measure of defense.[27] In a note of June 11, 1959, the State Department explained that the U.S. Government was sympathetic with the land reform program and recognized the right of a state under international law to take property for policy purposes on payment of prompt and adequate compensation. The Department expressed serious concern about economic aspects of the legislation, and the adequacy of provision for compensation to its citizens.

Ambassador Bonsal, in presenting the note (June 12, 1959), had his first real conference with Castro after his arrival in January. Castro appeared to regard United States concern over compensation as natural, but stressed that the revolutionary government was honest and would fulfill its promises to pay. His government wanted private enterprise, and he favored state industry only where private enterprise would not fill essential needs. He admitted that United States firms had played a constructive role, but pointed to the pitiful condition of the field workers, and wondered why these cane growers could not get higher yields in Cuba. Bonsal thought it a generally satisfactory conversation.

Next day Castro told a TV audience that opponents of agrarian reform were traitors in a "life and death" struggle and criticized the "reactionary campaign" against his plan.

Two days later the Cuban Government rejected the United States request for prompt compensation for the lands to be expropriated, and Castro said his government had adopted the manner of payment judged "most advisable to the supreme interests of the nation." In view of the traditional friendship and cooperation between the U.S. and Cuba, he hoped the United States would understand "the powerful reasons which justify the form of payment."

The 20-year 4½ percent bonds were never issued, hence land reform—actually land confiscation—remained one of the rankling issues in Cuban-United States relations.

While pushing his program on the home front, Castro extended his revolutionary activities to his Caribbean neighbors, immediately to Panama, Nicaragua and the Dominican Republic. This led to the Fifth Meeting of Consultation of Foreign Ministers to deal with Caribbean tensions. Herter led the U.S. Delegation committed to the principle of nonintervention in inter-American affairs. He did not expect much from the conference. No country was specifically on trial. After heated exchanges, especially between the Cuban and Dominican Republic representatives, also other discussions dealing largely in abstractions, and Herter's personal diplomacy, the conference adopted resolutions, which (1) expressed faith in the basic principles of the inter-American system (the Declaration of Santiago), (2) supported the sometimes conflicting principles of nonintervention and democratic government based on human rights, and (3) directed the Inter-American Peace Committee of the OAS to study and report on international tensions in the Caribbean.[28] Herter regarded the results as a blow to Castro, while Castro denounced the conference as a farce and ignored its resolutions.

United States-Cuban relations fluctuated, but they were becoming increasingly unfriendly. Castro's conflicting statements kept his friends off balance for many months. In March 1959, he affirmed Cuba's neutrality in the East-West struggle. In April he categorically stated in the United States that Cuba would the "neutrality" stance and, for a brief period, showed some independence of the communist movement.[29] But the Land Reform Law caused a break in the ranks of the 26th of July Movement, Castro's main support in his struggle for power. (The Movement took its name from the date of Castro's unsuccessful revolutionary landing in 1953.) The Communist Popular Socialist Party (PSP) strongly backed Castro, leading him to say, "We will never combat communism."[30] This period marked the flight into exile of many anticommunists and the disaffection of high-level moderates from the Castro regime, followed in July by the resignation of President Urrutia Lleo, Castro's personal choice as titular head of state.[31]

Meanwhile, Castro held Ambassador Bonsal at arm's length, refusing to discuss with him matters of great concern to the United States.

Herter took up this matter with Roa at the Santiago Conference, but Roa, who praised Bonsal for his approach to Cuban problems, could give Herter no hope for an early meeting, referring to Castro's busy program. Bonsal finally met with Castro on September 3, 1959, at Raul Roa's apartment, where they talked for over five hours. Castro was in a mellow mood. He expressed regrets about the delay in seeing the Ambassador and promised to see him thereafter within a maximum of a 48-hour delay. (Actually, Bonsal never had another conference with Castro.) The Ambassador expressed United States sympathy with objectives of the revolution but expressed concern over some aspects of it, such as communist influence, anti-American statements, and treatment of American private interests.

Castro said Bonsal was unduly pessimistic and gave assurances on many points raised by the Ambassador, while denouncing certain American newspapers and press services and stating that he accepted support of local communists because they helped him politically and in labor circles. Castro stressed the need for massive United States help to enable Cuba and other Latin American countries to industrialize. On the whole the meeting seemed not discouraging.

The hope of relaxed tensions marked only a slight and brief upswing of the downward curve of U.S.-Cuban relations. Shortly thereafter, in the United

Nations, Roa announced Cuba's adherence to a neutralist position comparable to that of Asian and African countries; and beginning in October 1959, events precipitated an unprecedented wave of anti-Americanism which swept Castro's government along toward total commitment to the communist camp. Theodore Draper calls this period the "point of no return."[32]

The imposition of an austerity regime caused by pinched economic conditions, repression of the press struggling for freedom of expression, the losing struggle of labor for independence, the arrest and imprisonment of Major Hubert Matos, a revolutionary hero and former aide to Castro, the flight of Major Diaz Lanz, former chief of the Cuban Air Force, over Havana in October in an unarmed plane from the United States dropping propaganda leaflets, the appointment of Castro's brother Raul as Minister of Armed Forces to check counter-revolutionary movements, the United States objection to the sale by Britain of jet planes to Cuba—all these contributed to climactic developments.

2

Secretary Herter in early November 1959, came to the conclusion that Castro's policies were, in effect, totally anti-American, and that there was no reasonable basis for hoping that Castro would voluntarily adopt policies consistent with minimum United States security requirements. He believed the prolonged continuation of that regime could have damaging ef-

fects on the U.S. position in Latin America, with corresponding advantages for international communism.
Therefore all actions and policies of the U.S. Government should aim to encourage, in Cuba and elsewhere
in Latin America, opposition to the extremist, anti-
American course of the Castro regime.

The State Department continued to probe the possibilities of an acceptable understanding with the
Castro government. A mild State Department note,
delivered by Bonsal on January 11, 1960, while not
questioning the right of Cuba to expropriate Ameri-
can-owned land, protested serious irregularities of
procedure in seizing land and reckless disregard of
legal principles, even of Cuban law. The note requested recognition of the legal rights of U.S. citizens. The Cuban Government brusquely rejected the
protest, affirmed its determination to accelerate agrarian reform, and continued its attacks on the United
States with greater intensity.[33] Secretary Herter appeared before the Senate Foreign Relations Committee, January 20, 1960, deeply worried about the
Cuban situation, and said Castro's speech on the previous day was the "most insulting" attack on the
United States since that leader came to power. It
was "insulting to the American Ambassador, the
American Government, and the American people,"
and he informed the committee he had ordered Bonsal back for consultation.[34]

After a careful review of the situation with Bonsal,
Secretary Herter, Assistant Secretary Rubottom, and
high officials from other agencies, recommended to
the President a moderate line, which Eisenhower ac-

cepted and embodied in an important statement of January 26. It ruled out reprisals and affirmed United States strict adherence to nonintervention in other countries including Cuba. It assured the Cuban people of our continuing friendship, recognized their right to undertake social, economic and political reforms, with due regard to obligations under international law, and expressed "confidence in the ability of the Cuban people to recognize and defeat the intrigues of international communism which are aimed at destroying democratic institutions in Cuba" and the traditional friendship between the two peoples.[35]

For a brief period there was hope of halting the deterioration in diplomatic relations, but this hope faded as Castro turned to the Russians. The first overt evidence of this was the 10-day visit to Cuba by Anastas Mikoyan, First Deputy Premier of the U.S.S.R., beginning February 4, 1960. Technically the purpose was to open the Soviet Exposition in Havana, but the visit opened new vistas of Cuban relations with the communist bloc and caused serious misgivings in the United States and elsewhere in the Western Hemisphere. There were some hostile public demonstrations, but Mikoyan was warmly welcomed officially, and Castro assured him that diplomatic relations with the U.S.S.R., severed since 1952, would soon be restored.[36] Agreements reached with Mikoyan began tying the Cuban economy to that of the U.S.S.R., and ultimately to the communist bloc, involving (a) a 12-year credit of $100,000,000, at 2½ percent interest for purchase of Soviet commodities; (b) Soviet purchase of 5 million tons of Cuban sugar over a period of five years, at the world market price; and (c) technical assistance for "the construction of plants and factories for the Cuban Government."

Efforts by the State Department to negotiate with the Castro regime failed, but Ambassador Bonsal after seven weeks in Washington returned to Havana following the Castro government's statement that it had no charges against him. Herter told Allen W. Dulles that if Bonsal were snubbed and insulted we would ask him to come out for good, and that this was our last effort at "reasonableness."[37]

Herter's venture in reasonableness was doomed by Castro's anti-American program which included closer ties with the communist bloc. The explosion of the French munitions ship *La Coubre* in Havana Harbor on March 4, 1960, with heavy loss of life, was a good illustration of Castro's determined anti-American bent. Although he admitted that he had no proof, and the dock workers' union expressed doubt that the tragedy could have been sabotage, and although Herter expressed furious indignation to the Cuban Chargé over charges of U.S. complicity, Castro built up an inflammatory propaganda case charging the United States with responsibility.[38] As Herter put it in a press conference on March 9, Castro tried to turn the grief of the Cuban people to animosity against the United States.

The question whether the Communist conspiracy was taking over was a matter of grave concern to Herter, the President, and other responsible leaders. In the preceding November, Herter had concluded that the Cuban revolution was totally anti-American, but official judgment in December was that Castro was not a communist, though he had the blessing of communist governments.

The question of remedies for a decaying political situation naturally came to the fore. Herter and the President wanted to rely on diplomatic methods as long as possible, but there seemed to be no common ground for negotiations, and Bonsal on his return to Havana could not change the trend of events.[39]

The problem most frequently discussed was what to do about the sugar quota allotted to Cuba under laws dating back to 1934 which, while aimed at stabilizing sugar prices and insuring sugar supplies, generally resulted in giving Cuban sugar a premium of two cents or more over world prices, a great boon to the Cuban economy—about $150,000,000 in 1959. Castro made frequent reference to this quota, calling it a weapon which the United States threatened to use. Herter and the President were anxious to avoid punitive action. In his speech before the National Press Club of February 18, 1960, Herter noted that the Cuban situation caused "very real concern." He pointed to obligations under the Charter of the OAS not to use either political or economic means to interfere in internal affairs of any nation in Latin America, and added: "We still have faith that the latent friendship between the Cuban and the American people will bring order out of the present picture without the extremes that may ensue."[40]

The Secretary's hope and patience wore increasingly thin as relations worsened. Castro had repeatedly threatened confiscation of American property in pro-

portion to the damage done to Cuba by reducing the
sugar quota. Already, reportedly, property seizures
amounted to $800,000,000, and much more than that
remained.[41] The Administration decided to send to
the Hill on March 15 a compromise measure proposing to extend the existing Sugar Act for another four
years, but giving the President discretion to change
the quotas as the national interest might require. The
President insisted in his news conference of March 16
that this was a request for stand-by power and not a
reprisal against Cuba. Herter doubted the value of
cutting Cuba's sugar quota, believing that sugar legislation alone would not solve the Cuban problem. Nib-
bling was no good, he thought. We should either take
actions that would hurt or leave well enough alone.
But he defended the measure before the Committee
on Agriculture of the House of Representatives on
June 22, emphasizing the importance of giving the
President discretion to make changes in quotas and
justifying the proposed law as a means to safeguard
U.S. consumers from interruptions in supply and
fluctuations in price.[42]

The Administration took precautionary measures of
a covert character, as the President on March 17,
1960, instructed the Central Intelligence Agency to
organize a program of training Cuban exiles for possible guerrilla action in Cuba and also to work with
the Cuban exile groups to develop political leadership. This project was destined to have a memorable
history.[43]

An important stimulus to passage of the sugar
quota law was Cuban seizure of the three major oil

refineries—British Shell, American Texaco, and Standard Oil. A demand by the Castro Government that they refine Soviet crude oil was rejected in early June 1960, on the claim that this was not called for by their agreements. Seizure of the refineries, which had been anticipated, was made at the month's end, thus bringing the entire oil processing industry into the hands of the Castro Government. The U.S. note of protest charging "relentless economic aggression" was rejected, as was also the British note. Castro bragged that he had "won every round" in his fight against the United States, and that he would continue to win against the aggression of Washington.[24]

The sugar quota act, passed by the Congress on July 6, 1960, fell short of what the President had requested. It gave him discretionary authority to fix, but not to increase, the quota for the remainder of 1960 and the first three months of 1961. It was a short-term policy for an interim period in which to observe developments in Cuba. On the day of enactment of the law, Eisenhower issued a statement reducing Cuba's quota for the remainder of 1960, from 700,000 tons to 39,752 tons. This was done, he said, "to reduce our reliance for a major food product upon a nation which has embarked upon a deliberate policy of hostility toward the U.S."[45]

Though several factors were involved in the reduction of Castro's sugar quota, the decisive reason for the change of policy was Castro's open swing to the communist bloc and his increasing reliance upon it for economic aid and cooperation. The new policy laid the U.S. Government open to Latin American charges of intervention, of which Herter had given warning, and caused hardship to the Cuban people, with serious political repercussions. Ambassador Bonsal opposed the policy. Herter had misgivings, but in view of Cuban developments and strong feelings in the Congress he nonetheless urged wide presidential discretion in determining quotas and a four-year extension of the law.

Repercussions were not long in coming. It seemed almost that suspension of the quota was the answer to Castro's prayers. He had already said he "would exchange the sugar quota for American investments," adding that "we'll take and take until not even the nails in their shoes are left."[46] He was ready with a more drastic policy of seizures of American properties, as announced on July 6, 1960, in the Nationalization Law, which applied exclusively to nationals of the United States. A U.S. note of July 16 charged that this law was discriminatory, arbitrary, and confiscatory and part of the Cuban "pattern of economic and political aggression." But the note was largely for the record, as a favorable response could not have been expected.

The temperature of United States-Cuban relations heightened with the abrupt entrance of Nikita Khrushchev into Western Hemisphere politics on July 9, with a pledge of fullest support for Castro by the Soviet Union and its allies. The Russian leader remarked that "figuratively speaking" Soviet rockets could support the Cuban people in case of Pentagon aggression.[47] Castro hailed the commitment as a guarantee of instant retaliation against the United States by Soviet missiles.[48] President Eisenhower immediately commented that Khrushchev's statement revealed "the close ties that had developed between the Soviet and Cuban Governments"—a situation which involved interference in the Western Hemisphere and the inter-American system. He said the United States, in conformity with treaty obligations, would not "permit the establishment of a regime dominated by international communism in the Western Hemisphere."[49]

In rejoinder Khrushchev taunted the President for thinking he could keep international communism out of the Western Hemisphere, and remarked that the Monroe Doctrine had outlived its time.[50] The State Department issued a bristling statement affirming that the "principles of the Monroe Doctrine are as valid today as they were in 1823" and denounced Khrushchev's naked menace to world peace.[51]

Castro appealed to the United Nations, charging "threats, intrigue, reprisals, and aggressive acts," but the Security Council adjourned discussion of the question pending action by the OAS. Mexico, Brazil and Canada offered their good offices. In response, with thanks, Herter emphasized to their envoys that the problem was primarily hemispheric rather than a disagreement between the United States and Cuba.

Khrushchev's dramatic interposition on July 9, 1960, in Western Hemisphere affairs with the promise of full support for Castro, sparked the call for another Meeting of Consultation of American Foreign Ministers to deal with the Cuban crisis. The conference was called by the OAS to meet immediately after the

Sixth Meeting already called on request of Venezuela, which had charged the Trujillo government of the Dominican Republic with acts of "intervention and aggression," including attempted assassination of the Venezuelan President Romulo Betancourt on June 24, 1960. The case against Trujillo was clear-cut and the wrath of other American Republics demanded condign punishment. Herter, while preferring and proposing measures looking to OAS-supervised free elections in the Dominican Republic, decided to accept the harsher terms demanded overwhelmingly by the Latin governments, including a diplomatic break, suspension of trade in arms, and study of other trade restrictions. Herter hoped thereby to get stronger support for his policy against Cuba.

While the Dominican Republic was in the dock in the Sixth Meeting, there was no direct confrontation with Cuba in the Seventh Meeting. Although Herter realized that sanctions against Cuba were out of the question, he met individually with Latin Foreign Ministers, with whom his relations were excellent (except Roa of Cuba), and urged that Cuba be found in violation of the principles of the inter-American system. The other members of the OAS were anxious to avoid pointing the finger at Castro, however strongly they felt against his policies. Hence the Declaration of San José, while not mentioning Cuba, did condemn "intervention or threat of intervention, even when conditional, by any extracontinental power" and stated that acceptance of such a threat by any American state endangered "American solidarity and security." It reaffirmed the principle of nonintervention and the incompatibility of totalitarianism with the inter-American system.

The conference was reported as "hectic, dramatic, and heartbreaking."[52] Although Herter did not gain all his objectives, he reported optimistically to the President on his return. He said the conference had indicted Cuba, but this interpretation was disputed by certain Latin American foreign ministers. Herter's personal diplomacy was an important factor in getting the relatively strong resolution which emerged from the meeting.[53]

After the San José Conference the chance of restoring normal relations between Cuba and the United States was minimal. Tempers flared on the Cuban front, and statements and policies were provocative rather than rational efforts to find solutions. Tempers in Washington remained under control. The Declaration of San José, with related resolutions, was a sweeping indictment, though indirect, of Castro's policies. But Latin American opinion was far from ready to give it legally binding effect. The Declaration was strong enough to infuriate Castro, but not enough to be a serious threat.

Supported by Khrushchev's July promise of assistance, reaffirmed by Foreign Minister Andrei A. Gromyko in late August 1960, Castro, in a nose-thumbing mood, scathingly forecast the overthrow of the Latin American governments that had signed the Declaration and charged them with being bought by the United States. He said Cuba would continue to rely on "rocket support" of the U.S.S.R. in case of attack.[54]

The increase of Cuba's ties with the communist

bloc continued. During the San José Conference, Castro on August 23 signed a trade agreement with Communist China involving purchase of 500,000 tons of Cuban sugar a year at world prices for the next five years, with provision that during the first four years the deal would be on a barter basis—Chinese merchandise for Cuban sugar. This was followed on September 3 by an announcement that Cuba would resume diplomatic relations with Communist China, at the same time withdrawing recognition from the Taiwan Government. The first ambassador from Communist China accredited to a Latin American country arrived in Cuba on December 28, 1960.[55]

The session of the U.N. General Assembly beginning in September 1960, gave Castro opportunity to strengthen ties with Khrushchev, as well as to use the General Assembly as a sounding board for charges against the United States. During his ten-day stay he exchanged embraces with Khrushchev several times, notably in the U.N. General Assembly where Castro and Khrushchev made a public display of close ties between their governments.

In his general policy speech to the Assembly on September 26, Castro poured his wrath on the United States in a speech of four and a half hours. He complained of treatment received, including travel restrictions which confined him to Manhattan (deemed necessary, owing to need for heavy police protection), and spread on the record a long list of charges, most of which he had made before to the U.N. or the OAS. He was applauded by nine Soviet bloc members and Guinea. One observer characterized it as a well-

known play presented before the world's most important audience. In a brief reply the U.S. representative
said a document would be circulated later which
would set the record straight. This document, a
10,000-word detailed indictment, was circulated to
U.N. members on October 13.[56]

Castro's expropriation policies emphasized his anti-
American course. He explained them as retaliation
against the "economic aggression" of the United
States. They hit American property hardest, but also
included increasingly Cuban and other foreign holdings. Speaking to a cheering throng of 30,000 Castro
announced the decree of August 7, 1960, saying it
provided for "forcible expropriation of all U.S. com-
panies in Cuba." Seizures of property accelerated,
culminating on October 14 in the most sweeping nationalization measures ever taken in the Western
Hemisphere. The U.S. Department of Commerce on
November 13 reported that U.S.-owned properties
seized by the Cuban Government totaled nearly one
billion dollars. This was book value. Market value
normally would have been a great deal more. This
estimate did not include other seized U.S.-owned as-
sets, such as the Nicaro Nickel plant of the U.S. Government. American notes of protest against the seizures were regularly rejected by the Castro government.[57]

During September 1960, the safety of American
citizens in Cuba became a matter of concern, and a
series of travel restrictions were issued by the State
Department.[58] The question of more drastic economic
measures came to the fore. Secretary Herter and

others had doubted the adequacy of the sugar quota bill. Restrictive economic measures, the Secretary thought, ought to be serious enough to be effective. He doubted that the sugar quota bill would be. There was also pressure from the Hill and by early October 1960, it was fairly certain that the trend of Cuban policy called for more stringent measures. The result was an embargo on exports to Cuba announced on October 19, applying to all commodities except medicine, medical supplies and a list of food products.

The State Department explained that discriminatory Cuban economic measures had injured thousands of American citizens and drastically altered the pattern of trade between the United States and Cuba. U.S. exports to Cuba were reduced to less than half of the figure for 1958, and payment was never received for about a fourth of the goods shipped after Castro seized power.[59]

While the embargo law was being prepared, Secretary Herter recommended to the President on October 16, 1960, that Ambassador Bonsal be recalled for consultation, with the announcement that he would not return for the reason that he could not function effectively under existing conditions. There had been no Cuban Ambassador in the U.S. since December 1959, and there were continuing rumors of a Cuban-initiated break in relations. Bonsal had not talked with Castro since his return to Cuba in the spring, and he seldom saw Raul Roa. There had been talk of negotiations, and Roa at San José had expressed Cuba's willingness to negotiate. In fact, since Castro had taken over the government the United States had made nine formal and sixteen informal offers of negotiation. The Castro Government replied only once to these—on the previous February 22, 1960—and it attached a condition that the United States could not possibly accept.[60]

The Ambassador was recalled on October 20, 1960, leaving Daniel Braddock as Chargé d'Affaires in the Embassy. The possibility of diplomatic dialogue during the current administration was at an end. From that time to January 1961, worsening relations were marked by Castro's frenzied charges of "invasion" by the United States, renewed tensions in the Caribbean, and Castro's efforts to consolidate his position at home.

Castro took his case against the United States to the U.N., charging "intensified plans of aggression and intervention" against Cuba. He knew that Cubans were training in Guatemala and elsewhere for guerrilla warfare. His complaint to the General Assembly on October 18, 1960, got nowhere. Nor did it fare better before the Security Council on January 4, 1961.[61]

Castro's continuing interest in spreading his gospel to Caribbean neighbors was indicated in November 1960, by simultaneous communist uprisings in Nicaragua and Guatemala. U.S. intelligence authorities believed the coordinated timing of the uprisings indicated outside direction. After the two countries got the insurgency under apparent control, they appealed for United States naval aid to prevent landing of reinforcements from Cuba. Herter recommended that the President instruct naval units to establish a discreet surveillance of Central American waters, keeping well out of sight of land. The exercise was to be merely precautionary. The President gave the orders, the patrol was established, calm was restored, and on December 7, the White House announced withdrawal of the patrol.[62]

The episode provided Castro with additional ammunition for use against the United States, enabling him to improve his domestic position by whipping up popular hates and fears of the "enemy" in a time of worsening economic conditions, guerrilla activities, revived opposition of the Church, tightening the communist screws, and the flight of thousands of professionals from the country.[63]

Castro's speech of January 2, 1961, accusing the U.S. Embassy of being the center of counter-revolutionary activities against the regime, and stating that the Embassy staff would have to be reduced to eleven persons within forty-eight hours, left the Eisenhower Administration no feasible alternative to breaking relations. Secretary Herter discussed the matter with incoming Secretary Dean Rusk, informing him of the situation and the impending break on January 3.

Before Herter's tenure ended, the break in relations offered one partial answer to the Cuban problem. Another answer, chancy and murky, was in the making. Although the United States had no plan to use its military forces in an invasion of Cuba, the fact had become known that Cuban refugees were training in Guatemala under U.S. direction.

The training, as first planned, was for guerrilla activities in Cuba. Beginning in early summer 1960, recruitment had built up a fluctuating force of about 1,200 exiles by year's end. During the autumn the objective of the operation changed from guerrilla activities to establishment of a formidable beachhead of at least battalion strength. It presumably would attract anti-Castro activists, encourage uprisings behind Castro lines, gradually enlarge the beachhead, and set up a provisional government. President-elect John F. Kennedy was apprised of this situation in December 1960.[64]

Confusion of leadership, organization, and training of the exiles, and growing restlessness and demands for action became embarrassing to President Miguel Ydigoras of Guatemala, who had freely agreed to the operation and who sought unsuccessfully to conceal the project's import. The State Department discussed the possibility of removing the group to another location; but it reached no agreement, and time was too short before the change of administrations.

The situation was explosive. Restlessness and frustration over delays were increasing among the exiles who felt they were becoming over-trained, and believed that with U.S. support, wishfully exaggerated, the venture could not fail. They were soon to learn that it could.

Cuba was a problem of major concern as Herter turned over his authority to his successor.

# CHAPTER ELEVEN

## INTER-AMERICAN RELATIONS: II

THERE WERE two problems, other than Cuba, involving United States relations with Latin America that were of special concern during Herter's secretaryship. One related to critical developments on the Panama front and the other to overall economic relations with Latin America.

### 1

The wave of anti-Americanism which swept Cuba and hit other areas of Latin America less severely struck Panama in 1959. Behind it lay extreme poverty of the masses (about 85 percent Negro, Indian, or mestizo) and concentration of wealth in the hands of a narrow political, economic, and cultural oligarchy which maintained forms of democracy by periodic elections, without disturbing its own control. The awakening spirit of nationalism was used by politicians and others who wished to explain or divert attention from economic and social evils by belaboring the United States. They attacked the terms and conditions of U.S. occupancy of the 10-mile-wide canal zone cutting across the heartland of Panama.

The newly independent Panamanians in 1903 were unhappy over the canal terms imposed by the United States—less generous than those offered to and rejected earlier by Colombia. Colombia had been asked for a 10-kilometer-wide (6¼ miles) strip on a lease basis (99 years, renewable on U.S. requst) whereas Panama was required to grant to the U.S. a 10-mile-wide strip in perpetuity, with "all rights, power and authority . . . as if it were the sovereign of the territory." The treaty also guaranteed the independence of Panama, which in effect became a protectorate of the United States.

Treaties in 1936 and 1955 made certain concessions to Panamanian objections, *e.g.*, regarding working conditions in the canal zone, commissary practices, and the annuity to Panama (increased in 1955 from $430,000 to $1,930,000).[1] Dissatisfaction with U.S. canal policies continued and in 1957 there was concern in Panama about the failure of U.S. legislation to implement the terms of the 1955 treaty. Acting Secretary Herter took up the matter with the President on July 29, 1957, and got congressional action that helped to avoid a crisis in 1957 and 1958.

In 1959 the repercussions of Castro's Cuban triumph were spreading around the Caribbean, and Panamanians saw a possible lesson in Nasser's seizure of the Suez Canal in 1956. There was little disposition to take over the Canal, but there were urgent demands for major changes in the terms of its control.

At the Santiago Meeting of Consultation in August, 1959, Foreign Minister Miguel J. Moreno, Jr., complained to Secretary Herter that in spite of repeated Panamanian protests the United States was still violating treaty agreements regarding equality of treatment in employment opportunities, purchases (*e.g.*, by the Commissaries) in the Canal Zone to be made only from the United States or Panama except where not "feasible," and the import of luxury goods in unfair competition with the Panama economy.

Meantime, the right, frequently requested, to fly the Panamanian flag wherever the United States flag was flown in the Canal Zone became the supreme issue. In May 1958, in a nonviolent "sovereignty march" students placed small Panama flags in the Zone. In July 1959, the ultranationalists began preparing for a huge "sovereignty march" on November 3 (the anniversary of Panama's independence) as a major challenge on the flag issue. In spite of American warnings, the November 3 demonstration was one of the worst explosions of anti-American violence in Panama's history.[2] Mobs rioted through the streets of Panama City for several hours without interference from the National Guard. Rioters destroyed property, and at the American Embassy pulled down the American flag, tore it up, and raised the Panamanian flag. In the Canal Zone they clashed with Canal police, and some 80 persons were injured. When the United States protested, the Panama Government brushed off the charges with counter-charges against the U.S. military for allegedly firing on unarmed Panamanians.[3]

The flag incident was the expression also of underlying issues, such as the claim for increased Canal payments, better working opportunities in the Canal Zone, and a more important part in the administration of the Canal Zone. Deputy Under Secretary Livingston T. Merchant, on a special mission, November

20-24, 1959, discussed problems of a mutual interest with President Ernest de la Guardia, Jr., and his Foreign Minister, including measures under study in the United States to improve Panama's economic well-being. But he emphasized that nothing could be done until normal conditions returned. He reaffirmed that titular sovereignty remained in the Government of Panama, and the President of Panama expressed determination to prevent further anti-U.S. violence.[4] When new riots broke out on November 28, causing damage to persons and property, the National Guard acted more decisively in getting the situation under control.

The Panama Government continued to press for the right to fly the Panama flag daily in the Canal Zone. President Eisenhower favored some form of visual evidence of Panama's titular sovereignty, and Herter on December 12, 1959, proposed that there should be a daily display of the two flags at two points in the Canal Zone, but that the Panama flag should not be displayed on transiting ships. Discussions on this subject were interrupted when the U.S. House of Representatives, on February 2, 1960, passed a concurrent resolution, 380 to 12, saying, in effect, that Panama's flag should not fly over the Canal Zone unless a new treaty provided for it. Though the Senate took no action on this measure, the State Department postponed further consideration of the proposal.

In the summer of 1960, Secretary Herter resumed efforts to secure action on the flag problem, anticipating the possibility that November 3, which loomed on the horizon, might witness further anti-American

demonstrations and violence. In spite of strong opposition in the House of Representatives and the Pentagon, the President accepted the recommendations of
Herter and the new Ambassador to Panama, Joseph S.
Farland, and issued a statement on September 17
permitting the showing of the Panama flag on a rou-
tine basis, along with the American flag.[5] The timing
of the statement, issued shortly after the close of the
Congressional session, was not a mere coincidence

The Panama flag was raised in the Zone along with
the American for the first time on October 1, 1960.
Panama President de la Guardia was absent from the
ceremonies, owing to insistence of the U.S. Government that the flag be raised by an American. In spite
of the bitter taste left by this aspect of the affair, the
reactions in Panama were generally favorable.[6]

The flag decision left a troublesome domestic "flag
pole" problem for certain U.S. Government agencies,
as there was confusion as to how the $1,500 bill for
the pole to fly the Panama flag should be met. The
Canal Company was strictly forbidden to pay the bill
by the Gross Amendment to the Department of Commerce appropriation bill. The State Department
wanted to avoid the expenditure, as it would be post-
reviewed by the critical eye of Congressman John
Rooney and his committee; but the Department finally was persuaded by Elmer Staats, of the Budget Bureau, to pay the cost out of its emergency fund, with
the assurance that, if questioned by Congress, the Department could say it was ordered by the President to
make the payment.

Economic problems with Panama tended to sharpen the conflict between the American "Zonians"—a privileged community—and the Panamanian employees in the Zone, owing to Panamanian demands for equal pay, greater access to white collar and supervisory jobs, restricting commissary purchases, and a voice in the administration of the Canal.

Purchasing policies of U.S. Zonal agencies had long been under fire, owing to charges of violating the terms of the 1955 agreements which forbade purchases from countries other than the United States and Panama, unless "not feasible to do so." The "not feasible" terminology led to broad interpretations which the State Department believed violated the terms of the agreements. Such "third country" purchases constituted only about five percent of total purchases, but Herter felt it was a question of principle, and that purchases from third countries should be made only in cases of real emergency. This caused difficulties with the Army which argued that the policy in Panama might have a worldwide impact on its commissaries, but the State Department held that the Panama restrictions applied to a unique situation— that the Zone had always been considered *sui generis*. During the first half of the year these arguments prevailed and third-country purchases by Canal Zone civil and military agencies were practically eliminated. The only exception was petroleum, since, at that time, there were no refineries in Panama.

Working conditions in the Zone presented more serious difficulties, owing to the traditional distinctions between Americans, who filled the supervisory, skilled, and "security" positions, and the Panamanians who were principally employed at the unskilled and semi-skilled levels. The Americans not only occupied the higher jobs, but they enjoyed a special 25 percent foreign-resident differential. The Panamanian workers' wage rates were considerably above those paid generally in Panama, but far below those paid Americans. A vivid illustration of frustrating discrimination was the pay increases of 1958, which totalled $2,000-000 for U.S. job categories and only $153,000 for Panamanian categories.

This situation, disturbing to the Secretary and the President, led to an Administration nine-point program announced on April 19, 1960, to improve wages and living conditions, including a 10 percent wage increase for unskilled and semi-skilled workers, and for teachers in the Latin-American schools in the Zone, as well as replacement of existing substandard housing, expansion of the apprentice program for Panamanians, and inquiry into the possibility of placing more Panamanians in skilled and supervisory positions.[7] This program was criticized in certain quarters of Congress and by Zonians, as "a sell-out," and in Panama as merely scratching the surface of the job discrimination problem.

Another serious aspect of U.S. relations with Panama, in the judgment of Herter and the President, was the dispersion of authority among three American officials—the Governor of the Canal Zone who, by statute, also wore the hat of the President of the Canal Company, the Commander-in-Chief of the Caribbean Command (CINCARIB)), later Southern Command, and the U.S. Ambassador. Thus the military played a triple role in the Zone vis-a-vis Panama—two of these in the dual functions of the Governor and President, and a third in that of CINCARIB whose function was to protect the Canal.

There was no prescribed means of coordinating responsibilities. Sometimes there were important disagreements on policy without any defined means of settlement. Milton Eisenhower studied the situation in Panama in the late summer of 1958. He said our Ambassador had no control over Zone affairs, and concluded that "the United States desperately needs a *single voice* in Panama. And that voice should be the Ambassador's."

Secretary Herter agreed with these views. In his judgment there was no longer any sound reason why the Canal Zone should be under a military governor, and he thought that if the Zone's government were "civilianized" by appointment of a civil governor, it would be more acceptable to the Panama people.

There was the related problem of the Board of Directors of the Panama Canal Company, on which all the members were businessmen, without any political representation. Herter felt that one voting member should be a State Department political adviser, with high rank to give him appropriate influence, since he would be a "Daniel among the lions."

These matters were threshed out with Defense during the following months. Defense argued that a political officer would be out of place in a board of high-level business-men running a "business corporation," but Herter insisted that one voice of the thirteen should be alert to the political implications of the

Board's actions. This proposal was finally accepted by Defense in August 1960, on the understanding, as stated by Secretary of the Army Wilber H. Brucker, that the representative would always be at the Under Secretary level.

Herter wanted the Governor of the Zone to be a civilian. Defense was concerned over the possibility of a run-of-the-mill politician becoming Governor, thus having two civilians—the Ambassador and the Governor—involved in relations with the Government of Panama. The Secretary wanted to reduce the "military occupation" aspect of the U.S. position in the Canal Zone. Agreement failed on this matter and attention turned more hopefully to assuring the Ambassador a position of primacy in Zone matters relating to the government and the people of Panama.

On this Herter was successful. Secretary Brucker agreed to the Ambassador's primacy over the Governor of the Canal Zone in matters affecting the relations between the United States and the Republic of Panama or any other nation. A comparable arrangement regarding relations with CINCARIB was not reached, but State approved a Defense proposal that a political adviser (POLAD) be appointed to CIN-CARIB.

Although Secretary Herter and the President, working closely in agreement, had taken important steps to improve U.S. relations with Panama, serious problems remained. One involved the future of the Panama Canal and U.S. Canal policy in the Caribbean area.[8] In a conference of February 15, 1960, Herter discussed with the President the desirability of reviving the project for a sea-level canal. Such a project, he thought, would have a moderating effect on Panamanian demands on the United States as well as serving the long-term interests of the United States and other countries. The existing canal was gradually being outdated, as already the modern aircraft carriers and a growing number of commercial vessels could not pass through the 110-foot-wide locks, and it was difficult to pilot large heavily-laden ore ships through the cut.[9] Questions of the future canal's location, its ownership and control, and the use of nuclear methods in its construction, were beyond the possibilities of early decision. Herter warned the President that the devices for nuclear excavation would have to be proven by full-scale experimentation before conclusions could be drawn, and he expressed a strong preference for a route through Panama. He felt certain that Panama would prefer an agreement for bilateral control, and thought any other arrangement would intensify friction in relations between the two countries.

At the San José Meeting of Consultation in late August 1960, Panama's Foreign Minister Miguel Moreno presented Herter with a memorandum on Panama's problems, as he had done at Santiago in 1959. He told the Secretary that in spite of some progress, or "intent of progress," working conditions were still in violation of treaty terms that called for "equality" of opportunity in employment." He emphasized the need for more economic aid, noting that in the new U.S. economic initiative in Latin America, Panama had been relegated to the lowest position among recipients of such limited economic assistance. The incoming President of Panama in 1960, Robert F. Chiari, played down emotional explosions, and in his inaugural address on October 1 called for a climate of "mutual understanding" while pointing to issues causing friction in relations with the United States.[10] In a letter of November 4 to Foreign Minister Galileo Solis (successor to Moreno), Secretary Herter expressed belief that the measures taken by the United States during the preceding months to improve economic and social conditions in Latin America (e.g., the Bogotá proposals), and to solve outstanding problems in the Canal Zone, indicated the importance attached by the United States to good relations. This policy was expressed also in November by loans of $5,300,000 by the Development Loan Fund for farm-to-market roads and $5,000,000 for budget support.

At the year's end U.S. relations with Panama seemed to have improved, thanks to the flag decision, new Canal Zone procurement policies, the Nine Point Program, and efforts of the newly appointed top U.S. representatives in Panama. Herter was aware that the Chiari Government faced serious domestic economic conditions and the urgent need for administrative and budgetary reforms which depended on financial assistance to restore fiscal order and greater liquidity in the nation's banks. For this the $5,000,000 budget support loan would be helpful. If the Chiari Government could survive the financial crisis there was hope for political stability and friendly relations between Panama and the United States and for the solution of other Isthmian Canal problems. Relations appeared to improve, but serious Canal Zone problems remained which were destined to lead to further crisis.

2

Since World War I the inter-American problem has been primarily economic, although as the Santiago and San José Conference demonstrated, the specter of intervention haunted Latin American minds. It was the economic argument that fired Fidel Castro's major onslaughts on the United States, and enabled him to arouse nationalistic anti-American sentiments among the Cuban people. It was the powerful political and economic position of the United States that enabled the ruling oligarchies in Latin America to shift the blame for widespread poverty and provided tinder for left-wing extremists to inflame passions against "Yankee imperialism," as well as against their own governments.

During World War II, interdependence of hemisphere countries was mutually appreciated. Unilateral and cooperative measures were taken to insure the security of the hemisphere and to minimize adverse economic effects of the war. Loans and technical assistance were made available by the U.S. Government to Latin American countries, and a coordinator of Inter-American affairs sought to insure prompt attention to Latin American problems in U.S. Government agencies.

The situation changed markedly after the war as the U.S. Government became preoccupied with the relief and reconstruction of war-torn areas of Europe and Asia, and with the defense of Western Europe and other areas threatened by communist aggression. The special agencies dealing with Latin American affairs were largely dismantled and experienced personnel transferred to other problems.

The change did not go unnoticed in Latin America, and especially in 1948, after the Marshall Plan for Europe was adopted, the Latin Americans sought comparable attention by the United States. Secretary of State Marshall told them that they were excluded from the Plan, which was designed only to rebuild war-shattered economies. He advised them to seek private capital for their development. This position was maintained by the United States for ten years in the face of increasing Latin criticism and discontent.[11]

By the middle of the 1950's storm warnings were visible in Latin America where economic conditions provided incentives for communist infiltration.[12] Conferences in 1954 and 1957 did not satisfy urgent Latin American requests for an Inter-American Development Bank and for U.S. participation in discussions looking to stabilizing commodity prices.[13] The United States was widely attacked for "neglect" of Latin America and for "taking its closest neighbors for granted." The disparity between the financial assistance given Latin America and that given Western Europe and the rest of the world was singled out. Total United States aid (economic and military) to Latin America was about 5½ percent of that of the rest of the world from July 1, 1946 to June 30, 1958—

$3,870,000,000 and $70,423,400,000. It was 8½ percent of that given Western Europe during those years. Economic aid to Europe totaled 10¾ percent.[14]

Vice President Nixon's good-will visit to eight Latin American countries, April 27 to May 15, 1958, dramatized the deterioration in the position of the United States in Latin America. The fury and bitterness of the attacks on the Vice President in Lima and Caracas, as well as the cat-calls and jeers mixed with the cheers in states previously visited, left no doubt that anti-American feelings extended far beyond the band of communists who were among the leading instigators. It was clear also that Nixon was primarily the sacrificial lamb.

The events of Nixon's trip hastened the pace of change in State Department thinking. In August 1958, reversing its long-standing opposition, the Department agreed to discuss stabilization of coffee prices, though the U.S. Government did not become a party to the agreement of September 27.[15] Economic aid for Latin American countries in fiscal year 1959 increased by $205,000,000 over that of fiscal 1958. Reversing a policy firmly stated in 1948, 1954, and 1957, on August 12, 1958, the Department promised U.S. support for an "Inter-American Development Institution," thus responding to the long-standing desire of the Latin American powers for an inter-American institution designed to promote the financing of accelerated economic development in Latin America.[16]

This announcement led to the signing of the charter in April 1959, and the establishment of the Inter-

American Development Bank in February 1960, with a capital stock of one billion dollars, to which the United States contributed $450,000,000. Of the capital stock, $150,000,000 could be used for projects socially desirable but not necessarily self-liquidating, and the loans could be repaid in local currency. It was a small start in coping with huge tasks, but it was a start and the funds supplemented those of existing credit institutions. It opened another important door.[17]

President Juscelino Kubitschek of Brazil meanwhile endeavored to solve Latin American problems by his plan, "Operation Pan America," brought out in August 1958, which aimed at overall development of Latin America and the "furtherance of the Pan American ideals in all their aspects and implications."[18] The proposal seemed to American officials to be a sort of Latin American Marshall Plan, hence they were wary of it, while recognizing that its objectives were laudable.

Milton Eisenhower returned to Washington in August 1958, after studying conditions in Central America and Panama for several weeks, full of a sense of urgency for action in what he described as "a continent in ferment." Reporting to the President on December 27, he urged speedy action in setting up an Inter-American Bank and called for action along various lines to promote economic and social development and a Latin American common market. He also urged that the President appoint a Latin American Council in the United States as an advisory body, with the Secretary of State as chairman.[19]

The year 1959 was a time of trouble for Latin Americans. Revolutionary outbreaks were reported from fourteen countries, as political consciousness and dissidence increased among disadvantaged groups.[20] An anti-Yankee outburst in Bolivia in March 1959, illustrated the sensitivity of the people and the hostility close to the surface. A report in the Latin America edition of *Time* magazine (March 2), that an American Embassy official in Bolivia had said, in jest, that the solution for Bolivia's economic problems was for "her neighbors to divide up the country and the problems," led to three days of rioting in La Paz and other cities. Crowds of angry demonstrators in the streets of La Paz shouted "down with imperialism" and "Bolivia will not be a Yankee colony." The American flag was burned and the Embassy and USIA were stoned and had to be evacuated. Eighteen hundred Americans were concentrated in two places, under police guard. Serious thoughts were given by U.S. officials to evacuating all Americans. Acting Secretary Herter assured the Bolivian Ambassador that it was impossible to believe that a member of the Embassy staff had made such a statement. He then faced the delicate task of trying to induce the editor of *Time*, Henry Luce, to express regrets and to say that some mistake had been made. Herter feared that if *Time* reaffirmed the story it would lead to serious consequences, since American lives were at stake.

Herter could not admit the Embassy's responsibility for the statement, and editor Luce felt that he could not admit an error in his staff's reporting. The March 16 issue of *Time*, however, carried a story saying that the "rueful jest" was only repeating what Bolivians and foreigners had said for many decades in the past. The incident was closed, but its violence and bitterness were all the more disappointing since the Eisenhower Administration had consistently provided substantial economic support for the revolutionary government that had come to power in Bolivia in 1952. As a political barometer it forecast unsettled conditions.[21]

Toward the end of 1959 United States relations with Latin America showed some improvement. The Inter-American Development Bank was being set up. The United States had been more disposed to discuss problems of commodity price stabilization, and had encouraged the movement in Latin America for establishment of free trade areas. A five-nation common market had been set up in Central America in 1958, and seven South American countries had reached a preliminary agreement in September 1959, to establish a free trade zone over a period of twelve years.[22]

President Eisenhower had made two spectacularly successful friendship tours in Europe and Asia, touching down in North Africa, and the question arose in Latin American quarters of extending his friendly tourism to the southern continent. The President was glad to go, taking with him members of the newly established Council on Latin America, including Secretary Herter, to emphasize U.S. concern for southern neighbors. In visiting the four countries chosen for his tour—Brazil, Argentina, Chile and Uruguay—he was warmly received in each of the capitals, though some demonstrators were occasionally in the offing.

In private discussions with top officials, interest centered chiefly on Cuba and on economic and financial problems. Eisenhower and Herter were frank in explaining the dilemma of the United States, faced by the evident drift toward Communism of Castro's policies, and the growing demands in the United States for action against the Cuban leader. President Kubitschek thought he was in a good position to talk with Castro, and Eisenhower assured both him and President Arturo Frondizi of Argentina that he would welcome anything the Latin nations could do to induce the Cubans to be more amenable. Both he and Herter, in their separate talks with top officials, were concerned to emphasize that the Cuban problem was an OAS problem and not merely a concern of the United States. This was not disputed, though it was scarcely accepted. President Alessandri of Chile, as well as other leaders, expressed approval of the moderate course of U.S. Cuban policies of that time, and all shared the view that great care should be taken in preparing any action safeguarding the principle of nonintervention. President Alessandri and his Foreign Minister, Taboada, favored "isolation" of Cuba rather than direct action. On crucial foreign policy matters Herter gave assurances of consultation.

During the tour the Secretary played an unobtrusive but important role in backstopping the President and in separate conferences with other officials of the respective governments. In Santiago he received cheers because of his fine performance at the conference the previous August.

In a Washington news conference on March 9, 1960, Herter forecast a follow-up to the tour, adding that Latin American leaders fully realized the need for both private and public capital.[23]

In a speech of April 20, before the Council of the OAS, the Secretary said drastic revisions in existing social, economic and political institutions would be required to satisfy the aspirations of the individual Latin American citizen, and stressed land distribution and credit facilities.[24]

An important change in U.S. official thinking, in process for some time, resulted from fuller appreciation of the deteriorating economic and political conditions in Latin America, emphasized by popular reactions to Kubitschek's Operation Pan America, the Nixon tour, the Bolivian outburst and, above all, the Castro revolution. These all pointed to new directions of economic policy toward Latin America. This new orientation was announced by the President from his Newport vacation retreat, after a conference with Herter. Noting that "in the Americas, as elsewhere, change is the law of life," and that "Latin America is passing through a social and political transformation," the statement proclaimed a "new affirmation of purposes" in cooperation with other American republics, looking to opening new areas of arable land for settlement and ownership by free, self-reliant men; improving the opportunities of the bulk of the population to share in and contribute to an expanding national product; and accelerating the trend toward greater respect for human rights and democratic government. The Secretary of State, he said, would confer with Latin American friends on those principles and purposes.[25]

The President asked the Congress to authorize funds totalling $500,000,000 to get the project started, and $100,000,00 for help to Chile after a devastating earthquake. Announcement of this program was inevitably regarded as a reflection of the Cuban crisis. In a news conference of August 9, 1960, however, Herter said "it had not been in any sense connected with the Cuban difficulties."[26] The requests were duly granted.

Under Secretary Dillon, chairman of the U.S. delegation to the ensuing conference at Bogotá, September 5 to 13, 1960, presented a draft agreement for an inter-American social development program for consideration of the Committee of 21. He said its purpose was to add the "new broad dimension of social development" to existing programs of "economic development" in a "conscious and determined effort to further social justice in our hemisphere." Dr. Alberto Lleras, President of Colombia, hailed the U.S. initiative and "the new way of seeing the heart" of their difficulties, but painted a somber picture, saying that Latin America was "on the edge of an economic and social crisis without precedent in its history." The Act of Bogotá was signed on September 13, 1960, by representatives of 19 inter-American states. (Cuba refused to sign, and the Dominican Republic was not represented.) It aimed "to meet the legitimate aspirations of the individual citizen . . . for a better life and to provide him the fullest opportunity to improve his status"; and it welcomed the decision of the United States to establish a special fund for social development.[27] The Act involved a new departure and a large commitment by the United States and demanded important contributions from Latin American peoples for social improvement in their countries. It was an act of faith, the justification of which depended on much that lay in the future. It pointed the way to a Promised Land, though the prospect of reaching that land depended on future policies and resources that would be hard to come by, in order to make available to the masses land, jobs, homes, schools, hospitals, and a fairer share in the products of their labor.[28]

The years 1958 to 1960 thus had witnessed a considerable change in the thinking of U.S. officials. By the end of the Eisenhower-Herter administration, much had happened to change perspectives and promote more realistic thinking on policy toward Latin America. Herter's attitude was well expressed in his speech of September 8, 1960, when he pointed to the need for social change in Latin America. A low standard of living, he said, combined with a high rate of population growth, a low level of technical and general education and, in some cases, outmoded economic, legal, and social systems, denied opportunity for improvement to a large part of the population. The result was frustration, social unrest, occasional violence, with threats to free democratic institutions. Our Government, in cooperation with the OAS, "was endeavoring to work out a program of social development that would avoid destructive social upheaval and its dangers."[29] The program was a challenge which the next Administration took up, though the Promised Land remained a distant vista.

# CHAPTER TWELVE

## ALLIANCES IN THE BALANCE: I

A s Secretary of State, Herter inherited a net-work of alliances—bilateral and multilateral—the nature and extent of which would have shocked the isolationist sensibilities of the pre-World War II generation. In 1959 mutual defense agreements existed with forty-two countries. The multilateral pacts were broader and more sensitive than the bi-laterals and therefore more important and of greater concern.

### 1

It was a time of testing for these alliances, though less so for the ANZUS agreement with Australia and New Zealand (effective in 1952) which lay outside immediate crisis areas and faced no serious challenge during this period. ANZUS was part of the Pacific de-fense system conceived along with the bilateral secur-ity treaty accompanying the peace treaty with Japan and the mutual defense treaty with the Philippines. The chief concern of the United States was the spread of communism. Its partners worried more over pos-sible Japanese policies.[1] Each party recognized that an armed attack in the Pacific area on any of the par-ties would endanger its own peace and safety, and agreed to "meet the common danger in accordance with its constitutional processes." There was no unequivocal commitment to render military assistance, but the relations between the three parties were growing increasingly intimate.[2]

Herter met in Washington with Ministers of other ANZUS states on October 26, 1959. They exchanged views on wide-ranging subjects and Herter reviewed highlights of the current international scene. He reported that Khrushchev's September visit was of doubtful value, as Russian policies had no "give" in them except possibly on the Berlin "ultimatum." Khrushchev, he said, was adamant in supporting Communist China against Taiwan; the Soviet leader's reason for desiring the postponement of Eisenhower's return visit to Russia was a mystery; De Gaulle was dragging his feet on the question of a summit meeting; the British regarded the summit as a safety valve, whereas De Gaulle considered it a court of last resort; "free Berlin," as proposed by the Russians, was unacceptable. U.S. policy regarding Communist China was not inflexible, but to change it then was not in the national interest. He said the United States was hanging on to its responsibilities abroad because it saw no feasible alternative.

Prime Minister Nash, of New Zealand, placed more confidence in Soviet aims and policies than did Herter. He was fearful of interfering in Laotian internal politics and of possibly maintaining in office a regime wanted by the United States rather than by the Laotian people. Foreign Minister Casey, of Australia, generally agreed with Herter's appraisals of political trends. A meeting of the ANZUS powers was not deemed necessary in 1960, or indeed in 1961.

2

The Southeast Asia Treaty Organization (SEATO) pact was originally conceived by Secretary Dulles in 1954 before the French military disaster in Indo-China. Its purpose was to strengthen French and indigenous resistance to communism. When signed in September, 1954, after the Geneva Conference agreements of July, the SEATO pact was an expression of lack of confidence in the Geneva settlement which Moscow's *Pravda* had hailed as a complete defeat of the "bankrupt" policy of the United States. U.S. Government leaders appraised its terms as the best possible under the circumstances.[3] General Bedell Smith uttered an eternal truth in saying that diplomacy had rarely gained at the conference table what could not be gained or held on the field of battle. Ho Chi Minh left no doubt as to North Vietnam's intention to "obtain unification, independence and democratization of all Vietnam" for which, he said, "the peoples and the soldiers of the north and south must unite to conquer victory."[4]

The SEATO pact did not include all noncommunist areas of Southeast Asia. Laos, South Vietnam and Cambodia (protocol states) were not eligible, owing to their commitments in the Geneva settlements. Burma, India, Ceylon and Indonesia preferred "non-involvement." This left Thailand and the Philippines as

the only Southeast Asia members of the geographically dispersed collectivity, including Pakistan, the
United States, Britain, France, Australia, and New
Zealand. Almost all effective political and military
power lay outside Southeast Asia. The wide dispersion of member states did not make for close-knit
organization, and the United States was not disposed
to spell out military obligations or to commit substantial military forces.[5]

Security commitments were not drastic or precise.
Each party agreed that armed aggression "against
any of the parties . . . would endanger its own peace
and safety," and that it would "act to meet the common danger in accordance with its constitutional
processes," as in the ANZUS pact. If any party were
threatened by subversion all would "consult immediately in order to agree on the measures . . .for the
common defense."[6] This left each party a good deal
of leeway in decision making.

SEATO had little military significance of its own,
but the treaty gave the United States a *locus standi*—
a treaty-grounded right, or commitment—to defend
the freedom of SEATO countries, including the three
protocol states, against communist aggression. The
commitment was individual as well as collective.[7] The
mobile striking power of the United States was the
mainstay of the pact, though individual or collective
power was relatively ineffective against the "soft"
methods of communist infiltration and subversion, as
became evident to Herter in 1959 and 1960.

Herter did not attend the fifth annual SEATO
Council meeting of April 8-10, 1959, as he was Acting

Secretary during the terminal illness of Secretary Dulles and was preparing for upcoming crucial East-West meetings. Under Secretary Dillon headed the American delegation to the meeting in Wellington. No burning issues were raised, though serious problems were looming up. The Council ministers expressed conviction that SEATO had served as a strong deterrent to overt aggression, but they agreed that communist subversion in all its forms was the principal immediate threat, and that countermeasures needed study. Secretary General Pote Sarasin reported that Chinese Communists were exerting pressure throughout the treaty area.[8]

The conference was disturbed because in South and Southeast Asia it was regarded in important quarters as being just a military organization. (The State Department had originally objected to the word "organization" in the title, because it suggested a false analogy with NATO. There was little organization in SEATO, but the "O" in SEATO seemed euphonically necessary.)[9] Although military security was primarily emphasized, the SEATO charter also aimed at promoting "economic progress and social well-being" and all agreed that they would have to convince their peoples of SEATO's genuine concern to promote social and economic development.[10]

SEATO narrowly missed a severe test in September, 1959, as Pathet Lao activities, supported apparently from North Vietnam, reached threatening proportions in late August. The State Department considered convening a special SEATO meeting as a deterrent to communist activities, and Herter on August 25 said the situation was very dangerous. He favored sending a U.N. team as observers. The U.N. did send a fact-finding committee, which, temporarily at least, took the heat off SEATO, where apathy prevailed among important members anxious to avoid involvement. Herter warned that a communist takeover in Laos would not stop there, but would present a threat to all Southeast Asia.The SEATO Council, meeting informally with Herter on September 28, 1959, hoped for U.N. success in solving the problem, but bravely expressed determination to abide by treaty commitments.[11] The report on November 3 of the U.N. Committee, which played down the North Vietnamese role in the Laotian crisis, gave SEATO members easy release from responsibility under their treaty commitments. Herter realized that the incident had disclosed cracks in the wall of SEATO security. These became more evident in late 1960.

The meeting of the SEATO Council in Washington, May 31 to June 2, 1960, came in the shadow of the aborted East-West summit conference in mid-May. Communist pressures in Southeast Asia had increased, and conditions in Laos and South Vietnam had deteriorated. Herter, as representative of the host country, was chosen as chairman of the meeting. In nominating him, Prime Minister Nash said Herter's year of service as Secretary of State had been marked with rapid changes and startling developments and Herter had "won their admiration for the calm and competent manner in which he conducted the foreign policy of his country." He was "a worthy successor to John Foster Dulles."

The overriding concern of the meeting was political, especially with the Pathet Lao insurgency in Laos, supported increasingly by the Viet Minh from North Vietnam. Herter sought to challenge and strengthen the determination of other members. While warning of dangers, he lauded SEATO as "a most effective deterrent to aggression and a vital link in the system of collective security." Other ministers spoke highly of SEATO's defensive value though with reserve as to the future. Khoman (Thailand) said SEATO had prevented Pathet Lao insurrection from becoming full-scale civil war. Couve de Murville exuded little optimism. The situation, he said, had deteriorated during the preceding year. Nash spoke of Communist China's threat to weak and disunited Laos. He said that country had been neglected, and means should be found to bring it into the family of nations. Selwyn Lloyd saw steady deterioration in the Laotian area. While SEATO should be prepared to act in certain circumstances, the U.N. presence in Laos, he thought, would be most helpful in halting communist influence.

Herter denied that the United States had ignored Communist China, as Nash had alleged, and pointed to extensive negotiations in Korea, in Geneva and in 197 ambassadorial talks which had made no progress. As to membership in the U.N., he noted that Communist China had made clear that complete abandonment of the Taipei Government was a prerequisite to acceptance of membership.

The Secretary then posed a question which he said he had asked himself many times: "What advantages have been gained by those countries who have recognized Communist China?" What advantages from points of view of intelligence information, concessions secured, trade, or "of anything that is tangible or morally helpful?" In a later spirited discussion Nash strongly advocated recognition, while other members, especially from the Philippines, Australia and Thailand, attacked Nash's arguments, and, in varying degrees, supported Herter's position.

The meeting closed optimistically, expressing "firm unity of purpose" and determination to maintain and develop capacity to meet "all forms of communist threats to the peace and security of the Treaty Area."[12]

When asked whether the U-2 incident had weakened U.S. alliances, Herter said on June 24 that this SEATO meeting indicated, if anything, stronger solidarity than ever.[13] In a statement for the use of the President on the sixth anniversary of the pact (September 8), he wishfully stressed SEATO's importance in "coordinating the efforts of its members in collective defense . . . against the threat of communist armed attack and subversion," and for other noteworthy accomplishments. The United States was proud to share in its accomplishments.[14]

SEATO's will power and sinews were tested when the Laotian Provisional Government of Prince Boun Oum (supported by Phoumi Nosavan) was established in mid-December, 1960. Herter sought British and French cooperation in securing SEATO recognition and support of the Boun Oum Provisional Government. Otherwise, he said, the Soviet Government and the Viet Minh could continue to supply the Pathet Lao on the pretext of aiding the constitutional government. The British and French demurred and rejected commitments. The British said a SEATO military operation would be offset by a corresponding effort of the Russians and Chinese. The French were indifferent.

Year-end reports of heavy infiltrations from North Vietnam and the formal Royal investiture of the Boun Oum Government on January 3, 1961, did not alter British and French aloofness from commitments. The SEATO approach was therefore futile, and further action was left to the next Administration. Herter later confessed to a massive loss of confidence in SEATO as an effective organ for the collective defense of national security in Southeast Asia. It nevertheless remained a basis for individual state action in cases of overt aggression, as later illustrated in Vietnam.

Herter's strangest "alliance" responsibility involved Turkey, Iran, Pakistan, Great Britain and, indirectly, the United States. The three "northern tier" states separated the U.S.S.R. geographically from the Arab world. Great Britain belonged because of its Middle East interests. The United States occupied the unique role of participating nonmember. Beginning in 1955 as the Baghdad Pact, to which Iran also belonged, the alliance was losing its only Arab member when Herter assumed responsibility at State, and it was gaining the more expansive geographical title, Central Treaty Organization (CENTO).

The United States was deeply interested in CENTO

because of its geographical coverage. In spite of its interest, the United States chose the ambivalent role of nonmember participant in order, hopefully, to avoid giving offense to the Arab world or to Israel, and also to sidestep the difficulty of getting a two-thirds approving vote of the Senate, as required for a treaty. The United States could still participate in the work of the major committees—Military, Economic, and Counter-Subversion—and attend meetings of the Council as an active "observer."

The commitments of the pact were loose—more so than those of ANZUS and SEATO. None was pinned down. The parties would "cooperate for their security and defense." The only organization specified was a Permanent Council at ministerial level. The commitments, such as they were, rested on an unstated common concern—the threat from the U.S.S.R. Pakistan, however, regarded India as an equal, if not greater, source of danger.

The vagueness of the commitments and American aloofness from membership did not avoid hostile reactions from Soviet or Arab sources, and the pact was a factor leading to Soviet arms deals with Nasser later in 1955.[15] The Iraqi defection from the Baghdad Pact in 1958 made the remaining members all the more anxious to have the United States become a full-fledged member, and they strove hard to bring this about. Instead of adhering to the pact, the United States entered into identical bilateral agreements with three regional members. These provided that in case of aggression the United States, in accordance with its constitution, would take "such appropriate action, in

cluding the use of armed forces," as might be mutually agreed upon," and as envisaged in the congressional joint resolution of March 7, 1957—the Eisenhower Doctrine. This joint resolution limited assistance to action "against armed aggression from any
country controlled by international communism."[16]
Turkey and Pakistan already had stronger security
guarantees under NATO and SEATO, respectively,
than those given by the bilateral treaties. Iran especially, therefore, was anxious for full-fledged American membership. The violence of Soviet propaganda
against Iran during much of 1959, for turning to the
West, increased that country's sense of urgency for
stronger American support.

This viewpoint was repeatedly urged on Herter.
Washington agreed to host the October 1959, meeting of the CENTO Ministerial Council, and Herter
headed the U.S. "Observer Delegation." With some
qualms (because of U.S. nonmembership) he also
consented to chair the meeting. The Pakistan Foreign
Minister, Qadir, told Herter it was imperative for
CENTO's future that the United States join, because
Iranians interpreted refusal as American disinterest
in problems facing Iran, and Soviet propaganda was
saying that the United States was afraid to join
CENTO.

Herter thought the bilateral agreements concluded
with the CENTO countries refuted these interpretations, but he pointed out that if the United States
joined CENTO the agreement would have to be sub-
mitted to the Senate as a treaty and would almost
certainly be disapproved. Selwyn Lloyd, looking

ahead to the October meeting, also expressed concern for CENTO's future without U.S. membership. He said Middle East members were worried. Furthermore, full membership would not add anything new to U.S. commitments. Herter said the entire matter was under review in preparation for the October meeting.

The review of the problem did not change Herter's position. To his news conference on October 6 he said: "We have decided that we can probably be of more assistance in maintaining tranquility and helping to develop that area by remaining as an observer rather than as a full member."[17] But the problem did not go away. The regional CENTO states were asking why they should have incurred the hostility of the U.S.S.R. and of other Muslim countries by joining CENTO, since the United States—which inspired it— was not willing to do so. The aloofness of the United States from full membership made the problem of providing for military defense all the more acute. This seemed to call for some form of military organization other than a mere military committee and a military planning staff. Something approaching the NATO model seemed to the regional members to be called for—a command structure, a Commander-in-Chief with staff, and probably a commitment of troops. The demand for this command structure was pressed strongly by the regional members and by Secretary General Baig at the October 1959, Council meeting.

Baig feared the existence of an inclination in some quarters (Anglo-American) to draw attention away from CENTO's defensive purpose and efforts, causing a lack of conviction that the treaty amounted to much. The problem was aggravated by Iran's concern about Soviet pressures, also by Arab nationalist subversion supported by the U.A.R. and "aggression by proxy" from Iraq, or from Afghanistan where the U.S.S.R. was building strategic roads and airfields.

Herter sought to give reassurance without over-committing the United States. He emphasized CEN-TO's importance in strengthening international peace and freedom, promised moral and material support of the United States, participation in defense planning, and assistance in economic programs, including telecommunications which would link the three capitals. Furthermore, he said the bilateral executive agreements made with the three regional states would "assure U.S. support in case of communist aggression."[18]

The regional members thought it impossible to have a defense pact without a command structure, and Britain was willing to agree if the United States approved. But Herter said it was premature to set this up, though contingency planning should be done for such a structure. Privately he feared that a defense structure would intensify pressure for increased U.S. military aid, including assistance for a CENTO "common infrastructure" which would be followed by assigning, or earmarking, U.S. forces. He pointed out to the conference that the United States would have to operate within the limits of the Middle East Doctrine which promised support only against threats from international communism, thus making it impossible to cover situations that might develop in Afghanistan.

Not wishing to press the matter at the time, yet fearing the danger of weakening CENTO's will to resist aggression, the conference referred the question of a command structure to the Military Committee for study and report to the next meeting of the Ministerial Council. Before the April meeting Herter exchanged views with the British Foreign Office and reached agreement that an announcement about setting up a CENTO command structure might have unfortunate effects on Soviet attitudes at the summit meeting. They therefore had the subject removed from the Military Committee's agenda. Its removal caused expressions of regret in the Council meeting, especially from Pakistan and Iran, which doubted the validity of the reasons given, feeling that Soviet aims and objectives did not change with apparent fluctuations in the cold war temperature.

At the opening session Herter said they were meeting "on the eve of the forthcoming summit conference," where the United States would pursue "its unswerving quest for peace."[19] He emphasized that it would take a firm stand, especially on inspection and control in disarmament negotiations, and on maintaining the freedom of West Berlin. He assured the conference members that the United States would not permit the summit to dictate the fate of the world, and that it would keep faith with its allies. Foreign Secretary Lloyd supported generally Herter's position, and the regional members expressed gratification at the reassurances, as well as support for the West's aims in the summit discussions. Herter gave assurances of support for certain economic projects, *e.g.*, railroad and telecommunications systems, though he pointed to limits of economic aid. He sought to calm Iran's anxieties regarding its military and economic problems.

In all his relations with CENTO, realizing the looseness of its ties, Herter sought to bolster morale, convince the members of CENTO's importance, and assure them of United States interest and support. In his opening remarks at Tehran he said: "There is no question of my Government's strong support of CENTO. It will continue—in the interests of the people of CENTO and . . . of world peace." In his departure statement he said, "We in the United States attach the greatest importance to the Central Treaty Organization."[20]

In stating this he was very sincere because the success of CENTO would not only strengthen the peace but would also mean the Westward orientation of the members. He paid CENTO the compliment of his attendance at both sessions of the Council during his Secretaryship, even going to Tehran for the April 1960, meeting in the midst of the strenuous preparations for the summit conference billed for two weeks later. He cabled the President that his going there was much appreciated. The session adjourned on the day before the catastrophic U-2 incident, which knocked the bottom out of hopes for improving East-West relations in the proximate future.

4

In the Western Hemisphere, as previously indicated, Herter also had alliance problems. The Organization of American States (OAS) was the oldest
multilateral alliance of the United States. It had
grown largely out of unique historical and geographical facts involving common experiences in breaking
away from European colonial tutelage and in sharing
the Western Hemisphere. These facts created presumptions—not too realistic—of special community
interests and, with tragic interludes, they led ultimately, through successive collective agreements, to
association for common defense and mutual cooperation in the OAS.[21]

Herter's concern with the OAS arose chiefly out of
the political explosion in Cuba, bringing Fidel Castro
to power and causing repercussions in other Latin
American areas. Castro's "war of nerves" against certain Caribbean neighbors in the spring of 1959 was
the *raison d'etre* of the Fifth Meeting of Consultation
of American Foreign Ministers in Santiago, Chile,
August 12 to 18, 1959. To his news conference Herter
expressed great concern about Caribbean problems,
saying that his Government regarded very seriously
the problem of intervention by one country in the
internal affairs of another.[22]

At the Santiago conference he gained all that he
could have hoped for, though not so much as he
would have liked.[23] The concern of Latin American

peoples for the sometimes conflicting principles of nonintervention, human rights, and representative democracy made collective decisions on Cuba very difficult. Castro was talking about democracy and "humanism," mixed with fulminations against American "imperialism," while his regime appeared to move steadily to the left.

Herter got from the conference a strong reaffirmation of faith in the principles of the Inter-American system and, more important, its call for a study of the whole problem of tensions in the Caribbean. The results of the conference, in spite of violent attacks on the United States by Cuban Foreign Minister Roa, were regarded as a personal triumph for Herter, whom Latin diplomats reportedly found to be more "simpatico" than his predecessor, and who conducted himself as "one among equals."[24] Castro's scorn for the Conference's work offered little hope for cooperative relations, and Herter's optimism of October 1959, gradually faded.[25]

Herter continued to look to the OAS for help in solving these problems. Speaking before the Council of the OAS on April 20, 1960, he followed his policy of encouraging, challenging, and warning American allies. He said the OAS had been an instrument of accomplishment in many ways and had become the concern of the whole American community. The pillars of nonintervention and collective action, he said, had become firmly cemented into the foundations of the tested and proved system of inter-American security.[26] By implication, the OAS, not the United States, must solve the Cuban problem. It was beyond the legal competence of the United States.

At the San José Conference, August 16 to 29, 1960, Herter tried to induce the OAS to take a hard line. That organization had blasted the Dominican Republic at the immediately preceding Sixth Meeting of Consultation by naming it and applying rigorous sanctions for its complicity in the attempted assassination of Venezuelan President Betancourt. These measures Herter supported, after much consideration, though they went farther than the United States wanted to go. He did so primarily to win overwhelming support for the case against Cuba. But the Cuban case was different. It was not clear enough against Castro, who was still denying communist intentions, though boasting of friendship with the U.S.S.R. and Communist China. Popular support in Latin America for the Castro revolution, regardless of its leftish tendencies, was a strong deterrent to firm action by governments.

At one point Herter reported that the prospect looked hopeless. In personal conferences he found each leading delegate unwilling to make direct charges against Cuba, but willing to "go the whole hog" in denouncing communism. On that basis the conferees reached agreement. The San José Declaration strongly condemned extra continental intervention in states of the region, denounced Sino-Soviet interference in domestic political, economic or social affairs, and any form of totalitarianism; and proclaimed the obligation of all regional states to submit to the discipline of the inter-American system.[27]

Was the Declaration a condemnation of the Castro

regime? Or did the OAS demonstrate its own futility? There were differing views. Herter thought the result was a condemnation. He viewed the OAS as a developing institution expressing the feelings and desires of member states and exercising a definite influence for closer cooperation among them. The Secretary's personal diplomacy at the Santiago and San José Conferences contributed to better understanding with OAS members and to their increasing willingness to take firmer action, as later evidenced by their expulsion of Cuba from OAS membership.

# CHAPTER THIRTEEN

## ALLIANCES IN THE BALANCE: II

O F ALL THE multilateral alliances which Herter
inherited as Secretary of State, the North Atlantic Treaty Organization (NATO) committed the
United States most heavily and was regarded as most
important to American peace and security during the
1950's. It was a landmark in the development of
American alliance policy, as it ran counter to presumptions of American diplomatic relations during
the preceding century and a half. It provided that an
armed attack against one would be considered an attack against all, and each party would forthwith
take such action as it deemed necessary, including
the use of armed force.[1] The other parties would not
be automatically at war, but the obligation to act was
unqualified.

When Herter assumed responsibility at State in
early 1959 NATO was undergoing severe testing.
The national and international situation had changed
markedly since 1949. With the help of the Marshall
Plan, Western European nations had made remarkable economic recovery and had stabilized their political institutions. Although cold-war confrontation
with the U.S.S.R. involved continued tensions, the
absence of overt hostilities or of immediate military
threat tended to lessen the sense of common interest
and loosen the bonds of the alliance. Many members

were failing to meet allotted contributions; NATO members in the "inner six" (the European Economic Community—Common Market) were at odds with those in the "outer seven" (the European Free Trade Area), and France's nationalistic reversion was beginning to threaten the principles on which NATO was built.

A special NATO committee (the "three wise men") had issued a warning in December 1956 that unity and strength were as essential then as in 1949, and urged improvement of "consultation"—political and economic—among all NATO members, to increase the sense of common interest and to dispel suspicions.[2]

East-West relations had greatly changed. In 1949 the Soviet's great preponderance in conventional forces was balanced by the American monopoly of the atomic bomb, and NATO strategy was based on the concept of the "shield" of NATO ground forces and the "sword" of American nuclear power. But the Soviet buildup of its long-range missile strength, which brought the United States within range of Soviet bombs, created a nuclear stand-off and raised doubts in important NATO quarters whether the United States would risk an all-out nuclear war by using its nuclear "sword" in defense of Europe.[3] It also raised questions whether NATO should not have nuclear weapons of its own.

The Soviet "ultimatum" of November 1958, demanding Western withdrawal from West Berlin within six months, was NATO's most serious external challenge. The NATO Ministerial Council at its December meeting denounced and rejected it unanimously. The final communiqué talked bravely of "effective shield forces" and "the manifest will to use nuclear retaliatory forces to repel aggression," though doubts existed about these within NATO circles, whose internal problems defied solution. The communiqué was said to be "all fancy wrapping and no substance."[4] The meeting of the NATO Ministerial Council in Washington, April 2-4, 1959, marked NATO's tenth anniversary. Acting Secretary Herter who headed the American delegation pointed to "splendid" achievements in the previous ten years, but he warned the conference members that they could not rest on their laurels. "Military strength, and the courage to employ it, if required," he said, "were the indispensable conditions for further progress."[5]

More important than the anniversary was the necessity for intensive consultation on the prospective East-West conference of Foreign Ministers, in which every NATO member was gravely concerned.

Herter reviewed Soviet policy during the preceding year and pointed to shifts and fluctuations on the surface with no real change in basic objectives. Firmness, cooperation and solidarity, he said, were essential. To these he pledged the United States. Selwyn Lloyd and Couve de Murville spoke in much the same vein.

Herter agreed with Chairman Spaak and others on the prime importance of full consultation, though he emphasized, as Spaak had noted, that it did not necessarily mean agreement on a common policy. The pressure of time and events had to be taken into account, but he said the fullest possible understanding of each other's views was of great importance, and there was no policy of the United States which he would not submit to NATO allies for discussion and common counsel and advice.

Herter had confidence in NATO as an "essential protective shield," and in a broadcast of April 5 he said that such military cooperation among 15 free nations in time of peace was unprecedented.[6] He was well aware of internal difficulties which were threatening that cooperation, *e.g.*, the continuing problem of unfilled military commitments of most NATO members—a problem which continually troubled him. More serious was the offensive against the NATO structure mounted by President de Gaulle, who was seeking a new *grandeur* and a larger role for France in world affairs.

After becoming Premier on June 1, 1958, with power to rule by decree for six months, De Gaulle lost no time in apprising Britain and the United States of his intentions to improve the world stature of France. Conversations of his Ambassador with Under Secretary Herter in Washington, and his own in Paris with visiting Prime Minister Macmillan and Secretary of State Dulles, outlined his thoughts: (1) France, in view of its great history, had to feel that it was playing a significant role in world strategy and that it was a world power. Otherwise, it would not throw itself so enthusiastically into the defense of the free world. (2) France was determined to become a nuclear power and American cooperation was very important. If France were given nuclear weapons, or if it produced them with United States assistance, that would be an economy and would reinforce the alliance. But France would not permit nuclear weapons on its soil if the order for their use had to be given by the United States or by SACEUR (Supreme Allied Commander Europe). France would have to control the custody and disposition of nuclear arms on its soil, though the United States could be associated with such control. (3) NATO was too limited geographically. It should be expanded to include the Middle East and North Africa. What was needed was a world organization directed by the United States, the United Kingdom and France. NATO was no longer adequate. Its command structure needed to be reorganized.

In September 1958, De Gaulle put in writing for the United States and Britain his grandiose proposal for a tripartite organization to take joint decisions affecting world security, especially nuclear policy. The three powers would be a kind of world directory, jointly planning international strategy and action.[7] De Gaulle regarded this program as indispensable. But if such a diplomatic blockbuster had been carried through, it might well have disrupted NATO. The American response, desiring not to offend French sensibilities, stressed the importance of extending NATO consultation beyond European limits and suggested that French objectives could be reached by informal conversations among the three powers. It observed that defense of the free world required the willing cooperation of many other nations, inside and outside NATO. The United States therefore could not afford to give other allies or other free world countries the impression that basic decisions affecting their vital interests were being made without their participation.

The clash of French and American views was highlighted by Herter's discussion with French Premier Debré on April 29 in Paris. Herter pointed out that unless the nine U.S. fighter squadrons in France were equipped with atomic weapons, they would be useless and would have to be moved elsewhere. Debré said France required satisfaction on three points: De Gaulle's request for tripartite consultation looking to the development of common world-wide policies; support for French interests in the Mediterranean, Algeria, and Africa; and cooperation in atomic matters, on which France wanted frank talks.

Herter protested the linking of atomic stockpiling with the other three subjects, saying he would gladly discuss them, but apart from stockpiling, which was our common emergency. He mentioned recent tripartite talks on Africa, saying the U.S. Government was glad to participate in them, but wished not to institutionalize such discussions. French policy on stockpiling remained unyielding, and the removal of American planes from France was completed early in 1960.

Herter saw serious problems in scheduling high-level meetings on a regular basis. Secrecy could not be maintained and such meetings would distress the NATO allies. He suggested that occasional three-power ministerial meetings could be maintained in Washington and that, for "more rarefied exchanges of views" on policy and strategy around the world, informal dinners during conferences, such as NATO, would be satisfactory.

While De Gaulle urgently sought to tighten bonds of consultation with Britain and the United States, looking to close agreement on global military, especially nuclear, policies, he was loosening French ties with NATO. Early in 1959 he gave notice of intention to withdraw the French fleet from the NATO Mediterranean command structure, in war as well as in peace. He wanted the French fleet to be as "free" as the U.S. Sixth Fleet. The official French position was that the essential mission of French naval forces was to defend and maintain communications between the French and North African coasts. Its mission was "national," especially "in the absence of a common policy" on the part of the alliance with respect to the problems of Algeria and North Africa.

Herter thought the reference to "absence of a common policy" looked like blackmail. The withdrawal of the French fleet, he believed, might give the impression that the NATO alliance was breaking up. When Ambassador Alphand informed him on March 3 that the withdrawal was taking place, Herter said the action was being taken without consultation, which was the antithesis of tripartism, which France had advocated. The United States was willing for the status of the French Mediterranean Fleet to be on an equal footing with that of Britain and the United States. But this assurance was of no avail. De Gaulle had committed France to "a gamble in *grandeur*."[8]

Pursuing his gamble, De Gaulle struck at the concept of military integration under NATO on the theory that integration would dilute the patriotic loyalty of the armed forces to their country. He therefore withdrew French Air Force units from NATO, and told the French Military School that "the system known as integration . . . has now served its turn."[9] His policy contributed to growing disillusionment regarding the future of NATO.

Herter faced this and other problems at the December NATO Ministerial meeting. A special problem of the United States was its deteriorating foreign exchange position creating a serious outflow of gold. It seemed that some American forces would have to be withdrawn from Europe and that European NATO countries, most of which were in arrears on their military contributions, would have to increase their share of the defense burden. Sharp differences of view existed within the U.S. Government, especially between Defense and State. Defense favored some withdrawal as the solution to the balance of payments problem. The President inclined to the view that the NATO shield could be symbolic, and did not require five-plus divisions. But General Lauris Norstad, Supreme NATO Commander, reacted violently to any suggestion of reductions. Herter at first was uncertain, but after thorough consideration with his able staff he concluded that any NATO reduction would have to be accompanied by some reduction on the Russian side, coupled with an agreement on a zone of inspection. Treasury Secretary Anderson, anticipating an unfavorable balance of payments for the year —possibly $4,500,000,000—favored some reduction of forces. Herter said that unless it were possible to obtain the agreement of General Norstad and other military people to a revision of NATO strategy, it would blow NATO higher than a kite. He told Secretary Gates in early December 1959 that an announcement of withdrawal of any air squadrons (then in question) would stimulate European fears that a significant change in U.S. policy was underway. The U.S.S.R., he said, would draw the same conclusion.

The controversy raised extremely important questions. Was the "shield" (strong conventional forces) to become only a "tripwire"? The "shield" concept assumed that NATO forces would be able to deal with local wars, and would delay a general attack while the "sword" of U.S. nuclear power was getting into action. The "tripwire" concept, which required smaller conventional forces, banished thoughts of local wars and relied more heavily on nuclear striking power. Was this a good thing? Herter thought not, and during the preceding year he had sought to reduce United States dependence on total war and to restore "balance" in the American military establishment. This called for full NATO ground forces as a basis for a rational and credible deterrent.

NATO was in trouble. It was eight and a half divisions short of the 30 divisions regarded as the irreducible minimum. Many European members fell short of their military commitments. Herter's urgings for additional contributions were of little avail. Nor did the West's current inability to reach any disarmament agreement with the U.S.S.R. spur NATO nations on to build up their vulnerable defenses. There were complaints of lack of unity, calls for firm United States leadership, and fears of a partial and dangerous American pull-out.

Herter's task was to bolster morale while pointing up problems and asking for additional allied efforts. French feelings were already smarting from General Twining's "diplomatic bombshell" sharply criticizing De Gaulle's noncooperative NATO policies. Herter sought to assuage, reassure and challenge. It was a difficult assignment.[10] East and West were agreed in principle on a summit conference some time the following spring, and the three Western occupying powers were agreed on broad objectives. Beyond that there was uncertainty. In a speech of December 15, 1959, Herter could make no promises of constructive results from the prospective summit meeting, but about NATO he said the United States still stood firm on its pledge of 1949. It had learned that it could not be self-reliant in the modern world. NATO must retain the principle of an integrated defense system, which was more important than ever. The United States believed it was being asked to carry more than a fair share, because Europe was then in a strong economic position. The long-range view needed more attention. The NATO Council should therefore undertake planning for the 1960's.

Herter also stressed the need for NATO to develop world-wide consultative practices, thus by implication answering De Gaulle's proposal for a tripartite global directory; and he urged maintenance of balanced forces that would make it possible to resist local hostile actions, in line with his opposition to the "tripwire" concept which relied largely on nuclear defense. Observers reported that Herter's speech restored a sense of purpose and American leadership to the alliance, especially by the assurance of continued American military presence in Europe and the proposals for 10-year planning.[11]

NATO problems remained. Herter's plea that European allies remedy the serious shortfall in fulfilling their allotted contributions to NATO defense forces aroused little enthusiasm. France was at odds with its NATO allies on military integration and global tripartism, and disagreed with the United States also on nuclear stockpiling, nuclear cooperation and Algerian policies. Herter thought military integration so important that he intervened in support of General Norstad's testimony. He said a closely unified defense system was essential because advanced military weapons had shrunk Europe so much that it was too small to be defended by national segments. Capabilities to react had to be almost instantaneous. He regarded a posture of collective defense as absolutely mandatory. But De Gaulle was reluctant to place any French air defense units under General Norstad's command. Differences of policy within NATO seemed to defy compromise, much less solution.[12] Fortunately there was unity in opposing the Soviet demands of November, 1958.

The foreign ministers of the three occupying powers reported to a roundup NATO session after the meeting of Heads of Government, in December 1959, and assured the NATO nonparticipating members of full consultation during the preparatory negotiations for the summit meeting. Herter took note of difficulties, but promised the nonparticipants that every effort would be made to maintain adequate liaison. In two communiqués (preliminary and final) the NATO Council reaffirmed confidence in NATO and expressed full support for the position adopted by the four governments, and satisfaction with arrangements for consultation in the preparatory negotiations.[13]

There was some feeling in the State Department that NATO powers, so concerned with the summit, neglected long-range planning and building alliance strength. Nevertheless, summit problems dominated the discussion at the Istanbul meeting, May 2-4, 1960. Herter said he approached the summit "with hope for progress," but with no "illusions." "Consultation" haunted all the discussions. Herter warmly endorsed the consultation principle, but noted the possibility of serious difficulties in maintaining close liaison at all times. One could not anticipate the precise points the Soviet might raise or the most appropriate Western response. The important thing, he said, was for all to be clear as to their basic principles.

On leaving Istanbul, Herter said the meeting had shown again "the extraordinary unity" among the 15 members of NATO.[14] His statement was overoptimistic, though the impending East-West conflict at the summit did impose a sense of unity. The rude disruption of the summit conference by Khrushchev in May contributed to holding the NATO powers together against the Soviet threat. But serious NATO problems troubled Herter throughout 1960.

De Gaulle continued his noncooperative attitudes

and his determination that France must become a world nuclear power. (Its first nuclear test was in February, 1960.) Anxious doubts remained in Western Europe about American purposes because of its vulnerability to Soviet missiles, Herter's talk of American trade imbalance, and his call for additional European contributions to NATO defenses. West Germany was becoming concerned to have a larger "say" in the use of nuclear weaponry, and an urge was developing in wider NATO circles to be less dependent on the United States.

Herter sought to allay NATO anxieties, and gave assurances that the United States would stay the course. He differed with De Gaulle on major policies and became convinced of the need to consider the German claim for a role in NATO nuclear strategy. He thought it important to endow NATO with a collective nuclear force, believing such a policy would curb nuclear proliferation and might even restrain De Gaulle's expansive designs.

The Secretary remarked to Eisenhower in August 1960 that other NATO nations were worried about the "tripartite business." De Gaulle nevertheless pressed on and outlined his major objectives in a news conference of September 5: times had changed, he said, since 1949; Western European countries, "especially France," had recovered and had become aware of their own strength; NATO should be brought up to date; the Big Three of the West must coordinate political and strategic organization elsewhere, as in Europe; military integration was outdated; the defense of Europe, carried out jointly, must have a "national character"; atomic arms, if stocked on French territory, would have to be in French hands. France could not commit her destiny to the discretion of others. He envisaged a "cooperative Europe" with atomic weapons of its own (presumably those of France), "with a voice equal to that of the United States."[15]

In a speech of September 8, Herter challenged De Gaulle's views. Modern weapons technology, he said, had substantially reduced the margins of time and space for military defense and made necessary a far greater degree of integration in planning, command and logistic support. Experience had shown that integration was possible without detracting from the sovereignty of independent, yet interdependent, members of the alliance. American policy, he said, continued to encourage integration in NATO.[16] Herter emphasized to newsmen a few days later (September 14, 1960) that integration was essential to an effective military operation, and that, although there had been some three-power meetings, tripartite global consultation had not been institutionalized, and he did not expect it would be.[17]

Herter had NATO problems also within the Government. He objected strongly, in August, 1960, to Defense proposals for a prospective cut of six squadrons from its NATO Air Force. He said there had been considerable concern about the effect of this cut. Norstad warned against any reduction in combat strength. Herter said the United States had set an example for the rest of its partners by meeting its commitments, and any United States reduction would have serious effects on the whole alliance. Defense assured him that no final decisions had been made.

Herter did not share the views of the President and Defense, which favored nuclear cooperation with France. He agreed with General Norstad and the AEC that concession to France in this area would have damaging consequences within NATO. He said others would also demand it, especially the West Germans. According to this view it was militarily unnecessary and would not "buy" any better French cooperation in NATO. Herter doubted that France would develop a *force de frappe*. In any case the Congress showed no sign of making such cooperation possible.

Herter's major NATO problem was how to satisfy the rising demand for a larger collective nuclear role. He had long regarded this as necessary to prevent proliferation of nuclear capability on an independent national basis. The determined push by De Gaulle for a French *force de frappe* and talk among Western European Union representatives in late 1959 about developing an independent European nuclear striking force, as well as concern among NATO members, emphasized the importance of decisive action.[18]

In the weeks preceding the December NATO Council meeting Herter and his staff, along with representatives from among other involved agencies, spent much time studying the problem and choosing a program feasible for presentation. Herter was anxious to present a plan that would improve NATO's collective nuclear capability and also carry out his 1959 10-year planning commitment. The President in October 1960 had approved a program offering an interim NATO force of five Polaris submarines committed to the control of SACEUR, who could order them to fire in case of a Soviet nuclear attack. These submarines would be regarded as a permanent contribution to NATO, but the U.S. would expect the other NATO governments, with American assistance, to develop a permanent NATO force of intermediate-range ballistic missiles (MRBM's) under multilateral ownership and control. The NATO Permanent Council would also develop a suitable formula for the use of the weapons, presumably under SACEUR authority.

This raised difficult problems. Could the President legally delegate such authority? Wouldn't it be necessary for the Congress to change the Atomic Energy Act? Shouldn't the approval of the incoming Administration be obtained before presenting the proposal to NATO? Was the proposed delegation in the national interest? Herter decided to proceed with the proposal, but also to consult the incoming Administration and appropriate members of Congress.

The Secretary's proposal soon encountered difficulties in Defense where strong objections were raised to delegating in advance firing authority to SACEUR. Reportedly there was a "misunderstanding." Defense had apparently thought the United States would retain a veto on the use of the MRBM force. There was opposition in some Defense quarters to any multilateral agreement. Herter agreed to submit the concept without this delegation of authority, particularly since there were legal problems. Some top staffers thought this omission would be regarded by Europeans as a retreat from United States defense commitments. Herter thought he still had a "saleable package." When an aide proposed that, in view of legal and other difficulties, the concept not be put before the December NATO meeting, Herter pointed to the months of efforts to develop a meaningful plan, and to possible loss of face if there were no significant proposals for the December meetings. He later expressed concern whether he would have a sufficiently strong statement without an MRBM proposal.

Conversations on the Hill were not encouraging, and President-elect Kennedy chose to make no commitments on foreign policy before the following January 20. Herter therefore presented the matter before the December NATO meeting not as an authoritative proposal but as "a new concept" of a multilateral force (MLF) which his Government viewed favorably and was exploring. He hoped the NATO allies would do likewise. The *raison d'etre* of the proposal, he said, was the belief that the creation of additional national nuclear weapons capabilities would have a divisive effect on the alliance, whereas the multilateral concept offered the best means of providing a collective basis for defense in the MRBM field.

Herter's proposal resembled the one approved by the President in October, though without surrendering the American "veto" over the use of the missiles. It offered five Polaris submarines as an interim force, and proposed a permanent multilateral MRBM force to be created by other NATO powers. Legislative approval in the United States and possibly elsewhere would be needed, and the Permanent Council might consider the delicate question of increasing the alliance's authority over the atomic stockpile—a problem ultimately unsolvable.

Herter struck hard on other problems, especially on shield forces, allied unity, and the international payments situation. He supported General Norstad in urging that shield forces be strengthened and that a balance be struck between conventional and nuclear weapons. A united alliance during the 1960's, he said, was essential to the success of the program. Agreement on political issues was necessary to the determination to use force when necessary. The international balance of payments problem was of primary importance. In a three-year period the United States had paid out over $10,000,000,000 more than it had received, and nearly half involved the outflow of gold. Though the alliance was vital to the United States as well as to the NATO allies, Europe had recovered and was far surpassing its prewar economy; but the United States did not intend to "lower its flag" in Europe.[19] He said he was expressing his government's view of things that ought to be studied seriously by the Council. He did not anticipate firm decisions at the meeting, and there were none.

His statements, especially regarding the MLF, were generally applauded, though Couve de Murville in guarded remarks said Herter had posed difficult problems for France, including the ownership and control of nuclear warheads. The problems ahead looked difficult, and the discussion took a pessimistic turn regarding both the U.N. and NATO. Canadian Foreign Minister Green deplored disparaging comments on NATO and the U.N. by various personalities and praised Herter for his "clearer view" of the world situation. Many members grabbed at the straw of consultation—"fruitful consultations"—as the best hope for all NATO relations. Von Brentano said these should be extended and enlarged. Spaak thought they should include all world problems. Wigny (Belgium) said he was extraordinarily impressed by the richness and the importance of Herter's suggestions, and thought that they pointed beyond the NATO defense perimeter. Herter said he welcomed frank discussion which indicated the desirability of political consultation well in advance of crises and of keeping the permanent representatives constantly advised and on the alert.

In a closing speech at the final session, Foreign Minister Mathias (Portgual) expressed regrets that it would be the last meeting that Herter would attend. He expressed the esteem of everyone for the Secretary's high moral and human qualities, and the value the Council members attached to his useful collaboration, always loyal, and so important for the progress of the alliance.

Herter noted with special satisfaction the frank exchange of views, the discussion of the long-range plan for NATO, the value of NATO as an organ of consultation and as a cohesive force, and agreement among its members that it should continue many years into the future.[20]

The Secretary had not hoped for much from the NATO conference, and not much came of it, as its colorless communiqué revealed. He was in an impossible position. He could only present as a "concept," somewhat vaguely defined, his multilateral ballistic-missile plan with all its potentialities for stabilizing peaceful relations. The British thought it "an offer," the West Germans considered it "a proposal," and a young American officer was quoted as calling it "a snow job."[21] At a time when American leadership was most needed he could not speak with authority, owing to the antiquated system of transferring power from one administration to another. He could only present, hopefully, in George Orwell's terms, "lame-duckspeak" ideas, and trust that the "concept" would ultimately become a political and military reality—a hoped-for reality that has continued to recede into the future.[22]

# CHAPTER FOURTEEN

## ALONG THE WAY

THE RELATIVELY BRIEF PERIOD of Herter's responsibility as Secretary of State (just short of two years, counting two months as "Acting") was crowded with crises involving every continent, as has been indicated. There were other problems, some of great importance.

1

The United Nations was significantly involved in most of the crises of the period, and Herter was always its supporter. Speaking to the United Nations Correspondents Association on September 22, 1959, the Secretary said, "If I seem to speak with overenthusiasm about the United Nations it is due to the fact that I happen to be one of those who had the utmost faith in the effort which was made in connection with the League of Nations after World War I. Very frankly, I left the Department of State with which I had been serving, when the Senate of the United States and Woodrow Wilson between them, in their entanglements over amendments, refused to bring the United States into that body. The United Nations is a second effort. I hope that as a peace mechanism it will be able to adjust itself to the inevitable change that we must look forward to in a constantly changing world, so that it will become a constant factor in the adjustment of those matters that unfortunately, through the mechanism of war, can become of tremendous danger to mankind."[1]

This point of view he maintained. His task was facilitated by excellent relations with Henry Cabot Lodge, U.S. Ambassador to the U.N., who was an old friend. Commenting later on their official collaboration, Lodge said they got along so well that it didn't make a good story." Herter also had good relations with Secretary General Dag Hammarskjold whom he firmly supported in his efforts to strengthen the peace-keeping arm of the U.N. Herter believed strongly "in some form of international police force" of sufficient strength to "be effective in maintaining the peace for all the world," and he went further than Hammarskjold in favoring a permanent force rather than an *ad hoc* arrangement like the U.N. Emergency Force.[2]

During the latter half of the 1950's the composition of the U.N. was changing and American influence in the General Assembly was declining. In the United Nations' early years the United States had a preponderant influence and the Assembly rolled up large majorities in support of U.S. positions. The Security Council had a built-in Western majority, though the U.S.S.R. freely used its veto. The Assembly membership, originally 51, by 1958 reached 82, of which the Soviet bloc had nine votes and the Asians and Africans had twenty-eight. This increase made it more difficult for the West to win the two-thirds majority necessary in voting on important substantive matters.

The sweep of nationalism in Africa resulted in adding 16 African states and Cyprus to the U.N. roster in 1960. Whatever qualms Herter may have had about the ability of the new members to carry their load, he welcomed them "wholeheartedly" in his Assembly speech of September 1960. He hailed the "dramatic expansion of freedom" which their independence represented, though he delicately suggested that "with freedom comes responsibility . . . for national development as well as for participation in the international community."[3] Meeting with the principal representatives of the African states (and Cyprus), the Secretary said the action of the General Assembly in admitting them "was universally applauded . . . We in America, who cherish independence, share your pride."

Herter was primarily concerned in 1959 with negotiations outside the U.N. on such matters as Berlin and Germany, Laos, Algeria and the banning of nuclear weapons tests. But he followed the discussions in the U.N., and spent a week in New York during the early days of the Fourteenth General Assembly where he met with key foreign ministers and on September 17 addressed the Assembly on United States policies. He expressed his "strong belief and firm faith in the United Nations," surveyed the major international policy problems and emphasized "constructive change through peaceful means."[4]

Khrushchev's disarmament blockbuster, dropped on September 18, 1959, demanding "general and complete" disarmament in four years, was troublesome because of its enormous propaganda content, in spite of its unrealistic character.[5] Herter said that "if it could be safely done" the proposed disarmament would be highly desirable for mankind. The great stumbling block was "the question of controls" on which agreement with the U.S.S.R. seemed impossible. Khrushchev had raised the flag of general and complete disarmament which no one dared to challenge, though the prospect of agreement on ways to reach the utopian goal remained dim.[6]

On disarmament and other trouble spots the Fourteenth General Assembly made little if any progress. It adjourned without improving or seriously aggravating East-West tensions.

The year 1960 was critical for the United Nations and for Herter. East-West relations reached a crisis level and American diplomacy was heavily involved on every continent in problems of great concern to the U.N. Secretary General Hammarskjold was alarmed at the trend of events and in the Introduction to his Annual Report for 1959-1960 he warned of the risk of a major war. With Herter's encouragement he sought to develop the authority of the Secretary General to use U.N. power to maintain peace and order in the developing countries. Having already antagonized Khrushchev by his interpretation of his role as Secretary General, Hammarskjold vigorously used in the Congo the authority granted him by the Security Council and further aroused Khrushchev's resistance, which led to internal crisis in the U.N. itself.

The Fifteenth General Assembly (1960) was expected to be explosive, coming as it did after the

Soviet disruption of the East-West summit in May and the disarmament discussions in June, followed by Khrushchev's announced intention to attend the session, and his request that all heads of government likewise attend so as to make it a U.N. summit meeting.

The session was hailed by the press as "the most remarkable and most critical session in its history," and "the largest collection of rulers, statesmen and diplomats since the Versailles Peace Conference."[7] In view of issues expected to arise at the Assembly, the buildup given it by Khrushchev, and the probable attendance of important heads of government, Eisenhower, accompanied by Herter, attended the session on September 22 and made the official statement of United States policy. The President appealed for hands off the internal affairs of African countries and for U.N. support of their security and development, promising increased United States contributions through the U.N. for these purposes, and also for the economic and social development in freedom of peoples in other areas. He deplored the Soviet walk-out from the disarmament conference and called for resumption of negotiation under proper controls. It was not a cold-war speech, and many neutrals praised it.[8] Regarding a private meeting between Eisenhower and Khrushchev during the Assembly session, Herter said he saw no prospect of such a meeting, or of any serious negotiations between the two.[9]

The next day Khrushchev went on a verbal rampage. After calling for immediate independence for all colonial and trust territories, and repeating his demand for general and complete disarmament, he turned his guns on Hammarskjold and the U.N. executive structure. He charged that Hammarskjold had used U.N. power to support the colonialist line and that the executive body of the U.N. did not reflect the actual situation in the world. He proposed to abolish the post of Secretary General and to set up an executive body of three representatives of the "three basic groups"—the Western powers, the socialist states and the neutralist states. He also proposed moving the U.N. headquarters out of the United States, perhaps even to Moscow.[10]

The Soviet Chairman got little support from noncommunist members of the U.N. These had just given Hammarskjold, in effect, a strong vote of confidence in an emergency session on the Congo and they did not want to see his position undermined.[11] Adverse criticism was widespread.

After Khrushchev's speech Herter went immediately to see Hammarskjold and asked whether under U.N. rules it was possible to call for an immediate vote of confidence in the Secretary General. It was found not to be possible. A separate resolution would be necessary, which would require normal procedure. An hour later, at a luncheon of the Foreign Press Association, Herter described Khrushchev's speech as "an all-out attack, a real declaration of war against the structure, personnel and location of the United Nations," an appraisal supported by the President.[12]

Khrushchev continued his battle to oust Hammarskjold and to set up a three-man U.N. directorate, each Secretary having a paralyzing veto. The problem of world disarmament could not be solved, Khrushchev said, until the problem of Secretary General was first solved. At a luncheon on September 21 for the newly admitted African delegates and one Cypriot, Herter warned his guests to beware of Khrushchev's plan for altering the structure of the U.N. The smaller states, he said, had a particular interest in seeing that the U.N. remained strong enough to protect their independence and territorial integrity.[13]

With encouragement from Washington and elsewhere, Hammarskjold resisted Khrushchev's pressure. He said it was "a question not of a man but of an institution." Khrushchev pounded his desk with his fists in anger. Later he brandished a shoe and banged it on his desk. But when he renewed his demand for the Secretary General's resignation, Hammarskjold in a hard-hitting statement on October 3 said that by resigning he would be throwing the U.N. organization to the winds, which he had no right to do. The Assembly responded with an ovation.[14]

Khrushchev had threatened to remain at the General Assembly until Christmas, presumably to win over the African delegations, gain control of the Assembly, reorganize the Secretariat, and move the U.N. headquarters from New York. In early October 1960, it seemed evident that he was not accomplishing his mission. He departed after a furious session on October 13. Soon thereafter, on November 4, the U.S.S.R. decided not to press for action in 1960 to reorganize the U.N. Secretariat, though Moscow did not abandon its campaign against Hammarskjold and the U.N. structure.[15]

There were other hot battles in the Fifteenth General Assembly over such problems as Algeria, the Congo, disarmament, and Chinese representation, but the battle for the integrity and effectiveness of the U.N. was of climactic importance. Speaking in observance of the fifteenth anniversary of the U.N., Herter sounded a note of warning. The U.N., he said, was under critical attack from one quarter and the proposed changes in its carefully constructed machinery would devitalize it. He said the U.N. needed to be stronger rather than weaker. A third of the world's inhabitants, involved in a revolution of rising expectations, looked to the U.N. as the guarantor of their independence, and the U.N. should help them mold a new life that would give Africa its rightful place on the international scene.[16]

Before he left office Herter could feel that the integrity of the Secretariat would be preserved, though Hammarskjold's personal relations with the U.S.S.R. had been damaged. An answer to the personal relations problem came with the tragic death of Hammarskjold in 1961, which removed the chief object of Khrushchev's wrath. The stubborn resistance of the noncommunist states to a tripartite Secretariat gradually convinced the U.S.S.R. of the futility of its troika project. It was therefore forced to rely on its earlier practice of checking U.N. peacekeeping activities not popular with the U.S.S.R. by refusing to contribute budgetarily to such purposes. Herter could only

pass along to his successor the complicated constitutional and political aspects of this disruptive policy.

2

The unfortunate circumstances in which Herter became Secretary of State were embarrassing to him,
but they did not impair his relations with members
of the Department or the Foreign Service, who had
become well acquainted with him during his two
years as Under Secretary. Working relations were ex-
ceptionally good, owing to his extensive reliance on
staff members and his friendly manner of dealing with
them. He enjoyed genuine respect in all Department
circles, where he was believed to possess essential
qualities of intelligence, courage, sensitivity, honesty,
firmness, pride and humility. In personal matters he
could dismiss a high-level officer when this seemed
called for, without passing the task to the top administrative official, Loy Henderson. In appointments to
high office his judgments were not always free of politics, which could sometimes lay a heavy hand.

Early in his secretaryship Herter's desire for good
relations with his former colleagues on the Hill led
to subsequent embarrassment. Three leading and re-
spected Senators, two of them from the same state,
called on him and secured his commitment to an ambassadorial appointment for an important Republican
personality who had large horse-racing interests and
a residence in the state of two of the Senators and a
business office in the state of the other Senator, as
well as personal connections with him. The hearing

before the Senate Foreign Relations Committee disclosed the nominee's meager technical qualifications
for ambassadorial appointment, though he was a
personable individual, a successful business man and
a collector of French contemporary and Italian Renaissance art. (He was also a heavy contributor to the
Republican Party treasury.) His poor showing in
answering Committee members' questions on personalities and problems relating to his assignment made
the headlines and led to protests by the Committee
Chairman regarding qualifications of nominees.
Though he won many friends during his ambassador-
ship, he resigned after a year's service, reportedly
because his wife was bored.

Herter sought to escape from a commitment made
to a leading Democratic Senator to find an appointment for a resident of New Mexico. He thought the
appointment would be "distasteful to our friends in
New Mexico." Herter got out the record and showed
it to the Democratic sponsor, saying that if any difficulty arose out of the appointment this sponsor might
blame the Department for not showing him the record. The sponsor jokingly said that if any such summary were done on himself it would be a lot worse,
and favored going ahead with the appointment, which
was done with reservations and subsequent regrets.

An Ambassador to a Scandinavian country wrote
to Herter in August 1960 proposing to resign at the
year's end because he thought he should have had a
larger post where his "experience could have been
put to better use," and because he had been "consistently in disagreement with the conduct of our for-

eign affairs," naming specific cases, such as the U-2 incident, lax policy toward Cuba, lack of long-term planning and poor personnel policies. Herter, in reply, said that so far as he was aware the Ambassador had not previously written him a single line complaining about the policies of the Department, but his letter indicated that he was not in accord with any policies of the State Department, which he should have known before accepting the appointment. "In blunt language," Herter said, "your action is incomprehensible to me . . . It is my own belief that holding the views which you apparently do . . . the President would accept your resignation, and the sooner you sever relationship with the Foreign Service, the better."

All Secretaries of State, especially since World War II, have had organizational problems. Herter had his, though he did not believe they called for a general overhaul of the State Department. He would have had no time for that, owing to the limits of his term and his absence on official business. In any case, Herter put more faith in topnotch staffing than in organization. Proposals for important organizational changes involving the State Department were nevertheless to the fore. On these Herter's views were divided. The President's Advisory Committee on Government Organization, chaired by Nelson Rockefeller, had become convinced that the technological revolutions in communications, industry and military weaponry, aggravated by the cold war, were complicating government operations, overburdening the President and the Secretary of State and endangering national security. This Committee reached agreement early in 1958 on the outlines of a plan to give the President more support in this area and to simplify and strengthen the organization for the administration of international affairs. This would call for integrating into a new foreign affairs organization the international economic and social, information, cultural and psychological, as well as diplomatic aspects of our international life. Most important, it would make necessary a new office—that of First Secretary of Government to assist the President in the overall direction of international affairs. The First Secretary would be personal adviser to the President on all matters of foreign policy and would supervise the planning and coordination of all government activities, even domestic, bearing on foreign policy. He would have an enormous range of power over government operations, along with an adequate staff, subject to the President's ultimate control.

There would be a new Department of State headed by a Secretary of State, and the Information Agency (USIA) would be brought back into the new Department. The Secretary would be in the Cabinet, but under the guidance of the First Secretary.

This scenario was placed before Secretary Dulles in March 1958, with word that he would be the first First Secretary. (It was inconceivable that a First Secretary could be imposed above him.) Loftus Becker, State Department Legal Adviser, explained the magnitude of the proposal. As Head of the Department of Government he would be the President's principal assistant in the coordination of national security, foreign policy, and domestic interests and activities. The presumption was that he would remain free to develop foreign policy, as distinguished from conducting it.

Dulles thought it over and admitted having qualms, but after a few days he expressed agreement. He said he had mentioned the proposal to Under Secretary Herter, whose initial view was unfavorable.

There was not time to put the plan through Congress in 1958, though the President hoped it would be ready for the next year. The President's Advisory Committee in December 1958, reaffirmed its support of the plan for a First Secretary, which was its primary concern, and gave assurances that his responsibilities would not impinge on, or reduce the individual responsibilities of the Secretaries of State, Treasury, Defense or other heads of departments or agencies. The assurances were not entirely convincing. The committee also repeated that the State Department should be given the strength and breadth essential to long-term planning, which would bring about effective coordination of information, economic and cultural activities with State's foreign policy functions, and also bring the USIA back to State. Herter was chiefly interested in the proposals to strengthen the State Department and relieve the pressures which had made the Secretary's task "an impossible job," and concentrated on efforts to improve the Department's status and its high-level staffing.[17]

The proposal that USIA be returned to the State Department encountered strong opposition; but the President's Committee, in a meeting of June 8, 1959, agreed that the union of political, economic, information, and cultural functions in State was essential to give that Department the strength and breadth to develop long-term plans. The U.S. Advisory Commission on Information, which worked closely with USIA, opposed the transfer and in its 14th Annual Report, released on April 7, 1959, restated the principles previously emphasized: that it "should be non-partisan, . . . responsive to policies established by Congress, and appreciative of its responsibilities to keep the Congress informed." (Persuasive words on the Hill.) Of course it "should continue to be an independent arm of the Government."[18] Dr. Mark A. May, Chairman of this Committee, stated on April 9 that USIA Director George Allen, as head of an independent agency, counseled the President, the NSC, the Secretary of State and others. This responsibility, he feared, would be lost by the proposed transfer.

Herter sought to remove or mollify such anxieties by assurances that USIA would retain almost complete operational independence within the State Department, and that the head of the Information Agency would be a member of the senior staff of the Department, with the title of Administrator and would rank immediately below the Under Secretaries, and above the Assistant Secretaries. Admittedly the Administrator's access to the President would be somewhat reduced.

The President in mid-1959 had doubts about proceeding with the transfer of USIA to State ahead of the over-all First Secretary program which he wanted to send to Congress in 1960. He feared that the USIA shift at that time would destroy the rationale of the First Secretary plan. But on being assured that such was not the case, he permitted consultations in Congress on the merger to proceed. Herter took up the matter with the President again in early February 1960, proposing to submit to Congress a program for State Department reorganization. He said State Department reorganization should be considered solely on its merits, and he wanted State's proposals to be on the record before Senator Jackson's Committee began its hearings later in the spring.

After a long discussion the President reluctantly approved the Secretary's request. Herter also sought approval from the Advisory Commission on Information. He wrote to Mark May, its Chairman, in October 1959, outlining gains in formulation of foreign policy which he said would follow the return of USIA to State. He said he had taken every appropriate measure that had been suggested to ensure the retention of the values of autonomy and independence for the information program. The Advisory Commission on Information was not moved. Its 15th Annual Report, in March 1960, blandly asserted that the State Department should continue its "traditional role" as a policy-forming mechanism, "unencumbered by cultural, educational or information operations. With obvious satisfaction it commented that the President's Draper Committee on the foreign economic assistance program "came to the same conclusions with regard to that program." The Draper Committee and the Information Commission, it said, "both recommend against retaining operations in a department which by tradition had been responsible for formulating the foreign policy of the United States."[19]

Herter found Maurice H. Stans, Director of the Budget Bureau, unconvinced in February 1960. Stans said the USIA seemed to be working quite well as an independent agency, and remarked that Director Allen in 1958 had made a very strong defense of USIA before one of the Appropriations Committees. Herter said his objective was to establish more effective overall machinery for development of foreign policy and conduct of foreign relations. He was also concerned to strengthen the authority of the Secretary of State. But forces marshalled against his proposals thwarted the move of USIA to State. The Brookings Institute added its opposing vote in a report in January 1960. It favored a Secretary for Foreign Affairs similar to the First Secretary of Government as recommended by the President's Advisory Committee on Government Organization (Rockefeller Committee), but proposed that Departments of Foreign Economic Operations, and Information and Cultural Affairs (USIA), be established at cabinet level on the same basis as the Department of State.[20] This view was shared by Director Allen of USIA. These influences and personal intervention with the President put an end to Herter's hope of strengthening the position of the Secretary of State by the return of USIA. Ended also was the prospect of improving the efficiency of the Department, and lightening the Secretary's load by better Department staffing. This was a special disappointment to Herter.

The "First Secretary of Government" Plan, which

the Rockefeller Committee advocated and the President ardently desired, was still alive. Its approval did not depend on the transfer of USIA to State, but events conspired against its realization. The death of Secretary Dulles removed the person chosen by the President for the job and made more difficult the problem of securing agreement among Cabinet members to the proposals. Eisenhower later recorded how difficult it was to win Dulles' approval.[21] Dulles was never really convinced, and during his final illness he warned Herter against the idea. Attorney General Herbert Brownell, active politically, thought it unwise in a Presidential election year.

A long series of hearings in 1960 by Senator Jackson's Subcommittee on Organizing for National Security facilitated the plan's demise. Herter expressed disapproval before the Jackson Committee in June. He thought the "so-called super Secretary of State with cabinet-level agencies reporting to him would not be desirable." He also objected to any plan that equated the information (USIA) and economic (ICA) functions with the diplomatic function. Obviously, in his judgment, diplomacy stood above the others. He still thought USIA should come back to the State Department in a status comparable to that of ICA (later AID).

The Secretary also expressed concern about lightening the load of the Secretary of State. The burden of attending Foreign Ministers meetings abroad was heavy. He had been Secretary of State for 414 days on June 10, 1960, and had been out of the country 156 of those days—38 percent of the time. Could a

Minister of Foreign Affairs, responsible to the Secretary of State, represent the Government for the Secretary? Herter thought not. He was convinced that the presence of the principal officer of the State Department at such meetings had become practically a requirement.[22] There should be fewer meetings of Foreign Ministers and two or three Ambassadors-at-large would be useful. He always came back to individuals and to "strengthening . . . career officials who give continuity and can give . . . advice to the political appointees . . . who are Cabinet officers and bridge over changes of administration."[23] Senator Joseph S. Clark applauded Herter's emphasis on the human elements in government—devotion, ability, and experience.

Nelson Rockefeller presented the case for the First Secretary of Government to the Jackson Committee in July, 1960, but most of the testimony before the Committee expressed skepticism. Secretary of Defense Thomas S. Gates agreed generally with Herter. He said he did not think our "very large and very complex" Government could be run "by creating . . . other superstructures or other superjobs."[24]

Senator Javits, on August 30, 1960, introduced a First Secretary of Government bill (S. 3911), which was duly referred to the Government Organization Committee; but it never got out of committee.[25]

The final report of the Jackson Committee concluded that "Our governmental system has no place for a First Secretary," and that "in the American system only one official has the constitutional and political power required to assume" the role of mediator and judge between differing government agencies and private groups. He was the President of the United States. The Committee suggested alternative ways in which the President's burden could be lightened, but the proposal for a First Secretary of Government to coordinate all problems of national security was laid to rest.[26] Herter could derive some satisfaction from the failure of the First Secretary gambit, though his hopes for a more prestigious and more efficiently staffed State Department were dashed.

3

During Herter's undersecretaryship armaments problems entered a new and more threatening phase. The U.S.S.R. orbited two sputniks in late 1957 and developed an operational intercontinental missile system in 1958. Herter had constantly on his agenda questions arising from these and other developments involving instruments of mass destruction. (Space permits only brief reference in these pages to this important subject.)

Herter had long seen armaments as a major obstacle on the road to peace, to which he had committed himself after his brother's death in World War I. The disarmament problem became more complicated when the United States opened the nuclear Pandora's box in 1945, but was unable to reach agreement with the U.S.S.R. to internationalize all nuclear processes. Herter labeled Soviet rejection of the United States "extraordinary proposal" as "one of the turning points of human history."[27] Before he became

Secretary, efforts to establish controls over the production and use of nuclear weapons had failed, and a conference on general, though not complete, disarmament under United Nations auspices ended in dismal frustration on September 6, 1957. The U.S.S.R. then rejected U.N. procedures for solving general disarmament problems, and for two and a half years efforts in this field languished.[28]

On October 31, 1958, an ad hoc conference of the three nuclear powers (U.S.A., U.S.S.R., and Britain) began a series of meetings to end nuclear weapons testing. This conference, carried on intermittently throughout Herter's secretaryship, constantly faced unsolvable problems, especially effective inspection and control, which the U.S.S.R., with its closed society and its inherent suspicions of Western motivations, could not bring itself to permit.[29] The U.S.S.R. wanted a test-ban agreement based on "good faith," but Herter said there must be no retreat from an effective inspection system, and good faith was not an adequate guarantee. The Secretary objected to placing a limit on the number of inspections permissible in a year, saying that if this were accepted there would be pressure to go lower and lower until inspections would no longer be an effective deterrent. He could not agree to the Soviet proposals to staff the control posts almost exclusively with host country nationals, or permit a veto on investigations of alleged violations.

The problem of general disarmament was revived by Herter at the Geneva Foreign Ministers meeting of 1959 and was taken up by the 10-nation conference early in 1960. But East and West positions remained far apart. Neither had any significant "give" in it. The Soviets tried to tie the West to general and complete disarmament within a short four-year period, as Khrushchev demanded at the U.N. in 1959; while the West insisted on moving toward general and complete disarmament, stage by stage, as quickly as possible, but with no fixed deadline. The shock of the summit fiasco in May 1960, seemed to harden the position of the U.S.S.R., and after three months of futile discussions the Soviet bloc delegates walked out and unceremoniously broke up the conference.

While frustrating negotiations on general disarmament were moving toward disruption, efforts to make some headway in banning nuclear weapons tests continued. Could agreement not be reached to cease nuclear tests in areas that could effectively be controlled by detection devices, *i.e.*, the atmosphere, the oceans, outer space to a certain altitude, and relatively large underground seismic events? This would leave smaller underground tremors uncontrolled until detection devices could be developed by a cooperative research program, thus making possible gradual extension of the range of controls.

Hopes were frustrated by the Soviets' refusal to accept an adequate quota of inspections for the larger seismic events (those above the "threshold"—4.75 on the seismic scale) and its insistence on a four- or five-year moratorium on testing earth tremors below the threshold during the research period. But the U.S.S.R. would continue the moratorium indefinitely even if the research program proved unsuccessful. The United States might thus have to rely on good faith, which was unacceptable to Herter, though he would accept a shorter moratorium.

Herter constantly confronted a policy dilemma: on the one hand, the extreme difficulty of setting up and maintaining effective controls owing to the immense resources required, the drain on professional personnel and financial support, and, on the other hand, the risk involved and the impossibility of gaining Congressional support for a comprehensive, but uncontrolled, test ban treaty with a closed society such as the U.S.S.R. The dilemma was beyond solution during Herter's term of office.

4

The November elections in 1960 made necessary the transfer of governmental authority to the Democratic party. In this situation the State Department paid greater attention to transitional details than would have been necessary if the outgoing and incoming administrations had been of the same party. In the view of Secretary-designate Dean Rusk, Eisenhower and Herter could not have been more cooperative in facilitating the process of transition. Rusk found his relations with Herter very easy and cordial. They had been friends since Herter's Congressional years. Herter made office space, with a secretary, available for Rusk immediately after his nomination by President-elect Kennedy. (This suite of rooms on the first floor came to be known as "skid row".) He also made a flow of telegrams available on all subjects of current importance. Rusk lunched with Herter on December 20, the day after Herter's return from the NATO conference in Paris.

The Secretary-designate began his consultations in the Department on December 16. He met with a wide range of upper-level officers of the Department with a view to familiarizing himself with policies and operations of the Department. He met also with leading personalities not directly connected with the Department, to broaden his perspective on policy problems. He found very useful a large black book, prepared by the Department staff, containing briefings on all important policy questions. There was also a related book explaining the Secretary's responsibilities and the administrative organization. Another smaller briefing book pointed up the most immediately urgent problems. Herter and Rusk had frequent conversations, by phone or in personal contact. Sometimes high-level staff members were present. Rusk also received frequent intelligence briefings from Hugh Cumming, Director, Office of Intelligence and Research.

The relation of the incoming team to questions of policy making was important. Both sides wanted to avoid a confusion of responsibilities. Eisenhower did not want to surrender the right of decision making before the following January 20, and Kennedy did not want responsibility for decisions before that date. But decisions on existing crises were of concern to both. Herter would have liked to have the incoming Administration's approval of his proposal at the December NATO conference to make five Polaris submarines available to NATO; but Kennedy withheld approval.

Kennedy and Eisenhower worked chiefly through their respective representatives—Clark Clifford for Kennedy, and General Wilton B. Persons for Eisenhower. Herter and Rusk frequently discussed policy problems. Although the rule of "no commitments" prevailed (Rusk would say neither "yes" or "no"), it is probable that in the discussions Herter became aware of the trend of Rusk's thinking. On the break of relations with Cuba on January 3, 1961, Herter consulted Rusk and alerted him to the fact that a break was contemplated, hence Rusk was prepared for it when it came.

The critical situation in Laos came to a head in January 1961, and led to a conference including staffs from State and Defense, in which the existing and prospective situations were appraised. There were questions of reactivating the International Control Commission in Laos and of appealing to SEATO to clear up the legal situation—which seemed hopeless. Herter said he did not want to take any action that would limit Rusk's freedom of action. Rusk raised questions and expressed opinions in the discussion, without making commitments. Herter observed that new initiatives regarding Laos could not be taken effectively in the three remaining days. Two days later Herter met with Rusk, Eisenhower and Kennedy for a final survey of this troublesome problem. There he gave his judgment as to future policy, concluding with counsel that the political solution depended largely on the military situation.

Time ran out on Herter, as Secretary of State, at noon on January 20. The President had previously accepted his resignation to take effect at that time. Under Secretary for Political Affairs Livingston Merchant became Secretary *ad interim* to fill the void caused by the delay in confirmation of Herter's successor. The confirmation of all Cabinet members was delayed a day by Senator Wayne Morse's objection to waiving the Senate rule requiring nominations to lie over for one day. Early practice had been for the Senate to act immediately on nominations to Cabinet posts in a new administration. In this case committee hearings had been held before the inauguration, and contingent approval had been given for the confirmation of Rusk and other Cabinet nominees. Kennedy sent the names to the Senate immediately after being sworn in as President on January 20. But Senator Morse exercised his right, as he had done in 1953, to call for the application of the one-day-delay rule, saying he wanted time to read committee reports on hearings.

During the day of delay Livingston Merchant, as *ad interim* Secretary, hosted a luncheon at Blair House for the Washington diplomatic corps, after which he repaired to the Department of State with a confessed feeling of loneliness. The next day he went to the Department, read the relevant telegrams, and sat it out, keeping watch on burgeoning crises. Happily none of these reached an unbearable pitch.

Rusk's day on the twentieth, after a morning conference with Herter, was filled with the inaugural ceremonies, a luncheon with fellow-Cabinet nominees, given by the Senate Foreign Relations Committee, the inaugural parade, a reception for Mrs. Franklin D. Roosevelt, another by Ambassador Biddle Duke, and the inaugural ball. The twenty-first he spent mostly in conferences, including one with former President Truman and a review of the situation with Merchant. Then at four o'clock in the afternoon —the Senate having confirmed the nominations— came the changing of the guard at the White House with the swearing in of all the new cabinet members. With it also came the formal end of the transition to the new Administration.

# CHAPTER FIFTEEN

## PERSPECTIVE

DURING MUCH of his tenure as Secretary of State, Herter was engaged in diplomatic holding actions. It was a period when powerful forces—nationalistic, ideological, and military—were on the offensive, struggling to change the distribution of power in the world, or gain recognition for newly awakened peoples, or otherwise to improve political positions. Herter was concerned to check dangerous moves, guide the forces of change, and bolster the position of the United States and its allies. The United States bore the brunt of diplomatic and other thrusts for power, and sometimes did not have the support of its allies.

When Herter took control at the State Department he said he would carry out the policies established by Dulles, and in large measure he did. Changes made were primarily in tactics rather than strategy. He approved of Khrushchev's visit in September 1959, though Dulles, tough-minded in such matters, might not have done so. More important, Herter encouraged the President to make goodwill visits to heads of foreign states as a means of improving relations by "personal diplomacy" without negotiations. The President told Herter that Dulles had frowned on such trips.

In the field of larger strategy Herter became concerned with the consequences of Secretary Dulles'

"massive retaliation" policy which primarily emphasized dependence on nuclear rather than conventional
weapons which Herter regarded as essential for limited wars. He thought such an unbalanced program
might cause "brush fires" to become general confla-
grations. He also opposed budgetary dictation of defense policy. As Under Secretary he expressed concern to Dulles in October 1957, shortly after the
U.S.S.R. put the first satellite in orbit. He said military
cutbacks were creating doubts in minds of peoples
abroad with respect to a shifting balance of power.
Cuts in the army then being planned down to 1961
would involve withdrawals from strategic areas. He
understood the Presidential decision, in effect, to be:
"Let's not worry about 1961, but make a decision in
regard to 1958 and 1959." Herter regarded as necessary a reassuring speech to allay anxieties caused by
the Soviet satellite, and believed that our friends,
allies, and the American people would welcome "a
clear-cut decision that the free world's security,"
rather than budgetary considerations alone, would
determine our defense decisions.

In late 1958, Secretary Dulles recognized that "massive retaliation" had a limited life expectancy, owing
to the developing nuclear stand-off between the
United States and the U.S.S.R., and he urged the
Joint Chiefs and Service Secretaries to start a re-
appraisal of policy. As Secretary, Herter continued
to press for this objective, and in 1960 a series of
reappraisals got under way to bring military capabilities into line with the balanced force concept which

would permit the use of force in limited wars without resorting to nuclear weapons—a concept later adopted by the Kennedy Administration.

The time available to Herter as Secretary of State was relatively short, and long-term planning was impracticable. (His NATO long-term planning gambit of December 1959 failed to get under way in 1960.) Formidable threats to American national interests confronted the Secretary throughout his tenure. Some of the threats were checked and contained, *e.g.*, the drive of the U.S.S.R. on Berlin and West Germany, its clamor for uncontrolled nuclear test ban and disarmament agreements, its disruptive incursion in the Congo, and its attack on the United Nations. In other cases, as in Southeast Asia, the Middle East, and Cuba, the situation remained fluid and ill-defined. East-West relations during this crucial period remained stalemated, though Herter could feel gratified that Western lines had held and that he, working with the President, had played a decisive role in the process.

There were disappointments. The disastrous U-2 incident which resulted in aborting the long anticipated Paris summit conference in May 1960, and disrupting the President's plans to visit the Soviet Union and Japan in June, were heavy blows to Herter and the Administration. Crucial issues to be negotiated at Paris were denied a hearing, the chance for peace-minded President Eisenhower to carry friendly greetings to millions of Russians was lost, and the opportunity to strengthen the American position with a key ally in the Far East was forfeited. These events made it impossible for Herter to negotiate further on matters of important East-West concern.

Herter enjoyed high public and official esteem throughout the trying times of his service. This esteem had roots in his service in the Congress, his governorship, and his two years as Under Secretary of State. After the striking vote of confidence by the Senate in confirming him unanimously as Secretary of State in record time—four and a half hours—and the widespread plaudits of the press, he left in late April 1959, for negotiations at Paris, knowing that he enjoyed the trust and support of the American people. An occasional question was raised regarding his "toughness," but very few voices questioned his fitness for the job.[1] In Paris, Geneva, Santiago (Chile), and elsewhere, his ability to get along with people proved a great asset. *Time* magazine wrote of his "genial, mellow, welcoming warmth along with known professional skill," and quoted a French diplomat as saying: "he knows his dossier." The *Daily Mail* (London) said "Mr. Herter is no brinkman . . . He starts off liked and trusted by his allies," and the *Daily Express* (London) reported that "Herter is a formidable figure. He has already won respect."[2]

At the end of his first year as Secretary there was a general appraisal of his role, often in comparison with that of his predecessor. It had been a trying year for the new Secretary, confronted by the Soviet diplomatic offensive and tensions in Southeast Asia, the Middle East, North Africa, and Latin America. Herter was flexible and willing to reexamine issues such as Berlin and disarmament. He did not see things in black and white, as Dulles often did, but he was firm in maintaining basic American positions.[3] The *U.S. News & World Report*'s international staff surveyed opinion in leading world capitals and reported a tendency among some important personalities to feel that American leadership had become less strong and clear-cut. Herter was highly regarded but there was concern that he might yield to pressures. This concern seems odd, as Herter had stood unflinchingly against Soviet pressures through several months of negotiations. The confusion in the West arising out of the Soviet diplomatic offensives placed Herter in the role of mediator between conflicting British, French and German positions and tended to obscure the firmness of his position.

Domestic opinion applauded Herter's first-year achievements, recognizing that while his successes had not been dramatic, they were important. He had improved the staff work and the confidence and morale of the State Department. To strengthen his advisory staff, regardless of criticism on the Hill, he had called back Ambassador Charles E. Bohlen from Manila, where he had been sent from Moscow by Secretary Dulles. Herter had also gained the confidence of the Western Foreign Ministers. *Time* magazine called him "*the unassuming American*," saying that though he lacked "the self-assertive flair of Dulles . . . or Dean Acheson, Secretary Herter's certainty of purpose has won growing respect from President Eisenhower, State Department aides and the capital's most critical press corps." Herter was regarded as a realist, promising no Utopia, forecasting no disasters. The *New York Times* said Herter was "not given to grandiloquent pronouncements or brilliant improvisations." He is "inherently a reasonable man who believes in talking out differences. . . . Altogether it has been a good year, and Secretary Herter deserves plaudits for the effectiveness with which he carried out his duties." All commentators agreed that Herter was "as firm as was Mr. Dulles in maintaining basic U.S. positions."[4]

Occasionally Herter unfolded his thoughts privately or publicly, on matters of personal interest and on the state of the world. In a conversation with David Schoenbrun in Geneva during July 1959 he said he found his job as Secretary of State much the most exacting of any he had held. He was wrestling with "the complete change that had taken place in the preceding 40 years," owing to the emergence of international communism, which was "a combination of an ideological and military problem." Germany was then the focal point of the discussion by East and West Foreign Ministers, but the problem was worldwide. Herter said comparisons were difficult, but so many millions of people were involved that perhaps it was also the most rewarding. Schoenbrun wondered how the Secretary got relaxation from the stresses and strains of his work. He said he thought reports of bridge games were but a cover-up for something else. Herter said the reports were accurate, commenting that Selwyn Lloyd, Couve de Murville and he got real relaxation from playing bridge. "It's a game I have loved all my life," he said. "Obviously it can't be a preoccupation, but it is a relaxation." He confessed also to liking detective stories and said he was working on one at the time—though it never got to the printer.

Herter told Assistant Secretary for Public Affairs Andrew Berding that he did not like formal news conferences as well as informal meetings with newsmen. Off-the-cuff answers in news conferences could sometimes be troublesome.[5] In answering a question after an address to the National Guard Association on September 29, 1958, he was reported as saying that the offshore islands, Quemoy and Matsu, were "not strategically defensible."[6] He was unhappy about this as he thought he had replied differently, though the Administration did believe that the islands could not be held against an all-out Communist Chinese attack. The incident stimulated letters of inquiry and of protest and these had to be answered.

At a news conference on November 12, 1959, Herter was asked about Indian charges of Communist China's encroachment on Indian territory. He said the United States had not taken a position and he did not believe the United States had ever backed the McMahon line of 1914. He assumed that the Indian claims were valid, but said the United States had no objective basis to go on. After the news conference he issued a statement condemning the Red Chinese use of force which, he said, was wholly wrong. Herter's statements were quite accurate, but questions raised in India caused him to call in the Indian Chargé d'Affaires the next day to assure the Indian government that the actions of the Communist Chinese were wholly abhorrent to the United States which strongly sympathized with India's attempts to resolve the issues peacefully.[7]

A remark at a luncheon of the Foreign Press Association in New York in September 1960, when the Secretary was replying to a question about Kwame Nkrumah, Prime Minister of Ghana, caused some repercussions. He said Nkrumah's left-wing speech in the U.N. Assembly, and his fawning on Khrushchev after the latter's speech, indicated that Nkrumah was bidding for leadership of the left-wing group of African states and that he had "marked himself as very definitely leaning toward the Soviet bloc."[8] The statement was doubtless quite accurate, but Nkrumah complained, and there were other criticisms. Herter remained convinced of its truth and was not very regretful over having said it.

Herter's absences from Washington were a factor in reducing the number of his news conferences. He was away 277 days during his incumbency, which was about on a par with Dulles' absences during a comparable period. He had a total of thirteen regular conferences, but he made speeches fairly frequently. He preferred backgrounders where he was more at ease because his remarks were not for attribution. He also met informally, from time to time, with groups of newsmen in evenings at some residence. In such background meetings he was said to be superb.

Looking back from April 1960, to the previous year, Herter did not brag about its accomplishments. He said it was not too easy to say what had been accomplished. Methods of doing business had changed, beginning with the visit of Macmillan to the U.S.S.R. in February 1959. This had inaugurated a series of high-level talks. The Khrushchev visit had changed the picture of negotiations considerably. The result was that the impending crisis was being held in abeyance and the United States was hoping to find some common ground with the Soviets. Unhappily, events soon overran this hope.

Herter spoke to Andrew Berding of the improvement in his relations with the President. He noted that his secretaryship began unhappily because the loss of Dulles was a hard blow to the President, to whom Dulles was very close. His own relations had been "fouled up" also because of the requirement for him to take a physical examination before the President could announce his appointment. It was an awkward start, but he said relations had become "infinitely better." He went to the White House several times a week and was in contact with the President by phone many times during the week. Sometimes this was through General Andrew J. Goodpaster when the President was busy. Herter's staff thought Goodpaster played too prominent a role as telephone intermediary with the President. This situation reflected the fact that during his two short years as Secretary, Herter did not enjoy as close personal relations with the President as did his more assertive predecessor during his six-year tenure. Nevertheless, trust and confidence had developed between them. In accepting Herter's resignation in January 1961 the President said in his letter, which had the ring of sincerity: "I pay tribute to both your ability and devotion. . . . For your steady hand and wise counsel throughout our service together, and for the privilege I have had of working with you in close association, I am deeply grateful."

In an off-the-record review of the international scene in the closing weeks of his Secretaryship, Herter was less than optimistic about the future. He viewed the free world as a heterogeneity of peoples, a "spectrum of disparity and antagonism" which the communists were constantly trying to exploit. The cold war focused largely on the underdeveloped and uncommitted world with its enormous material and human resources, including more than two billion people with per capita incomes of less than $100 a year. The leaders of the underdeveloped peoples, he said, regarded economic growth as essential and they wanted benefits from both the United States and the U.S.S.R. They desired not only economic benefits but also peace and elimination of the threat of nuclear warfare.

Herter said United States political and military strategy rested on belief that the United States could live in the same world with communism and, barring nuclear war by miscalculation, could prevail without resort to war. Apparently Khrushchev believed his system could triumph in the global struggle for the allegiance of the underdeveloped world—an attitude that forecast a ruthless, protracted, world-wide competition over a long period of time. The Communist Chinese, he said, believed that peaceful coexistence did not accord with the pure doctrine of Marx and

Lenin. They thought a communist victory called for warlike measures. The West must maintain adequate political and military strength and demonstrate that underdeveloped societies could develop successfully within the framework of democratic institutions, and should avoid general war if possible, but must prepare for that contingency. He regarded an invulnerable nuclear deterrent as vital to a strategy of peaceful competition with communism. Also essential were arms control with adequate inspection and a flexible and mobile military capacity to meet effectively all forms of non-nuclear violence.

The U.S.S.R., Herter said, preferred to fight its wars by proxy and it would like to embroil Red China with the United States. Likewise Red China would like the U.S.S.R. and the United States to devastate each other. He emphasized the importance of the growth of Western European power and expressed concern that the fissioning process in Africa was giving birth to new nations which assumed independence prematurely without economic or administrative strength to sustain themselves in a modern democratic way. They also affected the balance of power in the United Nations.

In the long run, he said, much depended on the United States. It would require the economic strength necessary for world leadership—a role which unhappily it had inherited, and which it had to fill in the absence of other comparable and responsible free world power. The decisive factor might well be the internal strength and determination of the United

States to conduct what might be a long-drawn-out, very difficult type of warfare, whether hot or cold, limited or global.

Herter thought he saw one ray of hope— an apparent evolution going on in Soviet Russia. He admitted that many people might not live to see this development reach a point of mutual trust where both countries could work together for the benefit of mankind. The evolution of Red China he thought was more doubtful and farther away. If that evolution in Russia did not take place, 1960's children's children were going to face a very dangerous world.

In a final roundup a week before leaving office Herter said he had found his secretaryship completely engrossing. It had been demanding physically and involved a tremendous amount of reading merely to keep up with current material. There were innumerable things to be done for the President, including clearance of everything that went to him from the Department. Another factor had been the travel which U.S. alliances made necessary. If the Secretary went to meetings only of some alliance partners, the others would feel downgraded. He had traveled officially 123,987 miles to foreign countries and 9,420 in the United States. The foreign travel of Secretary Dulles in the two years preceding Herter's takeover totalled 175,909. His domestic travel totalled 22,270. The need to travel would continue unless some other formula could be found. He recalled that Dulles had gone to the Latin American Foreign Ministers Conference at Caracas in 1954 and had stayed only three days, in order to get one resolution through. He, Herter, went to the Santiago Conference in 1959 and stayed two weeks, which, he said, made more impression on the other Foreign Ministers than anything else he did. The value of such travel was demonstrated at the San José (Costa Rica) conference in 1960 where he found that he had already met all but two of the foreign ministers attending.

Herter said the world was worse off than two years previously. The major problem facing the world was population expansion, which exceeded economic growth.

His most satisfying experience was the fact that the Department had functioned as a unit better than he thought possible. There had been unspectacular but most effective team work. He thought the staffs had to work too many hours a day. He did not think all top jobs should be filled by professionals. The Department should have a law that would allow retirement after fifteen years at 2 percent of salary per annum. This would make possible more effective thinning out. An officer could then retire while young enough to get another job.

He gave his view of the "compleat" Secretary of State: flexibility of mind, allowing him to apply his talents to the many facets of his job, such as relations with the President, the Congress, his colleagues and the public, and then tackle all the specific problems that came up to him for decision, many of which are not connected with foreign policy. A sense of humor. Lack of it could make him a crusader, but would eventually make difficulties. Refusal to be forced off course "by the other guy." Good relations with the

President. The Secretary of State was the only Cabinet officer acting solely as the agent of the President. Everything the Secretary did was delegated by the President. Would the world get worse before it got better? That, said Herter, depended on the degree to which the Communists made it worse.

As Herter stated, his secretaryship had been physically demanding. The stormy period of 1959-1960 would have been hard on any Secretary of State. It was harder on Herter because of arthritis which affected his legs and hips. Talking with several friends in November 1959 he said he usually went home at 7:30 if he had a dinner appointment, or at 7:45 otherwise (which meant a fairly long working day), and he did not feel like working later in the evening. He said he intended to retire at the end of his term—January 1961—and he wanted then to get his legs straightened out.

Although arthritis impeded his movements, his close associates said it did not affect the quality of his mind, which remained sharp at all times. Everybody agreed that he had great courage in meeting his physical problem.

At a farewell Foreign Service Association luncheon for Herter shortly before he left office, Livingston Merchant introduced the Secretary as "a patriot and a great gentleman," saying, "His is a cool lucid mind, with a sense of history, courage and selfless devotion to America, to principle and to his friends. Here stands the whole man that Greek philosophers delineated, part Stoic, part Epicurean in relish for life, and even part Pythagorean in his insistence on facts and figures."

In collaborating with Western colleagues in international conferences Herter never sought to impose his leadership. This was well expressed by Foreign Minister von Brentano who said he was "a splendid person, quiet and precise . . . very cautious and unpretending, but everyone knew where he stood. He was a good negotiator with the Russians, as he knew how to be patient with firmness. . . . He was modest and did not assert or claim his leadership of the West, but this made him all the more effective as that leader."[9]

On Herter's final day at the State Department, Senator Mike Mansfield, Majority Leader, but of the opposite party, told his colleagues that he would not want the occasion to pass without noting that "Mr. Christian Herter, whom the Senate confirmed by a unanimous vote as Secretary of State, has warranted that expression of confidence in every way. His tenure of office as the first officer of the Cabinet has been marked by courage, steadfastness, wisdom, fairness, and dedication."

Although Herter looked forward to retirement and to improving his health, his concern for the United States position in world affairs led him, later in 1961, to accept the chairmanship of the Committee on Foreign Affairs Personnel—a subject of special interest to him. The blue ribbon committee's report in December 1962—Personnel for the New Diplomacy—illuminated many personnel problems of the service and made recommendations which were stimuli for further thought and action.

Herter also accepted President Kennedy's call in December 1962 to serve as the President's Special Representative for Trade Negotiations. He continued in that work under President Johnson until death claimed him in December 30, 1966, after a "lifetime of selfless and brilliant service," a "wise, gentle, and wholly dedicated patriot," as national leaders put it. He was outwardly "the personification of gentleness, but possessed of inner toughness," with "kindly eyes under a fierce thicket of eyebrows."[10] "When you just look at him," Eisenhower once said, "you know you are looking at an honest man."

In a career devoted almost entirely to public service, his four years as Under Secretary and then Secretary of State were the climactic period of Herter's life. His personality and policies suited very well the period in which he served. It was no time for thundering pronunciamentos or strident diplomacy. Aggressive forces—nationalist, ideological, and imperialistic—were forcing the pace on other continents, and it was the task of the United States and its allies to block aggressive designs, help developing nations, and strengthen international cooperation for the promotion of peace and justice. It was a time for quiet but firm diplomacy. This Herter employed. It was well said that few men in public life did more than Herter "to put an end to the sterile isolationism of the years between the wars."[11]

Neither diplomacy nor arms could stem the tide of crises evolving in Cuba, Southeast Asia, Arab-

Israeli relations, the Congo, burgeoning nuclear and other armaments, East-West tensions topped by the U-2 incident, and the aborted summit meeting. Yet Herter stayed the course as a confirmed internationalist. He had a clear view of dangers ahead, a conviction that these dangers must be confronted, and a patient optimism as to the ultimate outcome.

# NOTES

The following notes represent mostly points of reference, almost all from published sources, which may prove of interest to readers. The present study is based largely on the papers of the late Mr. Herter. In the last years of his life he kindly made these available to the author. In addition, he talked privately at length about his secretaryship, on many occasions. He also read and commented on drafts of a majority of this book's chapters. Because of the assistance of Mr. Herter, and Mr. Livingston Merchant, as earlier explained, and the nature of the detailed notes that follow, the usual bibliographical essay is not appended to the present study.

## CHAPTER ONE

1. *New York Times*, Apr. 23, 1959. Hereafter cited as NYT.

2. *Department of State Bulletin*, May 11, 1959, p. 671. Hereafter cited as DSB.

3. *State Department Register: 1918*, p. 121.

4. *American Journal of International Law*, vol. 13 (1919), 406-449.

5. Henry F. Pringle, in *Saturday Evening Post*, Feb. 14, 1948, pp. 26-27, 125-126.

6. *Current Biography: 1947*, p. 298.

7. *Ibid.: 1958*, p. 192.

8. *Ibid.: 1947*, p. 298.

9. *Ibid.: 1958*, p. 192.

10. *Congressional Record*, vol. 93, p. 9761.

11. *Current Biography: 1947*, p. 298.

12. Henry F. Pringle, *op. cit.*, pp.26-27,125-126.

13. NYT, Jan. 6, 1948.

14. 80th Congress, 1st and 2nd Sess., *Hearings before the House Committee on Foreign Affairs,* Jan. 12, 1948, pp. 23-29; Robert H. Ferrell, *George C. Marshall* (New York, 1966), p. 124.

15. 80th Congress, 1st Sess., *Hearings before the House Committee on Foreign Affairs,* Dec. 17, 1947, pp. 1-26.

16. See Robert H. Ferrell, *op. cit.,* for further discussion.

17. *U.S. News & World Report,* Dec. 21, 1956, p. 20.

18. U.S. Statutes at Large, vol. 62, pt. 1, pp. 137-158; Felix Belair, Jr., in NYT, April 3, 1948.

19. *Congressional Record,* vol. 94, pt. 11, p. A3040.

20. *Ibid.,* vol. 93, pt. 3, pp. 3822-3825.

21. *The Nation,* Feb. 11, 1955, pp. 111-112.

22. *Congressional Record,* vol. 98, pt. 11, p. A4434.

23. *Ibid.,* vol. 98, pt. 7, p. 9688.

24. *Boston Herald,* Nov. 6, 1952; Jan. 23, 1953; May 14 and 24, June 6, July 24.

25. Francis W. Tully, Jr., ed., *Addresses and Messages to the General Court, Proclamations, Public Addresses, Official Statements and Correspondence of General Interest of His Excellency Governor Christian A. Herter,* pp. 22-26, 48, 54-75.

26. *Christian Science Monitor, Dec.* 7, 1956.

## CHAPTER TWO

1. *Newsweek,* Oct. 17, 1955, p. 34.

2. NYT, Feb. 10, 1959.

3. *Ibid.,* Jan. 13, 1956.

4. *Ibid.,* March 12, 1956.

5. *Ibid.,* Aug. 23, 1956.

6. Conversation with Herter, Dec. 8, 1962.

7. NYT, Dec. 9, 1956.

8. James Reston, *ibid.,* Dec. 10.

9. Conversation with Herter, Dec. 8, 1962.

10. *Saturday Evening Post*, Sept. 12, 1959, pp. 31, 81-84. See also Emmet Hughes, *Ordeal of Power* (New York, 1962), p. 253.

11. NYT, Feb. 10, 1959.

12. *American Foreign Policy: Current Documents, 1956*, pp. 1264-1265. Department of State Publication, 6811.

13. *Ibid., 1957*, pp. 1536-1543.

14. DSB, Nov. 25, 1957, p. 831.

15. Unpublished report of Francis J. Colligan, Special Assistant to Assistant Secretary of State, Bureau of Public Affairs: "Programs of International Cultural Cooperation and Technical Exchange of Agencies of the U.S. Government and Related International Organizations," November 1957, p. 10. Policy Review and Coordination Staff, Bureau of Educational and Cultural Affairs, Department of State.

16. Herter statement of July 9, 1958, before Senate Foreign Relations Committee, mimeographed, Department of State.

17. *The Operations Coordinating Board, National Security Council*, Feb. 1957.

18. Dale O. Smith, in *Foreign Service Journal*, Nov. 1955; Roy M. Melbourne, in *ibid.*, March 1958.

19. Conversation with Herter, Oct. 21, 1965.

20. Conversation with Karl Harr, Oct. 11, 1965.

21. Conversation with Jerry O'Connor, State Department Coordinator, June 27, 1963.

22. NYT, Sept. 1, 1957.

## CHAPTER THREE

1. Department of State Publication, 6972, *Background of Heads of Government Conference: 1960*, pp. 295-313; DSB, Dec. 15, 1959, p. 948.

2. *Ibid.*, March 9, pp. 333-343.

3. *Background of Heads of Government Conference: 1960*, pp. 329-330.

4. C. L. Sulzberger, NYT, Mar. 18, 1959.

5. Arthur Krock, *ibid.*, March 26.

6. *Background of Heads of Government Conference: 1960,* pp. 335-336.

7. NYT, Mar. 31, 1959.

8. *Ibid.,* April 5, 1959.

9. Committee on Foreign Relations, U.S. Senate, *Documents on Germany: 1944-1961,* pp. 444-445.


## CHAPTER FOUR

1. Drew Middleton, NYT, May 11, 1959.

2. State Department publication, 6882, September, 1959. *Foreign Ministers Meeting, May-August, 1959, Geneva,* pp. 63-88. Hereafter cited as *Foreign Ministers Meeting.*

3. A. M. Rosenthal, NYT, May 17, 1959.

4. Sydney Gruson, *ibid.,* May 19, 1959.

5. James Reston, *ibid.,* May 24, 1959.

6. Drew Middleton, *ibid.,* May 27, 1959.

7. Herter backgrounder, June 20, 1959.

8. NYT, June 11.

9. *Foreign Ministers Meeting,* pp. 328-331.

10. DSB, July 6, 1959, pp. 43-45.

11. *Ibid.,* June 28, 1959.

12. Harry Schwartz, NYT, June 30; *ibid.,* July 1, 5, 6, 12; Kozlov radio talk, *ibid.,* July 3, 1959.

13. W. J. Jorden, *ibid.,* July 3, 1959.


## CHAPTER FIVE

1. *Foreign Ministers Meeting,* pp. 349-361.

2. James Reston, NYT, July 12, 1959; C. L. Sulzberger, *ibid.,* July 13, 15, 1959.

3. *Foreign Ministers Meeting,* pp. 381-386.

4. *Ibid.,* pp. 439-456.

5. Sydney Gruson, NYT, Aug. 2, 1959.

6. DSB, Aug. 24, pp. 265-279.

7. Sydney Gruson, NYT, Aug. 5, 1959.

## CHAPTER SIX

1. DSB, May 23, 1960, p. 817.

2. *Ibid.*, p. 818.

3. *Ibid.*, pp. 817-818. See also 86th Congress, 2nd Session, Hearings before the Committee on Foreign Relations, U.S. Senate, May-June, 1960. *Events Incident to the Summit Conference*, May 27, 1960, pp. 4-5.

4. *Ibid.*, pp. 5-11.

5. *Ibid.*, pp. 104-105.

6. DSB, May 23, 1960, pp. 818-819.

7. *Events Incident to the Summit Conference*, pp. 12-17.

8. *Ibid.*, pp. 27-45.

9. *Ibid.*, pp. 17-19.

10. NYT, May 10, 1960.

11. Thomas P. Ronan, *ibid.*, May 9, 1960.

12. Reports from the U.S. Embassy in Stockholm. Department of State.

13. May 5, 1960.

14. May 13, 1960.

15. W. J. Jorden, NYT, May 10, 1960.

16. David Wise and Thomas R. Ross, *The U-2 Affair* (New York, 1960), pp. 91-92.

17. *Events Incident to the Summit Conference*, p. 28.

18. Chalmers M. Roberts, *Washington Post*, May 27, 1960.

19. The Russian news agency, Tass, first reported Khrushchev's arrival statement without the references to "influential quarters seeking to revive the cold war." Tass later made the correction, which indicated that Khrushchev's altered remarks were tougher than those handed out to Tass in advance.

20. DSB, June 6, 1960, p. 904.

21. Dwight D. Eisenhower, *The White House Years: Waging Peace, 1956-1961*, p. 554.

22. NYT, May 17, 1960.

23. *Events Incident to the Summit Conference*, pp. 225-226; DSB, June 6, 1960, pp. 904-905.

24. Actually it was ambiguous.

25. DSB, June 13, 1960, pp. 955-962; Lodge statement and Council resolution; *U.S. Participation in the U.N.: Report by the President to the Congress for 1960*, pp. 80-82. Hereafter cited as *U.S. Participation in the U.N.*

26. NYT, June 22, 1960.

27. Dwight D. Eisenhower, *op. cit.*, pp. 560-563.

28. DSB, June 13, 1960, pp. 955-961; *United Nations Review*, July 1960, pp. 6-9, 38-50; Quincy Wright, "Legal Aspects of the U-2 Incident," *American Journal of International Law*, Oct. 1960, pp. 836-844.

## CHAPTER SEVEN

1. DSB, July 15, 1957, pp. 91-95.

2. *Ibid.*, April 13, 1959, pp. 514-515; NYT, April 19, June 21, 1959; *U.S. Participation in the U.N.: 1960*, pp. 50-52.

3. DSB, Sept. 28, 1959, p. 447.

4. *Ibid.*, Oct. 5, p. 489.

5. *American Foreign Policy: Basic Documents, 1950-1955*, pp. 775-787.

6. DSB, Aug. 2, 1954, pp. 162-163; *American Foreign Policy: Basic Documents, 1950-1955*, pp. 787-788.

7. DSB, Nov. 14, 1954, pp. 735-736.

8. *Ibid.*, May 27, 1957, pp. 851-852.

9. *Ibid.*, April 27, 1959, pp. 579-583.

10. NYT, Apr. 29, May 1, 1960; Amry Vandenbosch and Richard Butwell, *The Changing Face of Southeast Asia* (Lexington, Ky., 1966), p. 177.

11. DSB, July 27, 1959, pp. 115-116.

12. Dept. of State, *Threat to the Peace: North Vietnam's Effort* (Washington, 1961), Part II, pp. 1-2.

13. "The Legality of U.S. Participation in the Defense of Vietnam," DSB, Mar. 28, 1966, p. 483.

14. *American Foreign Policy: Basic Documents, 1950-1955*, 787-788.

15. Amry Vandenbosch and Richard Butwell, *op. cit.*, pp. 205-211; Tillman Durdin, in NYT, May 18, 1958, Aug. 9, 1959; Arthur J. Dommen, *Conflict in Laos* (New York, 1964), pp. 114-118.

16. Amry Vandenbosch and Richard Butwell, *op. cit.*, p. 206.

17. Arthur J. Dommen, *op. cit.*, p. 104.

18. Dept. of State, *The Situation in Laos* (Washington, 1959), pp. 16, 18; NYT, Feb. 12, 1959.

19. Dept. of State, *The Situation in Laos,* pp. 19-20.

20. The Pathet Lao had excluded the ICC from territory under its control. *United States in World Affairs: 1960,* p. 308 (hereafter cited as USWA); Tillman Durdin, NYT, Aug. 9, 1959; Osgood Caruthers, *ibid.,* Aug. 18.

21. News briefing, Aug. 11, 1959; John Finney, NYT, Aug. 12.

22. E. W. Kenworthy, *ibid.,* Aug. 25.

23. DSB, Sept. 14, 1959; E. W. Kenworthy, NYT, Aug. 27.

24. *Ibid.,* Sept. 5.

25. E. W. Kenworthy, *ibid.,* Sept. 5.

26. *Ibid.,* editorials in Oct. 4, Nov. 8, 1959.

27. *U.S. Participation in the U.N.: 1959,* pp. 43-44.

28. DSB, Nov. 30, 1959, pp. 783-784; Teltsch, NYT, Nov. 7.

29. *Ibid.,* Jan. 3, 1960; Arthur J. Dommen, *op. cit.*, pp. 125-128.

30. *Ibid.,* p. 145.

31. Tillman Durdin, NYT, Aug. 19, 1960.

32. *Ibid.,* Aug. 17.

33. Jacques Nevard, *ibid.,* Aug. 30, Sept. 1, 2.

34. *Ibid.,* Sept. 12; Nevard, *ibid.,* Sept. 17; Arthur J. Dommen, *op. cit.*, pp. 150-154.

35. Nevard, NYT, Sept. 6, 1960.

36. *Ibid.,* Sept. 29; Associated Press (AP) report, NYT, Oct. 1, 1960.

37. Nevard, NYT, Sept. 28, 1960; Amry Vandenbosch and Richard Butwell, *op. cit.*, p. 209.

38. AP report, NYT, Oct. 8, 1960.

39. Nevard, NYT, Oct. 16, 1960.

40. Arthur J. Dommen, *op. cit.*, p. 160.

41. NYT, Oct. 16, 1960; Nevard, NYT, Oct. 17 and Oct. 28, 1960.

42. NYT, Nov. 18 and 19; Arthur J. Dommen, *op. cit.*, p. 164.

43. AP report, NYT, Nov. 23, 1960.

44. Nevard, NYT, Nov. 27, 1960; AP report, NYT, Nov. 27.

45. Arthur J. Dommen, *op. cit.*, pp. 165-170; NYT, Dec. 16, 1960.

46. DSB, Jan. 2, 1961, pp. 15-17.

47. NYT, Jan. 1, 1961.

48. DSB, Jan. 16. pp. 76-77.

49. *Ibid.*, Jan. 23, pp. 114-115.

50. Arthur M. Schlesinger, Jr., *A Thousand Days* (Boston, 1965), p. 163.

## CHAPTER EIGHT

1. Halford L. Hoskins, *Current History*, Apr. 1962, pp. 193-199.

2. *Washington Post*, Jan. 1, 1957; articles by Walter Lippmann.

3. For interesting close-ups on the episode, see Charles W. Thayer, *Diplomat* (New York, 1959), pp. 1-37; Robert D. Murphy, *Diplomat Among Warriors* (New York, 1964), pp. 397-409.

4. DSB, Sept. 29, 1958, pp. 494-495.

5. *U.S. Participation in the U.N.: 1958*, pp. 74-88, pp. 36-49.

6. DSB, July 9, 1959, pp. 111-112; *ibid.*, Sept. 17, p. 468; Thomas J. Hamilton, NYT, July 29, 1959.

7. R. P. Hunt, NYT, March 14; USWA: 1959, p. 223.

8. *Current History*, Feb. 1959, p. 83.

9. Senate Resolution 294, Apr. 23, 1958; *Congressional Record*, 85th Congress, 2nd session, vol. 104, p. 6992; House resolution 546, Apr. 23, 1958, *ibid.*, p. 7069.

10. Seth S. King, NYT, April 10, 1958.

11. *Ibid.*, April 19, 21-24.

12. *U.N. Year Book: 1959*, pp. 37-43; NYT, Dec. 10, 1959.

13. *Ibid.,* Nov. 20, 1960.

14. *U.N. Year Book: 1957,* pp. 35-36, 42-48; Thomas J. Hamilton, NYT, May 31, 1959; Jan. 3, 1960.

15. J. S. Raleigh, "The Middle East in 1960, a Political Survey," *Middle Eastern Affairs,* XII (Feb. 1961), 34-35.

16. DSB, Feb. 29, 1960, pp. 321, 324; *ibid.,* April 11, 1960, pp. 551-552.

17. Thomas J. Hamilton, NYT, Feb. 21, 1960.

18. Eric F. Johnston, "A Key to the Future," NYT, Oct. 19, 1959; USWA: 1955, pp. 171-173.

19. State Department Press statement, Mar. 7, 1960, NYT, March 8, 1960.

20. *Ibid.,* March 9, 12, 21, 27, 1960.

21. *Ibid.,* Nov. 7, 1960.

## CHAPTER NINE

1. Vernon McKay, *Africa in World Affairs,* (New York, 1963), pp. 7-17.

2. April 16, 1959.

3. DSB, Oct. 5, p. 486.

4. *Ibid.,* Oct. 10, 1960, p. 589.

5. *Ibid.,* Sept. 26, 1960.

6. *Ibid.,* June 19, 1950.

7. *Ibid.,* Nov. 16, 1953, pp. 655-660; Vernon McKay, *op. cit.,* pp. 343-347.

8. DSB, May 5, 1958, p. 729; NYT, Apr. 19, 1958.

9. Robert Doty, NYT, Dec. 16, 1958.

10. William Blair, NYT, Aug. 24, 1959.

11. *Ibid.,* Sept. 17, 1959; *American Foreign Policy: Current Documents, 1959,* pp. 1096-1099.

12. NYT, Sept. 19, 1959.

13. DSB, Oct. 12, pp. 503-504; NYT, Sept. 23, 1959.

14. DSB, Oct. 26, p. 578.

15. NYT, Nov. 22, 25, 1959; DSB, Dec. 14, 1959, pp. 865-866.

16. *U.S. Participation in the U.N.: 1959,* pp. 16-19.

17. Parrott, NYT, Dec. 6, 1959.

18. *U.S. Participation in the U.N.: 1959*, pp. 30-34.

19. NYT, Oct. 4, 24, Nov. 2, 4, 1960; USWA: 1960, pp. 169-174.

20. NYT, Oct. 28 and 30, 1960.

21. Robert Doty, NYT, Nov. 5, 1960.

22. *U.S. Participation in the U.N.: 1960*, pp. 35-39; Doty, NYT, Jan. 9, 1961; USWA: 1961, p. 122.

23. Catherine Hoskyns, in Colin Legum, ed., *Africa: A Handbook* (London, 1965), p. 165.

24. *U.S. Participation in the U.N.: 1960*, p. 43.

25. *U.N. Review*, vol. 7 (August 1960), p. 46.

26. Henry Tanner, NYT, July 18, 1960.

27. *American Foreign Policy: Current Documents, 1960*, p. 535; NYT, July 24, 1960.

28. DSB, Aug. 8, 1960, p. 206.

29. *Ibid.*, Aug. 15, pp. 245-246.

30. King Gordon, *U.N. in the Congo* (New York, 1962), p. 31.

31. *U.N. Review*, vol. 7 (Sept. 1960), pp. 181-185.

32. USWA: 1960, pp. 185-192; NYT, Sept. 1, 4, 1960.

33. DSB, Sept. 19, p. 437; NYT, Sept. 2-4, 1960.

34. *U.N. Review*, vol. 7 (Oct. 1960), pp. 8-13; *U.S. Participation in the U.N.: 1960*, pp. 49-51.

35. NYT, Sept. 18, 1960.

36. DSB, Oct. 3, pp. 517-520.

37. King Gordon, *U.N. in the Congo*, pp. 56-57.

38. *U.N. Review*, vol. 7 (Nov. 1960) pp. 15-25; (Dec.) pp. 24-36.

39. NYT, Oct. 30, 1960.

40. *U.S. Participation in the U.N.: 1960, p. 54.*

41. King Gordon, *op. cit.*, pp. 86-89; *U.S. Participation in the U.N.: 1960*, pp. 54-56.

42. Colin Legum, "The Republic of South Africa," in *Africa: A Handbook*, pp. 335-338, 342-343.

43. *U.S. Participation in the U.N.: 1960*, pp. 46-49.

44. DSB, Dec. 28, 1959, p. 948.

45. *Ibid.*, April 11, 1960, p. 551.

46. *Ibid.*, pp. 551-552.

47. NYT, April 1, 1960.

48. *American Foreign Policy: Current Documents, 1960*, pp. 75-77.

49. DSB, Apr. 25, 1960.

50. *U.N. Review,* vol. 8 (Jan. 1961), p. 7. *U.S. Participation in the U.N.: 1960*, pp. 39-41.


CHAPTER TEN


1. USWA: 1957, p. 270.

2. *Ibid.*, p. 258.

3. 86th Congress, 2nd session, Senate Committee on Foreign Relations, *United States and Latin American Relations: Problems of Latin American Economic Development*, Committee Print No. 6, pp. 1-19.

4. USWA: 1957, p. 260.

5. See Matthews, *The Cuban Story* (New York, 1961), p. 45; also his accounts in NYT, Feb. 28, March 1, 17, 1957.

6. Earl E. T. Smith, *The Fourth Floor* (New York, 1962), p. 68.

7. David D. Burks, *Cuba under Castro*, Foreign Policy Association Headline Series, No. 165 (June 1964); Earl E. T. Smith, *op. cit.*, p. 107.

8. Theodore Draper, *Castro's Revolution: Myths and Realities* (New York, 1962), pp. 16ff.

9. Herbert L. Matthews, *The Cuban Story*, p. 79.

10. Earl E. T. Smith, *op. cit.*, p. 166.

11. *Ibid.*, pp. 170ff.

12. NYT, Dec. 27, 1958.

13. *Ibid.*, Jan. 11, 1959.

14. DSB, Jan. 26, 1959, p. 128.

15. NYT, Jan. 3, 1959.

16. *Ibid.*, Jan. 23, 1959.

17. *Ibid.*, Jan. 24, 1959.

18. *Ibid.*, Jan. 22, 1959.

19. *Ibid.*, Feb. 21, 1959.

20. Dwight D. Eisenhower, *op. cit.*, pp. 520-523.

21. NYT, Mar. 1, Apr. 4, 1959.

22. Statements of Filipe Pazos, June 8, and Roy R. Rubottom, June 11, 1959, in interviews. See Theodore Draper, *Castro's Revolution* (New York, 1961), pp. 157-159.

23. Interview with Senator J. William Fulbright, June 19, 1965.

24. NYT, April 18-26, 1959.

25. *Ibid.*, Apr. 25, 1959.

26. Conversation with Filipe Pazos, June 8, 1959.

27. NYT, May 29, 1959.

28. Department of State, *Inter-American Efforts to Relieve International Tensions in the Western Hemisphere: 1959-1960* (Washington, 1962), pp. 7-9; Nicholas Rivero, *Castro's Cuba: An American Dilemma* (Washington, 1962), p. 110; USWA: 1959, pp. 351-359; NYT, Aug. 16, 1959.

29. Conversation with Filipe Pazos, June 8, 1965.

30. NYT, May 31, 1959.

31. *Ibid.*, July 13 and 18, 1959.

32. *Ibid.*, Sept. 29, 1959; Theodore Draper, *op. cit.*, pp. 65ff.

33. NYT, Jan. 17, 1960.

34. *Ibid.*, Jan. 22-23.

35. *Public Papers of the Presidents: Dwight D. Eisenhower, 1960-1961*, pp. 134-135.

36. NYT, Feb. 12, 1959.

37. *Ibid.*, Mar. 23, 1960; DSB, Apr. 4, p. 523.

38. NYT, Mar. 8, 1960.

39. Tad Szulc, NYT, Apr. 12, 1960.

40. DSB, Mar. 7, 1960, p. 359.

41. NYT, June 25, 1960.

42. 86th Cong., 2nd Session, *Hearings before the Committee on Agriculture*, on H.R. 12311 and 12534, June 22, 1960.

43. David Wise and Thomas B. Ross, *The Invisible Government* (New York, 1964); interview with Allen W. Dulles, July 26, 1965.

44. NYT, July 8, 1960.

45. DSB, July 25, 1960, p. 140.

46. NYT, June 26, July 3, 1960; Theodore Draper, *op. cit.*, p. 109.

47. NYT, July 10, 1960.

48. *Ibid.*, July 17, 1960.

49. *Public Papers of the Presidents: Dwight D. Eisenhower, 1960-1961*, pp. 567-568, July 9, 1960; NYT, July 10, 1960.

50. *Ibid.*, July 13, 1960.

51. DSB, Aug. 1, 1960.

52. *Caribbean Tensions*, pp. 53 and 368ff; Tad Szulc, Sept. 4, 1960.

53. USWA: 1960, pp. 308-315.

54. R. Hart Phillips, NYT, Aug. 31, 1960.

55. Phillips, NYT, July 24 and Dec. 29, 1960.

56. NYT, Sept. 28, 1960; Sam Pope Brewer, NYT, Sept. 27, 1960; *U.S. Participation in the U.N.: 1960*, p. 59; DSB, Oct. 31, 1960, p. 690.

57. NYT, Aug. 8, 1960; Phillips, *ibid.*, Oct. 16, 1960; NYT, Nov. 14, 1960.

58. DSB, Sept. 19, 1960, p. 441; *ibid*, Oct. 17, 1960, p. 603; W. J. Jorden, NYT, Sept. 30, 1960.

59. DSB, Nov. 7, 1960, p. 715.

60. E. W. Kenworthy, NYT, Oct. 21, 1960.

61. *U.S. Participation in the U.N.: 1961*, pp. 87-89.

62. Paul Kennedy, NYT, Nov. 20, 1960; DSB, Dec. 12, p. 888; *ibid.*, Dec. 19, 1960, p. 924; *ibid.*, Dec. 26, p. 958; Tad Szulc, NYT, Dec. 7, 1960.

63. Max Frankel, NYT, Dec. 22, 1960.

64. Arthur M. Schlesinger, Jr., *A Thousand Days*, pp. 220-240; NYT, Nov. 19,1960.

## CHAPTER ELEVEN

1. DSB, Feb. 7, 1955, p. 237.

2. NYT, Nov. 8, 1959.

3. DSB, Nov. 23, p. 759.

4. NYT, Nov. 5; Paul Kennedy, NYT, Nov. 26, 1959.

5. DSB, Oct. 10, 1960, p. 558.

6. NYT, Oct. 2, 1960.

7. *Ibid.*, Apr. 20, 1960.

8. See 86th Cong., 2nd Session, *Report on U.S. Relations with Panama by the Sub-Committee on Inter-American Affairs of the Committee on Foreign Affairs.* House Report 2218.

9. Hanson W. Baldwin, NYT, Aug. 12, 1960.

10. *Ibid.*, Oct. 9, 1960.

11. Karl M. Schmitt and David D. Burks, *Evolution or Chaos* (New York, 1963), pp. 33ff.

12. John C. Dreier, *The Organization of American States and the Hemisphere Crisis* (New York, 1962), pp. 50-53.

13. USWA: 1957, pp. 280-285; Juan de Onis, NYT, Nov. 29, 1959.

14. Agency for International Development, *Overseas Loans and Grants and Assistance from International Organization: July 1, 1945 to June 30, 1964.*

15. *American Foreign Policy: Current Documents, 1958,* pp. 413-415.

16. DSB, Sept. 1, 1958, pp. 347-348.

17. See Robert Cutler, "The Inter-American Development Bank," *The Business Lawyer* (Nov. 1960); C. D. Dillon, in DSB, March 21, 1960, p. 436.

18. *American Foreign Policy: Current Documents, 1958,* pp. 380-381, 404-408.

19. DSB, Jan. 19, 1959, pp. 89-105.

20. Tad Szulc, NYT, Feb. 21, 1960.

21. *Ibid.*, Mar. 8, 1959; *Time* magazine, Mar. 16, 1959.

22. USWA: 1959, p. 368.

23. DSB, Mar. 28, 1960, pp. 471-473, 487.

24. *Ibid.*, May 9, pp. 754-757.

25. *Ibid.*, Aug. 1, pp. 166-168.

26. *Ibid.*, Aug. 29, p. 310.

27. *Ibid.*, Oct. 3, pp. 533-537; Juan de Onis, NYT, Sept. 7, 1960; *ibid.*, Sept. 6; DSB, Oct. 3, 1960, pp. 537-540.

28. *Ibid.*, Sept. 26, p. 469.

## CHAPTER TWELVE

1. USWA: 1952, pp. 218-221.

2. *American Foreign Policy: Basic Documents, 1950-1955,* pp. 878-885.

3. *Ibid.,* pp. 750-788.

4. USWA: 1954, pp. 255-256.

5. *Ibid.,* p. 258.

6. *American Foreign Policy: Basic Documents, 1950-1955,* pp. 912-915; USWA: 1954, pp. 259-261.

7. Southeast Asia Treaty Organization, *Manila Pact and Pacific Charter,* p. 6.

8. DSB, Apr. 29, 1959, pp. 605-614.

9. Dana Adams Schmidt, NYT, Sept. 8, 1959.

10. *American Foreign Policy: Basic Documents, 1950-1955,* pp. 912-915.

11. DSB, Oct. 19, 1959, pp. 564-565.

12. *Ibid.,* June 29, 1960, pp. 986-987.

13. *Ibid.,* July 11, 1960, p. 41.

14. *Ibid.,* Sept. 26, 1960, pp. 499-500.

15. J.M. Mackintosh, *Strategy and Tactics of Soviet Foreign Policy* (London, 1962), pp. 122-127.

16. *American Foreign Policy: Current Documents, 1957,* pp. 829-831, 1020-1022; 85th Cong., House Joint Resolution 117, Mar. 9, 1957.

17. DSB, Oct. 26, 1959, p. 576.

18. *Ibid.,* Oct. 26, 1959, pp. 583-585.

19. *Ibid.,* May 16, 1960, pp. 801-802.

20. *Ibid.,* pp. 802-803.

21. 81st Cong., 1st Sess., *A Decade of American Foreign Policy: Basic Documents, 1941-1949,* pp. 411-445.

22. DSB, July 27, 1959, pp. 108-109.

23. *Ibid.,* Aug. 31, 1959, pp. 299-306; *ibid.,* Sept. 7, p. 342.

24. Dept. of State, *American Opinion Report,* Aug. 13, 17; Chalmers M. Roberts, *Washington Post,* Aug. 17; DSB, Sept. 7, 1959, pp. 343-344; USWA: 1959, pp. 352-359.

25. DSB, Oct. 26, 1959, p. 576.

26. *Ibid.*, May 9, 1960, p. 570.

27. *Ibid.*, Sept. 12, pp. 395-408.


## CHAPTER THIRTEEN

1. *A Decade of American Foreign Policy: Basic Documents, 1941-1949*, pp. 821-825; 81st Cong., 1st Session, Senate Document 123; USWA: 1949, pp. 75-79.

2. DSB, Jan. 7, 1957, pp. 18-28.

3. Drew Middleton, NYT, Oct. 19, Dec. 7, 1958; C. L. Sulzberger, NYT, Dec. 20, 1958; Henry A. Kissinger, NYT *Magazine*, Mar. 8, 1959.

4. DSB, Jan. 5, 1959, p. 4; Robert Doty, NYT, Dec. 18, 1958; James Reston, NYT, Dec. 21; Editorial, *ibid.*, Dec. 21, 1958.

5. DSB, Apr. 20, 1959, pp. 543-547.

6. *Ibid.*, p. 545.

7. Dwight D. Eisenhower, *op. cit.*, p. 427; C. L. Sulzberger, NYT, Feb. 2, 1959; Robert Doty, *ibid.*, June 4, 1959; James Reston, *ibid.*, June 18, 1959.

8. Robert Doty, *ibid.*, Jan. 8, Mar. 14, 22, 1959.

9. Sydney Gruson, *ibid.*, Nov. 30, 1959.

10. Editorial, NYT, and Associated Press report, Dec. 12, 1959; *ibid.*, Dec. 13 and 14.

11. Sydney Gruson, also Drew Middleton, NYT, Dec. 16, 1959.

12. C. L. Sulzberger, NYT, Dec. 16 and 19, 1959.

13. DSB, Jan. 4, 1960, p. 3; *ibid.*, Jan. 11, p. 43.

14. *Ibid.*, May 23, pp. 840-841.

15. NYT, Sept. 6, 1960.

16. DSB, Sept. 26, 1960; Dana Schmidt, NYT, Sept. 9, 1960.

17. DSB, Oct. 3, 1960, p. 516.

18. Robert Doty, NYT, Nov. 30, 1959.

19. Drew Middleton, NYT, Dec. 17, 1960.

20. DSB, Jan. 9, 1961, p. 41.

21. Middleton, NYT, Dec. 20, 1960.

22. C. L. Sulzberger, NYT, Dec. 24 and 31, 1960.

CHAPTER FOURTEEN

1. DSB, Oct. 12, 1959, pp. 502-504.

2. *Ibid.*, pp. 503, 508.

3. *Ibid.*, Oct. 10, 1960, p. 589.

4. *Ibid.*, Oct. 5, 1959, p. 467.

5. NYT, Sept. 24, 1959.

6. DSB, Oct. 12, 1959, pp. 503-508.

7. NYT, Sept. 18-19, 1960.

8. *Ibid.*, Sept. 23, 1960.

9. *Ibid.*, Sept. 20, 1960.

10. *Ibid.*, Sept. 24, 1960; *American Foreign Policy: Current Documents, 1960*, pp. 35-38, 715-718.

11. DSB, Oct. 10, 1960, pp. 583-589; *U.S. Participation in the U.N.: 1960*, pp. 49-50; USWA: 1960, pp. 343-345.

12. NYT, Sept. 24, 1960.

13. *Ibid.*, Sept. 25-26.

14. *Ibid.*, Sept. 27, Oct. 3, 1960.

15. W. J. Jorden, *ibid.*, Nov. 5, 1960.

16. DSB, Nov. 14, 1960, pp. 739-740.

17. Arthur Krock, NYT, Apr. 19, 1959.

18. *Fourteenth Report of the United States Advisory Commission on Information* (Washington, 1959), p. 15.

19. 82nd Cong., 2nd Sess., *Fifteenth Report*, House Document, 369, pp. 29-30.

20. *U.S. Foreign Policy: The Formulation and Administration of U.S. Foreign Policy.* Brookings Institution (Washington, 1960).

21. Dwight D. Eisenhower, *op. cit.*, p. 637.

22. *Organizing for National Security*, I, pp. 699-702, Committee on Government Operations (Washington, 1961).

23. *Ibid.*, pp. 713-714.

24. *Ibid.*, p. 737.

25. *Congressional Record*, Aug. 30, 1960, pp. 18262-18263.

26. *Organizing for National Security*, III, pp. 19-24, 99.

27. DSB, Mar. 7, 1960.

28. Dept. of State, *Documents on Disarmament, 1945-1959* (Washington, 1960), pp. 7-16.

29. *Geneva Conference on the Discontinuance of Nuclear Weapon Tests*, pp. 356-358, Department of State Publication 7258 (1961).

30. A. M. Rosenthal, NYT, Mar. 13, 1960; Roscoe Drummond, *Washington Post*, Mar. 16, 1964.

31. *Documents on Disarmament, 1960*, pp. 83-86, 124-125.

## CHAPTER FIFTEEN

1. Department of State, *Daily Opinion Summary*, Apr. 28, 1959.

2. *U.S. News & World Report*, June 8, 1959.

3. Francis B. Stevens, *ibid.*, Apr. 18, 1960.

4. Department of State, *American Opinion Reports*, Apr. 18, 1960.

5. Andrew Berding, *Foreign Affairs and You* (Garden City, N. Y., 1962), p. 171.

6. NYT, Sept. 30, 1958.

7. DSB, Nov. 11, 1959, pp. 782-783, 786; NYT, Nov. 13-14.

8. *Ibid.*, Sept. 24, 1960.

9. Personal interview.

10. NYT, Jan. 1, 1967.

11. *Washington Post*, Jan. 1, 1961.

# INDEX